Greetings,
   May you look, listen &
stay positive along life's way.

                    Sunshine & Smiles,
                    Karen Johnson

Let us take you for a walk through
rural America and we hope that you
will enjoy the journey

                    Bill Johnson '94

Once Upon A Farm

How To Look, Listen, Laugh, And Survive

By Bill and Karen Johnson

Sigler Printing & Publishing
Ames, Iowa

Illustrations and cover art by Karen Johnson
Cover design by Sigler Printing & Publishing

© 1993 Bill and Karen Johnson. All Rights Reserved.

Johnson, Bill (1941-)

    Once upon a farm: how to look, listen, laugh and survive / Bill and Karen Johnson. -- 1st ed. -- Ames, Iowa : Sigler, 1993.

    A collection of true stories, poems, jokes, and journal entries of the authors' thoughts and recollections of people and events that they've encountered during their half-century of living on Iowa farms.
    Includes Glossary.

Library of Congress Catalog Card Number 93-84973
ISBN 0-9635812-1-X

    1. Farm life--United States--Middle West. 2. Agriculture--Economic aspects. 3. Iowa--Rural conditions. 4. Autobiographies. I. Johnson, Karen (1948-), joint author.

630.92--dc20

Dedicated With Love,

To Our Children,

Alan, Kristin, and Jerod

With Special Dedication To Very Special People

* Jerod Johnson

* Duane and Michael Johnson

* The people of the rescue squad/ambulance crews of the towns of Shelby, Avoca, and Harlan, Iowa

* The Life Flight Helicopter Team; General Surgeon Dr. Ronald A. Hinder; Specialists Dr. Joel N. Bleicher, Dr. Lynn A. Crosby, Dr. Euclid J. de Souza; and the many other doctors, intensive care nurses, and floor nurses, all at Saint Joseph Hospital in Omaha, Nebraska

* Dr. Antonio P. Manahan and the rehabilitation staff at Immanuel Medical Center in Omaha, Nebraska

With deep gratitude, appreciation, love, and blessings to all who helped save Bill's life and thus make this book possible.

Special Thanks...

...to Alan Johnson for his contribution to the author's cover biography and his proofing; to Kristin Johnson for proofing; to Pastor Robert Kruempel for sharing his computer know-how; to Walt Herreid, our reader, for his helpful comments; to Dr. Roy Schultz, D.V.M. for his technical information, and to the "Writer's Bloc" for listening.

Contents

Section I Who Are These People?
A Tale Of Old 3
The Breeze Blows By 4

Section II What's In It For You?
How This Book Came About
    And What's In It For You 7
How To Look, Listen, Laugh, And Survive 9

Section III A Collection Of Recollections
Sound Impressions 13
Sour Krauts And Wienies 14
Another Threshing Story 14
It's Mine In Deed 15
A Piece Of The Rock 16
Daily Debut 17
The Explorer 18
The Daus 19
Rule Of Thumb 20
Hollering Up The Stairs 21
Just Twice A Day 22
Omaha Stockyards 23
Once Upon A Farm 24
Lean, Mean, Cuisine 27
 Summer's A Better Time For Birthdays 28
Brighton No. 8 29
Grandmas And Grandpas 32
The Visitor 34
Kidnapped 34
Figuring Income Taxes 36
Footprints 38
Thur Apr 12 40
Our Wishbook 42
Saturday Nights At The Acova 43
Making Memories At The Acova 45

Section IV   Journal Journey

Journal Journey 49
1968 49
1969 50
1970 50
1971 54
1972 56
1973 60
1974 63
1975 66
1976 71
1977 72
1978 84
1979 88
1980 95
1981 100
1982 108
1983 114
1984 117
1985 124
1986 132
1987 139
1988 148
1989 158
1990 174

Section V   A Laugh A Day Keeps The Doctor Away

First 185
My 4 Speed, Posi-traction, 4 x 4 Truck 186
Potpourri 187
Potluck 190
In 191
A Fractured Fairy Tale 192
Kids Say And Do The Darnedest Things 193
Cutting Remarks 195
Delicious? 196
Daffy Definitions 196
Things That Are Spotted 197
Mary's Kitchen 199
It Must Come From Your Side 200
My Kingdom, ... Come 200

It's All Mine 201
Mystery Lunch 202
The Joys Of Being A Farm Wife And Mother 202
Hide! I Can't Let My Cornflakes Sog! 205
I See You 206
Things Parents Used To Say 206
Over The Hill? 208
Cents Of Christmas 209
The Night After Christmas 210

Section VI   Observations And Thoughts

Savor It 213
First Exposure 214
See The Shape Things Are In 214
Journey Just Before Dawn 215
The Old Folks At Home 216
The Hands Of Time 217
Pinnacles Of The Prairie 218
Consumed In The Night 219
Gone !!?? 220
The Best Laid Plans Of Man And Cows
    Often Go Awry 221
We're Pulling For You 222
Dress? 223
The Scheme of Things 225
My Least Favorite Job 226
A Tear, "So What?" 227
Treasures 228
The "Doctor" 229
Oohhh, It's DRY 230
Déjà Vu 230
When It Rains ———? 231
Dirt Farmer 232
Peace Unquiet 233
The Key 234
When The Dust Settles 235
The Harvest 236
Dance With Destiny 237
Harvest Time ... Down Time 238
The Seasons Of Life 239
A Farm Sale 240
Where Did The Farmer Go ? 241

ix

Section VII The Nature Of Things

Pull The Wool Over My Skies 245
Passing The Reins ? 246
Fork In The Food Chain 247
Oh! Isn't It Pretty. What Is It? 248
SURPRISE 249
Windrowing Alfalfa 250
The Old Maple In The Middle Of The Farm 251
Shhhh, The House Is Bugged! 252
Leptocoris Trivittatus 253
Amaranthus Retroflexus
   (Tumbleweed) 254
In Silent Servitude 255
The Little Raindrop 256
The Safety of Similarity 257
Walk Down The Lane One Time For Me 258

Section VIII Some Serious Selections

On Dad's Funeral Day 261
Shorted By Alzheimer's 262
On My Own 263
Where Are You Goin', Grandma? 264
Ronnie 265
1900 hrs E.S.T. Jan 16,1991 266
Harvest Angels 267
Lonely 268
Loneliness 269
Simply Renewed 270
Ode To Farmers 271
Critical List 272
As I Saw It 273
Positively Yours 276

Epilogue 277
Glossary 281
Title Index 287

Section I

Who Are These People?

A Tale Of Old

by Karen Johnson

Once upon a farm, long, long ago, I was a little dark haired, brown-eyed girl who lived with my mom and dad, big brother Calvin, and younger sister Sherry in a white house with a big swingset out front (Dad had made it for us with his welder). We kids swang and sang and learned to "skin a cat" on its bars.

We built tree houses in the grove, bale houses in the barn, and snow houses in big snow banks. We had tea parties in the yard, made dams and caught crawdads in the creek, and made mud pies in a fabulous mud pie house. We fed chickens and gathered eggs, helped feed pigs and cattle, helped make hay and straw, and walked corn fields for cockleburs.

We had lots of fun but we knew our chores had to be done before we could play or go anywhere, and we were satisfied with a few simple material possessions.

There were lots of get-togethers with family and neighbors; and for us, just going to school was fun. Since I was small for my age, my classmates nicknamed me "Half-pint," but I didn't mind because I was lively and pretty easy going. I had a dear country school teacher who wrote on my 1st grade report card, "Karen is like a little star that shines all the time".... Ah, those were the good old days.

***

- Born Karen Kay Bornholdt Aug 3,1948
- Grew up on a farm east of Marne, Iowa
- Watched Mickey Mouse & the Mouseketeers after school
- Went to Brighton #8 Country School (S.E. of Marne) 7 yrs
- Graduated from Atlantic High School 1966
- Iowa State University Textiles & Clothing 1 1/2 yrs
- Married Bill Nov 30,1968. Work with him on our farm & have 3 children: Alan William (6-14-70); Kristin Kay (6-28-72); & Jerod James (7-8-77)
- All 5 of us are members of Shelby United Lutheran Church
- Past Member Shelby County Porkettes: education Chairman 5 yrs
- 4-H leader 5 yrs Shelby Superstars
- Shelby County 4-H Aide 1982-1984
- Love to design, sew, draw, read, write, and refinish
- Enjoy houseplants and flower gardens
- Collect snow globes, Mickey Mouse items, old jewelry (especially pins), and kitchen and sewing items
- Work daily to keep my family from driving me crazy

The Breeze Blows By

by Bill Johnson

I grew up in a strict home environment on a farm, in a small community, where if you got your work done, you still didn't get to go anywhere.

We as a family weren't burdened with excessive material wealth, so we created our own fun: in the haymow; grain bins; on the easy tree; in the fields and creeks; and in winter and evenings, parlor games, cards, etc. We had an old upright Edison (phonograph) with thick records so we knew tunes that the other kids in school didn't (popular?).

There are pros and cons to the timing of everyone's existence. I feel one great asset to mine was that the farming community was slowly evolving into mechanization. I was involved in the hard way of doing things, but an easier way was soon to come; and still, I could hear the stories firsthand from the folks who had carved their existence from a virgin prairie; and in those days, we had a little more time to listen.

There were five kids in our family and out of necessity, hand-me-downs were commonplace. Having two older sisters and two younger brothers, you can readily see why I really didn't mind staying home.

***

Born William James Johnson Oct 3,1941
Almost died Aug 23,1989
    revived later that day
Graduated from Shelby Consolidated School 1959
Army National Guard 1965-1971 Red Bull Division
A member of the Clodbusters tug-o'-war rope pulling team 1976-1984
Took 2nd place in the National Monster Arm Wrestling Competition (men's middle wt.) 1983
Won both corn & soybean yield contests in Shelby County 1984
Shelby County Pork Producers Board 1984-1987
Shelby-Tennant School Board 1980-present
Born on, now live on and farm land that has been in the family over 100 years
Grew a beard once
Collect antiques and primitives
Enjoy competition if I can choose the competitors
Took some creative writing classes
I'll play a hand or two of cards if I'm dealt in

Section II

What's In It For You?

How This Book Came About
And What's In It For You

We've both written pieces for a number of years and I have kept a journal for over twenty-four years. About five years ago we vowed to put our writings together in a book.

This book is made up of eight sections: (the first one telling you about the book's authors) and this section is some of how the book came about and what you can find in the rest of the book. Next **"A Collection Of Recollections"** contains stories and poems about the good old days of threshing and railroads; and happenings from our lives as kids on the farm like choring, making mud pies, and going to country school; as well as some of more recent past farm events.

In Section IV you can go on a **"Journal Journey"** with us thru highlights from my daily journals from 1968 thru 1990 to see what life on our farm was (or is) actually like.

To change the pace somewhat the next section **"A Laugh A Day Keeps The Doctor Away"** may bring you a smile or two with humorous pieces about a variety of thoughts and things from chickens, to pickups, to people that brought us a laugh during our years on the farm.

"Observations And Thoughts" is made up of pieces about people, events, and such that we've thought of or observed.

"The Nature Of Things" is about cows, coyotes, weeds, weather, and things in nature.

Finally **"Some Serious Selections"** of people and events in our lives, including Bill's account of his Aug 23,1989 tractor accident in which he was critically injured, are in section VIII.

The book closes with an epilogue, followed by a glossary of terms from the book that may not be familiar to non-farm folks, and may not be in most dictionaries.

The organization of the book began forming in my mind as I disked or windrowed or unloaded grain at harvest. Many of our pieces began in such places, as well. Bill wrote some of his poems on a parts sack, or whatever was handy to balance on his knee, as he was going thru the fields in his combine.

I wrote the stanzas for "Windrowing" (in section VII) while windrowing alfalfa. As I maneuvered the huge machine thru the field, I repeated the lines over and over in my mind, changing words for better ones as they came to me, counting syllables on my fingers to get the rhythm right, and repeating stanzas as they formed to embed them in my mind. Later that evening when I had finished the field, I hurried to the house to write down the poem.

My poems "The Shape Of Things" and "Dance With Destiny" (in section VI) came to me as I was hauling in corn at harvest. I used a cornstalk "cigar" to write lines and stanzas in the dirt on the sides of the metal gravity wagons that I was hauling corn in. The next day I went back with a pad and paper, copied down the material, and later wrote the poems.

Sometimes we get up in the middle of the night to write, as an idea leaps from our subconscious minds and wakes us. Bill did this once and quickly wrote down over three pages of stories he had been forming in his mind as he slept. His story "First" (in section V) was part of that episode.

Bill even wrote poems while he was in intensive care in the hospital after his 1989 tractor accident (these poems are in section VIII).

Ideas can come at strange times and in strange places, but over the years we've jotted notes and tried to preserve our thoughts on paper. This book is a collection of thoughts and recollections of people and events that have entered our minds and touched our hearts during half a century of living on a farm.

When I began in earnest to type our pieces, and rewrite and revise my notes, Bill worked on revising his pieces, as well as dreaming up new ones.

We spent a lot of time listening to or reading each other's works. We critiqued each others pieces, although I had trouble with Bill being objective and/or serious about my contributions. For example, Bill's first comment after reading my "Simply Renewed" (in section VIII) was, "You never did find the cows!"

And so it goes...

Bill hopes the book will inspire the younger generation to ask about the way things used to be, while there's still someone left who can tell them.

And I hope the stories, poems, and such in this book will bring back memories, or make you laugh, or even cry. (Crying is not all bad, you know; it can show you care, and can help relieve stress.)

As you read the book to see for yourself how we look, listen, laugh, and survive on a farm, maybe we can make a difference in your lives.

How To Look, Listen, Laugh, And Survive

How you survive depends on how you look at life and what goes on around you. You've got to be observant: **look for details,** notice the details. You've got to "look" before you can "see."

It's the same with listening: you've got to **listen for details,** pay attention to what's being said. Whether it be your heart, your conscience, the land, or other people who are "talking," you've got to "listen" before you can hear.

Finally, you've got to **laugh.** A laugh a day keeps the doctor away.
* Laughing helps you cope
* helps break a tense moment
* relieves stress
* lightens your heart
* brightens your day
* helps keep your attitude POSITIVE !

You've got to laugh to survive!

Look, listen, and laugh; and you too can survive, on a farm or anywhere else.

Section III

A Collection Of Recollections

Sound Impressions

Remember the rooster who got you up when the dew was pearly?
In my estimation, he was two hours early.
Or the coyotes who kept the dog up all night,
Willing to bark, but too cautious to fight?

When the first streams of milk hit the clean, dry pail;
Or when old Bossie wrapped your neck with her cold, wet tail?
Then the clanking of the pail rolling across the barn,
When you unknowingly touched the teat, freshly torn.

Nothing, to my ear, was quite as forlorn,
As the coo of the dove in the early morn';
Or were you ever frightened by the pheasant's whir,
As he left your feet in a sudden blur?

There was that thump— thump— thump of yet another ear,
That always came in the fall of the year;
And later, the most mechanical sound you would ever hear,
When Dad eased that first 2-M picker in gear.

As a hard rain fell on a shingled roof,
You had to look in a bucket to measure the proof.
Now we hear an incessant din,
As a few raindrops fall on the tin.

Do You remember the squawk of the hayrope pulley,
That was hooked to the sill of the old feed alley;
And when the hayfork tripped right inside the door,
Almost sending its load through the haymow floor?

I could hear the quiet whisper of the windmill wheel,
Until a fin came loose; then it was steel on steel.
That's when that stately old tower lost its poise,
And a peaceful sound became a "noise"!

Sour Krauts And Wienies

Back in the era of the threshing ring, whole neighborhoods would work together. They moved from farm to farm during the heat of the summer; for that is when the small grain crop ripened, was cut, shocked, and when dry, was threshed. Usually one family would own the steam engine and threshing machine, or separator, as it was called. They would receive a few cents a bushel for the grain they threshed, but the rest of the work was pretty much traded off between neighbors. It was hot, hard work; but no one thought twice about it because that is the way it was.

The wives and daughters of the men would take care of feeding this hungry crew, and would set a table comparable to any Thanksgiving feast you have ever seen.

But all was not just work; these guys were as hard as nails and reveled in a little friendly competition from time to time. On our ring, there were a couple of young German lads who touted they could hold anyone's horse with their bare hands. Grandpa's brother Henry had a stud horse on his team, and he thought just maybe he could pull these boys.

The two guys would lay down behind the 6 x 6 sill in a barn door, and wrap a hay rope once around their waists, and clench the loose end with their hands to the rope that was fastened to the single tree behind Hank's stud. Since stud horses are a little harder to handle, Hank talked the boys into allowing him to lead the horse's teammate alongside, to keep him calm.

Well, Henry knew his team, and he knew his stud always pulled just a little ahead of the other horse, and that he would pull himself blind to retain that position. When they said go, Henry made sure he had the second horse just a little ahead of the stud. It wasn't long at all until there was "Kraut" all over the barnyard.

***

Another Threshing Story

My dad, Walt J. Johnson, was the separator man on our neighborhood's threshing ring. In the mornings, he would get the threshing machine separator ready, just as the engineer would fire the big steam engine.

Before the racks of bundles would get in from the field, they would belt the engine to the separator and test run. The big endless belt between the two would be twisted once so it would not flop up and down. Where the belt crossed itself, Dad said he used to grip it with both hands and he could prevent the big steamer from turning its drive pulley.

It didn't take long though, for the engineer to direct the steam to the other end of the piston, reversing the pulley and whipping the belt and Dad ten to fifteen feet into the air.

Of course, there had to be revenge! The man on the threshing machine always had a bucket of grease to fill the hard oilers. If he would place a handful of grease on the drive belt, imagine who would have grease in their ear when that handful of black stuff passed between the belt and the drive pulley on the engine.

I doubt if it all ended there.

***

It's Mine In Deed

The United States Government deeded alternating sections of ground along a proposed railroad right-of-way to the companies who would lay the grade and install the tracks.

If you have ever seen an abstract of title to land near a railroad track, you will have seen a name like "Chicago, Rockland, and Pacific Railroad Company" listed as owner, second only to that of the U.S. Government.

Much of this ground was used to pay the men who built the endless tracks that tied our eastern cities to the new frontiers.

The names of these men then are listed on the titles as subsequent owners, and that is how much of this rich prairie was deeded from the U.S. Government to private ownership.

Without the railroads, can you imagine how the prairie land could have been settled and the commerce of this great nation could have developed?

Many of the local spur lines, along which small town Iowa sprang up and was nurtured, were built in the 1870 to 1900 period and are now nothing but a scar through the countryside. I wonder when they will be back.

***

A Piece Of The Rock

The Rock Island railway passed through our farm and Dad had many stories to tell of its existence.

My great-grandpa, John Johnson, helped to haul the hills into the valleys, leveling the roadbed so the track could be laid.

Although seeming level, the stretch of track connecting Avoca and Shelby was touted to be the steepest grade in the Rock Island network. On those big trains, it took three or four engines and all the pressure in their boilers and all of the traction that they could muster to make that grade.

One day, Dad and some of the boys thought it would be fun to put a little grease on the rails so they could see if the engines would spin a little. They applied the grease and then took position in the attic of a house where a window overlooked the track, and there was a pool table there to shorten the wait.

Well, spin a little it did. After three attempts, and backing nearly to Avoca on the third; the boys were relieved to see the train go over the hump and on to Shelby.

They knew for sure that there would be a "Railroad Dick" watching the house so it was well after dark when they got home for chores.

Dad also used to tell of how during the 30's, things were tough all over. The trains would usually have a few cars loaded with coal, and enterprising folks thought it would help the train get over the hump if they'd climb aboard and throw off as much coal as they could before it got to the top. Then they'd jump off before it got going too fast.

Not being wasteful, they would of course pick the coal up and carry it home with them.

***

Daily Debut

We'd hear the whistle,
    Most days, the very same time;
And we'd seldom miss dinner,
    Living by the Rock Island line.

We kids would count the cars,
    There would be a hundred or more;
And patiently wait and see
    What they all had in store.

There would be cars and trucks
    And coal and posts.
About whatever in our town
    They needed the most.

A few years the flat cars
    Would carry bombs and tanks,
With banners to "Buy war bonds"
    To support the Yanks.

As it passed by on down the track,
    It's hard to describe just how we'd feel
Watching it clack-clack, clack-clack, clack-clack,
    Weaving down those shiny ribbons of steel.

The Explorer

Grandma would hold me in front of her and utter the darnedest things. Since then, I've heard other grandmas speak that same language, but never between themselves, always to little babies. Then, seemingly out of nowhere, came Grandma's teeth. The very person who would scold Grandpa for scaring little Billy. What could be more scary than someone who could bite you from a distance!

I remember standing beside Grandpa on the couch. He would have his arm around me; and I would be following the pathways of his ear with my finger, in and out, over and over. He had the softest ears, but I could bend them down, and they would spring right back up again. Eventually I would explore too deeply, and he would move me around to the front and we'd talk.

He seemed to understand me but I didn't follow a thing he said. Here though, I had lips and a nose to play with. This lasted until I found his dirty old pipe in his shirt pocket, and priorities put me on the floor.

As I grew taller, more doors would open up to me. Do you remember when you could put your finger into a keyhole and explore? Eventually you could reach the door knob. It would be a while before you could actually turn the knob. Then you would pull the door into your toes and it would pop shut again. It did no good to get a chair until you learned to space it back far enough to prevent the same reaction. Then there was the opening at the back of the door that inevitably got too small for tiny fingers.

There were kittens, baby chickens, pigs, and all sorts of soft fuzzy things to touch and experience. There was one thing that was even softer than my proverbial butt and that was the nose of a horse. I never did get to know a horse well enough to trust one from either end, but for those darting touches on its soft nose.

Mom would let us guys have a little dough when she baked bread. It was way better than the Play–Doh® the kids get now because we could eat it if it didn't get too dirty. I can remember those soft white rolls of dough laying in the bread pans when we went to bed. In the morning they stuck up out of the pans as big as my head. When they were baked, Mom took them out of the Kalamazoo stove and buttered what stuck out of the pan. They would set shining on the cupboard and when I knocked on them with my little fist, they seemed as hard as a turtle. Sure was good dipped in hot cocoa.

The Daus

Our old neighbors, John and Alice Dau, lived back in the field three fourths of a mile. They did things the hard way right up until they died. Well, it wasn't "the hard way" when they started, it was the only way. As things changed on the farm for others, John and Alice kept right on doing what they had known all of their lives, and I guess "that way" served them adequately.

I know that our relationship with those hard working people gave us kids an insight into "the good old days" that most our age never experienced. I only wished we had spent more time over there.

There was no electricity; and when there was no wind to turn the windmill, water was pumped by an old John Deere single-cylinder, water-cooled gas engine into a wooden supply tank just outside of their house; and of course, the in house was out.

Alice kept her house spotless even when, in later years, some raccoons lived under the floor. My brother Duane and I would help them bale hay on occasion and would eat dinner there. Alice was getting so bent over from years of hard work that she could barely see into her cooking pots on the old cookstove. The pots were old and bent and the spoons she stirred with were worn flat where they had rubbed on pot bottoms daily for years. The food was always good and there were plenty of potatoes and gravy. Alice always had dessert for us, but I can't brag on her blueberry pie. It had half an inch of bottom crust, half an inch of blueberries, and half an inch of top crust: not quite enough juice to allow for easy swallowing. There was plenty of powdered milk to wash it down though.

John had tractors: his old D John Deere was probably one of the earliest in the neighborhood; but he kept his horses longer than anyone in the neighborhood. Those old timers took real good care of their horses because they depended on them. Until farmers finally accepted tractors to do work as well as the horses did, the team was almost as important as the cook. To some, they were probably more important, and were treated accordingly.

When plowing was first done with horses, a one-bottom plow was used. They would cut from an eight inch to an eighteen inch furrow, but fourteen or sixteen inch plows were most common. John would relate that when he got his eighteen inch plow, the neighbors could tell he was getting something done!

I'd see John at the sale barn once in a while and he would be standing by a pen of straight Hampshire pigs. He'd offer to anyone close that they were Missouri pigs, and in those days, that meant they weren't too good.

When the auction started and those Hamps came in the ring, John would buy them no matter what and take them home, just as proud as he could be. They had to be better pigs than John let on though, because they got by on the barest of necessities for the next year of their lives.

Most times when I'd visit with John, he'd tell me what I'd heard before; and then, as if out of the depths of his memory, he'd come with a story that made it all worthwhile. Old people are like that and there is a lot to be gained by spending some time listening to them.

He'd usually come with a line in German, always the same line, and I'd ask him what it meant. He'd say he "couldn't say it on American," and he'd laugh. I never did find out what it was. As I think back, maybe it meant, "why don't you nosey little guys ever go home," but I doubt it. John and Alice didn't have any children, and I believe they enjoyed us as much as we were intrigued by them.

Well, John would pull out his pocket watch, flip it open, and tell me I had better get home for chores. When the sun went down it got pretty quiet back there in the trees ...

I suppose.

***

Rule Of Thumb

We all know that the ruler the teacher carried around the classroom wasn't there just to see how we measured up. I guess in olden times also, a man was entitled to correct his wife on occasion; but he could use a stick no bigger in diameter than his thumb. That wouldn't be so bad if he found it laying on the ground and didn't pull it fresh from the tree. Anyway, that's where we get the expression, "rule of thumb."

Dad had his "rule of thumb" in the form of a razor strap hanging in the closet beneath the stairs. It kept us kids pretty sharp most of the time. He must have been very fond of that old strap because he'd get really mad when it came up missing for some reason.

You can imagine how us boys felt when we were drug into Glen Hendersen's barbershop for our first "store-bought" haircut. He had one of those razor straps hanging right there on his intimidating big chair. Every once in a while, he'd look us right in the eye and smile as we sat across the room, and he would sharpen that strap with his razor. I noticed the old guys in his chair would change the subject pretty often when he did that.

***

Hollering Up The Stairs

Dad always hollered up the stairs at 5:30 sharp. It seemed we kids had an appointment with those old cows each a.m. In Summer, we knew he'd call twice and we could sneak a few extra winks. After Labor Day, though, we had a second appointment and it required that we be even more punctual than the first.

At 7:40 a.m., give or take sixty seconds, the big yellow and black school bus would be at the mailbox, honking. It always seemed one of us five kids could get there in time to hold the taxi while the rest of us were taking a final forkful of pancakes, putting lotion on our rough chapped hands, or trying to find the books we had dropped somewhere the night before. (Oh, the two girls would have done a little peeking into their books, as they were in competition with the other brains in the class for first or second.) (About all the wear my books received was in the transportation.) ... (Too bad though — about the books, I mean. It seems like now I wonder more than I should.)

But anyway, we've still got the farm, still got the cows, and the big yellow and black bus still stops at the mailbox.

Now the calves milk the cows,
and I do the hollering up the stairs.

***

Just Twice A Day

There was the barn to clean and the stalls to bed;
Throw the hay from the mow that had to be fed.
Then we'd break the corn ears in the milk cows bunk,
And empty the slop to the hogs. Oh! how it stunk.

Of course, the milk cows were nowhere to be seen.
They had to be here, the pasture, or the cornfield between.
If it got late, we chased them home a little faster;
But if we got too close, we flirted with disaster.

As soon as the cows were all tied in their stalls,
We grabbed a stool from the floor and a pail from the wall.
We sat down right of Bossie for a "teatious" chore,
And if she liked our work, we wouldn't land on the floor.

Then we'd carry the milk to where the separator stood;
If Sis didn't want to crank, I said that I would,
Put the cream in the ice box, skim milk to the hogs,
After we fed the calves, the cats, and the dogs.

Wait! Turn the chickens perched on the water tank,
And dip off the droppings before they sank.
Then chase the broilers out of the box elder tree,
Before the coons decided on a main entree.

We'd gather the eggs and feed the old hens some corn;
After that, the rest of the day was our own.
At last, a holler for supper; and when dishes were through,
Not once did we say, "I have nothing to do."

Omaha Stockyards

We used to go to the yards,
    And ride the elevators up and down,
        When Dad would bring his cattle in;
            And the buyers would run them in the ground.

"There are a few way too fat,
    And a couple that aren't quite done."
        The darn fools tried to buy them,
            Like they were born, one by one.

"That one's got some horns;
    We'll have to have a couple dollars off for that;
        And look at that damn 'red neck,'
            The sucker's gobby fat!"

"What's the story on that old heifer?
    The one walking behind.
        I wonder how many calves she's had;
            Her bones are harder than mine."

We didn't figure on topping the market that day;
    For our cattle, that would be kind of steep.
        When you try to pass a 'stein or two,
            The buyer has to be hungry or asleep.

Art would tell them they belonged to the kids,
    That we'd worked all year for them,
        And, by gosh, it seemed to work;
            They left them in the pen.

Then Art would start his "spiel,"
    And he would usually say,
        "If you want that pen of baldies,
            You'll have to take Walt's along today."

Then we'd go up to the office,
    Cause we had to have our pay,
        So we could stop at Johnny's,
            And that would make our day!

Once Upon A Farm

With my parents and brother and sister, I experienced life on the same farm two miles east of Marne, Iowa, for sixteen years.

We raised cattle and hogs and always had a milk cow: "Matilda" was our main source of milk and cream for lots of years and then her daughter "Tillie" took her place. We had a rat terrier named Teeny Tiny who used to sleep next to Matilda in the barn to keep warm in the winter time. During decent weather she slept in her dog house with cats.

Since we had a milk supply, we had cats, as many as 40 at one time. There was Puddin, a huge dark golden yellow tom who used to purr super loud and "knead" with his front feet when we petted him. Sometimes when we held him on our laps to pet him he'd get carried away with his "kneading" and sink his claws into our legs causing us to let out a "YEOW!" and cast him off of our laps — as soon as we could get his claws all loose from our jeans. There were also Gracie and Sixtoes (she actually had six toes on each of her front feet) who always had at least ten kittens a piece each spring. There was Huckleberry (a beautiful big black tiger cat) and Boo Boo, and Midnight, and Spooky, and Fluffy: they were all named and were all good mousers as was Teeny Tiny.

Mom also raised chickens. We kids hated chicken chores! We had a hen house with a high fenced scratch pen (for the older, meaner birds) and a brooder house & pen for each spring's fuzzy new baby chicks. Here they would live until they reached adult size and either started laying or could be dressed (butchered) for eating. When my mother determined the time was right, we carried the pullets by dark of night, upside down by their feet, one or two birds in each of our hands, to the hen house where they would continue their laying careers (and develop their mean dispositions).

My sister and I often carried a stick when we did chicken chores, to defend ourselves against the big ol' rooster. He'd appear from nowhere, strut up behind us, and then suddenly fly at us with a flash of beating wings, and scare the pants off of us! The stick also served to hold the neck and head of the mean old hens over to the side of the nest while we quickly, but reluctantly, reached under them to retrieve their eggs, before they pecked us. The stick didn't always work, as the old biddies were not only mean but quick: they'd scrunch their necks down and free their heads from our stick's hold, and give us a sharp enough peck on the hand to bring tears to our eyes, and reinforce our dread of, and hatred for chicken chores!

We raised crops of corn, oats, and alfalfa on our farm. Dad used to give us a penny a piece for each cocklebur we pulled or cut, as we walked the corn fields for such.

At harvest it was our job to kick ear corn down in the hoisted wagons as Mom unloaded it into the elevator for the corncrib or corn piles. When the crib got full, we'd help Dad set up a circle of snow fence to form the bottom ring of an outside corn pile. It was then our job to help rake the corn to the outside of the big ring until the floppy snow fence had enough corn up against it to stand upright. When this ring got full, Dad would come in from the field and we'd all help boost another ring of snow fence up on top of the first one; he'd secure it good and tight to the ring's two tall pole supports; and we'd set to raking corn up against it until it stood on its own. We'd repeat the procedure for a third and final ring on top of the other two, and when it was peaked up nice with corn, we'd start another pile until the corn was all harvested.

It was also our job to fill the water tanks for cattle, break corn ears into bunks for them, and mix oats into mash to feed the hogs.

Dad used to combine oats with a pull-type Massey combine; and we'd help to make the straw into bales, haul them in on skids, then mow them away in the barn. The neighbors helped us make ours, and then we helped them make theirs.

One year, long before my tractor handling expertise was perfected (I guess I was maybe eight or nine), Dad set me to raking straw into windrows, for my first time, with a B John Deere tractor and side delivery rake. I was scared but started off through the field, trying to do all the things he had told me to do. After I had gone a ways I felt I was doing pretty good and thought, "Wow! This is a piece of cake!" ...

Wrong! ... No sooner had that pleasant thought entered my mind than I heard the tractor start to pull down, as I started up a hill in the field. I glanced back, only to see a huge mountain of yellow straw between my tractor and rake. Their was such a gigantic mound of straw that my rake was nearly totally obliterated from view.

I quickly yanked on the clutch lever, knowing that if I killed the tractor I couldn't start it again, as it took Dad's power to turn the fly wheel to restart it. Next I decided I'd have to back up some to be able to get the giant wob of straw free. I put the gear shift in reverse and pushed the clutch lever ahead; but I was on an incline; and the steering wheel proved to be more than I could control (no power steering then). My tractor reeled back abruptly until the big back tire smacked right into the rake tongue and bent it. The tractor slugged and died.

I walked to the house, "sweatin" and "sobbin" all the way, knowing I'd have to tell Dad what I'd done.

He didn't scold, just told me, "get me a wooden post," and he took me back out to the field ... He used the post to wedge under the tongue of the rake and pry it up until it was straightened to his satisfaction. He started the tractor, helped me take care of the giant wob of straw, gave me a few instructions, and set me to raking straw again.

There was hay making too, and my uncles helped us: one of them ran a John Deere tractor with a hay buck to push piles of hay up as they went down a windrow of hay in the field. Dad would come along with another John Deere tractor with a huge contraption mounted on the front of it, and with the big tines of the Jayhawk (hay stacker), he'd pick up the mounds of hay that my uncles had pushed up. He'd maneuver this big grasshopper-looking machine, with a big mound of hay out in front on its tines, to the center of the field, where he'd raise it way up, and dump it on what became a huge hay stack. More of my uncles and my brother would fork the loose hay around to make a nice even stack of hay.

They'd continue doing this until the stack got as high as Dad could reach with his Jayhawk. He would then get up on the stack too, and help the boys fork the last dump of loose hay around, and lay it just right to "top off the stack" to make it shed rain as good as possible to keep it from spoiling.

As the year progressed, the cows would be allowed to eat from the stack; eventually they would "eat" tunnels into the stack in several directions. These made great "homes," "forts," and "hide-outs" for us kids and we spent many hours playing pretend games out in the field by the big haystack.

***

Lean, Mean, Cuisine

When the Jayhawk wasn't being used for making hay, it served as the west wall of our mud pie house; the hog yard fence was the east wall. Although this area was a "house" only in an imaginary sense, we did have a genuine wooden cupboard and a working stove.

My big brother helped us build the stove from cement blocks, stacked two high, like an open cube. He dug a fire hole under the stove, and we used an old furnace register between the layers of blocks as our oven rack; and an old steel sign for the top or grill portion of our stove.

Our cupboard held orange and black Tone's spices cans of ingredients: cattle mineral was "chili powder"; ground wood (like bugs chew up around dead trees) was cinnamon; dirt was "pepper." Colored water in bottles became our "vanilla" and flavorings. And we had makeshift dishes, pans, an utensils in our house, some that were cast-offs of Mom's.

Here we had great fun making lovely cakes and pies with dirt, and ground corn for texture and color. We even made instant chocolate frosting, from the crickles that the sun forms on top of a mudhole as it dries it: when put on top of cakes and sprinkled with water, voilà! a creamy frosting was created! We boiled dried crushed leaves in water to make "tea"; and carefully-stripped corn shucks boiled with red cobs became sauerkraut and wieners. Once in a while Mom'd give us some old flour and eggs, and we'd make pancakes on our griddle. After pretending to take bites, and exclaiming how delicious they were, we'd delight the cats by serving them — of course, they actually ate them.

The pigs got the mud pies and gourmet dishes after we had "sampled" them, and they especially liked the ones we made with corn. (We had a little cousin who actually tasted our mud pies, after she saw us "pretending" to eat them. We still tease her about it.)

Once my brother shot a pigeon and we pulled its feathers off and cooked it in a pot of water on our stove. We kept the fire going under it all afternoon. I remember the water turned really green (you see, we hadn't removed his innards)! Anyway, when we deemed it to be done, we flaked the tender meat apart with a stick and the cats loved it!

After we got tired of making mud pies we'd maybe go watch some TV, like *The Adventures Of Spin And Marty,* or *Tom Terrific And His Wonder Dog Manfred,* or *Rootie Kazootie,* or *Rin-Tin-Tin*; and then it'd probably be time for chores.

Summer's A Better Time For Birthdays

One of the most common forms of entertainment, when I was a kid, was going to friend's or relative's birthday or anniversary parties, also known as get-togethers. Entertainment at these affairs was in the form of visiting; eating lots of good food; playing games with cousins and friends, and exploring different places; or playing ball outdoors, which even the adults would join in on.

Since I was born on my brother's second birthday, we often had some really neat double parties, and our summer birthday was at a good time for picnics. Our party was often quite large, since my dad had nine brothers and sisters; mom had one of each; plus we had two sets of grandparents, a great aunt, other extended relatives, and all our country school mates who usually came to ours.

Calvin and I usually had a big birthday cake with appropriate candles for each of us, and Mom would take a special picture of us with it. There were always neat presents too.

Now our sister Sherry's birthday was a different story. She was born (2 1/2 yrs. after me) on December 15th, which was not a good month for parties: the weather was often bitter cold, with snow and bad roads for travel; and it certainly wasn't fit for big, fun outdoor picnics.

Another problem was that it was close to December 25th: relatives, not wanting to buck the bad weather, would say, "Well, it's only a few days till Christmas, and we'll see her then." Of course "Christmas" always took priority in the thinking at the traditional Christmas day dinner at Grandma Bornholdt's, and Sis' birthday was often lost in the bustle. She never got as many presents either, because it was so easy for people to just give her one present, and say it was for Christmas and her birthday both.

Summer is just a better time for playing outside, and having picnics, and birthday parties.

***

Brighton No. 8

In the fall of 1953 I started primary (kindergarten) at a one-room country school southeast of Marne, Iowa. Wide wooden steps led up to an open porch on the west side of the school, and a door then opened into a hall where coats and lunch buckets were kept. There was a table here that held a wash basin and a crock watercooler, and on the wall was a small cabinet, with cubbyholes for each pupil's water cup.

Since the school had no running water or indoor plumbing, each day one of the oldest kids would walk a short jaunt kitty-cornered across a road, to the nearest farm house, to carry a cream can full of water back for the days drinking and hand washing.

There were two outhouses, one for girls, and one for boys, that sat way east of the school — quite a long walk (or run as the case may have been) when nature called.

The hall was where students got sent to sit by themselves if they misbehaved, but getting "sent to the hall" could also be a treat: the first older student to finish all his/her lessons for the day could take the younger kids to the hall and read them stories or help drill them on phonics or new words.

The porch is where we stood each day to ring a brass bell to call the other kids in from recess. Sometimes there were fights over who should get the privilege of ringing the bell, so the teacher usually had us take turns.

Another privilege or treat for getting lessons done was to be allowed to go to the basement. Here there was a five foot square sand table up on two foot legs, in which we enjoyed building roads, farms, castles, etc. in its sand. The biggest room in the basement was also great for roller skating at recess, or for games of blindman's bluff, tag, or whatever other contests we dreamed up.

A big old oil furnace in the basement was the heat source for the building. We could bring a foil wrapped potato and lay it on a ledge inside the furnace door, when we got to school in the morning; and it'd be piping hot and done for our dinner. In the big main room there was a three foot square floor register above the furnace, that also served as a place to warm soup or whatever culinary delights came to school with us in our metal lunch pails. The register was also a popular spot for everyone to hover over to warm up, after coming in from outside (and the object of a little peeking prank that I once overheard the boys talking about: seems there was a tiny hole in the furnace, that if squinted through just right would provide a look up through the register to whatever, or whoever was on it).

Tall windows along the porch wall to the west and all along the south wall flooded the big main room with light. It was near these windows that parallel rows of desks for all grades sat north and south, in graduated sizes, from smallest on the west to biggest desks farther east.

Each school year everyone got to pick a new desk; and it was really neat to get to choose one of the biggest ones, because being one of the "big kids" was special. I always wanted to move to that east row of desks, like the kids my age finally got to do; but even though I picked out a big one when my turn came, I had to very reluctantly move to a smaller one, because the top was too high for me to write on comfortably, and my feet didn't begin to reach the floor. This sort of thing is why I got nicknamed Half-Pint.

Over by the porch windows there was a long table where we ate our lunches or worked on art projects, like making valentines from the pretty pages of a wallpaper sample book, or decorating dozens of Easter eggs. Art, on Friday of each week, was the favorite day of most of the kids.

Friday was also a day for another favorite event: the 3rd Friday each month was an evening potluck supper for all people of the community, even those with no school children. We'd hurry with our studying on school supper days; then sweep, and dust the school to make it nice for the evening.

The teacher would call each grade up to her desk for our lessons, and then we'd practice our writing, spelling, math, etc. on big black boards on the north and east walls. And yes, we did get a good education from just one teacher.

Each year the fathers would come in and move the teacher's desk aside, string no. 9 wire, and hang big purple cloth curtains. This became our stage for our Christmas program of memorized recitations from each child, a play with costumes and props, and songs for all the community people.

I was to do a solo song one year and I was so excited! The big purple curtains opened and I was center stage, in my new red plaid dress, singing my song, when a little three year old girl dashed up front by me and chanted over and over, "Mommy, I want a dolly for Christmas." I kept singing, but I felt crushed, as my solo singing debut was ruined.

The only other bad memory I have of country school is once when my teacher gave me a slap across the mouth, because when she was reprimanding a classmate, I was telling someone else that I didn't think she was being fair.

Other than this one time, this teacher was kind, caring, and understanding and we all liked her. She was an excellent teacher and loved her students dearly. (She bought us all Christmas gifts each year: mine once was a beautiful baby doll.) However Mrs. Andersen died of cancer, at age 49, when I was in 3rd grade. There were eight of us in school then, my brother being the oldest. We then had two or three other teachers before the school closed at the end of my 6th grade year.

Though we were few in number (10 at the very most), we knew how to have fun. We had swings to play on at recess but more original fares usually caught our fancy. There was the long grass that had grown all summer in the schoolyard, and was mowed before school started each fall: we had gobs of grass to pile for jumping into, and for making into forts and pens. There were sticks to build into houses, and trees to climb. During winter a steep hill north of the school offered a perfect place for sleigh riding, and there were road ditches for digging great snow houses in ... our imaginations gave us toys and games galore.

As long as the weather was nice, we walked home from school each day (about 3 mi.) with neighbor kids, the Miller kids; and we usually had fun on the way. One day though, as we were heading up the first big hill on our route home, so was a farmer with a tractor and lowboy of bales. He was going quite slow so, unknown to him, we hopped on the back of his wagon to get a free ride up the steep hill. Well, when he got just over the top of the hill, he quickly shifted gears, and surprised us with a lurch forward, that knocked us all off. Becky Miller, our littlest school mate, hit her head hard on the ground. She was hurt and crying and we carried her the rest of the way home on our backs. Her mother was furious with us all; and we got a good scolding there, and another one when we got on home.

We never caught any free rides home again, but there was another time when we decided to take a short cut across a field: when we were part way across, a big bull came up over a hill and scared us; we ran like crazy across the field and ducked under a fence. I went bawling all the rest of the way home because I'd torn a hole in my dress hurrying through the fence. We never tried this again either.

Our country school wasn't much to look at, and may not sound like much either, but we got a good education in an atmosphere filled with imagination and excitement. I always thought town kids missed out on "something special" by not getting to go to a country school like Brighton No. 8.

Grandmas And Grandpas

Staying at my Grandma and Grandpa Bornholdt's farm when I was a little girl was always a real treat for me.

My grandpa, Orville (1894-1979), was a tall man who always wore blue chambray work shirts and striped overalls, and always had a smile for us. He called me and my sister both "Sister," and he called our brother "Sonny."

Often when we'd go there he'd be sitting in his spot at the end of the big dining room table, and he'd put out his long arm to beckon us for a squeeze while he said, "Well, hello there Sister. How are you today?" And we'd visit some. Grandpa rolled his own cigarettes and he'd have us blow out his match after he got his smoke lit. We enjoyed following him around the farm to help him with chores.

Margaret Mary Brink Bornholdt (1901-1992), my grandma, was a friendly, caring, loving person and very special to me. She and Grandpa married on 12-31-1919 and raised ten kids. The oldest is my Dad, Carl (born 12-01-1920), and there are twenty-three years between him and my aunt Darlene, the youngest of the children.

My mom, Mickey, told me that when she and Dad got married, she came down with mumps on their honeymoon; and they went home to Grandma and Grandpa's. Grandma had kids having mumps for weeks afterwards, but my dad never did get them.

Our cousins and us used to have great fun playing at Grandma & Grandpa's. Grandma had a store room upstairs that she'd sometimes let us explore in: there were old books that we'd read and play school with. There was a huge black board in the basement where we'd draw pictures and play cat and mouse for hours. Downstairs here also, we'd help Grandma do laundry with a wringer washing machine. She used cakes of homemade soap that I always thought smelled icky and so did their water! (It tasted yucky too!)

We delighted in making mud pies in their grove. There was even a genuine old kitchen stove that sat up against a tree there, where we could "bake" pies in its oven, or "cook" coffee on its burners.

My grandma was a good cook, and of course with ten kids, she got plenty of practice. She made the most delicious bread I've ever tasted (with potato water) and the biggest slices I've ever seen! She baked her bread in a huge round white enamel dishpan. She'd plop three giant rounds of dough into it, let them rise way above the pan, and then she'd bake the huge loaves. The slices would be about twice as big as my grandpa's huge hands when she'd set a plate of it out.

We'd have a slice of Grandma's good bread and go off to play again.

Maybe we'd play house or good guys and bad guys, in their brick cob house; or we'd pick hollyhocks in the garden and make dolls with beautiful gowns out of the blossoms. In winter we'd have fantastic sleigh riding sprees on the two steep hills on either side of their driveway. While in summer we'd walk down to the bottom of the west hill to our "home" up under the east end of a bridge, where we made lovely cakes and pies or floated stick and leaf boats in the creek. Sometimes one of us would be the mean troll and try to leap out and catch whoever was stomping over our bridge.

We'd help Grandma hunt eggs and feed chickens, and pick strawberries in her huge patch, or cherries. Another of our jobs was to set the table. Her cupboard held all different kinds of dishes, some light green milk glass, some plain white, some pink, some white with gold rims and flowers; her silverware was a mix too. One side of her buffet held stuff for the table like salt, butter, jam, and always Hershey's chocolate syrup (in a can) (that we never had at home). We'd make big glasses of chocolate milk that were so good! It didn't taste anything like chocolate milk does today. It was deliciously different! She had a blue Shirley Temple pitcher that she'd let us use if we were careful with it.

Grandma had a way of making us behave, and feel special; and before we would leave for home, she'd slip us a little money for "being so good to help her with chores."

My other grandparents were John H. Marxen, Sr. (1893-1977), and Lola May DeBord Marxen (1904-1982). The year I was born they moved from the farm to town. They were every bit as special as my other grandparents; however beings they lived in town where there wasn't as much for lively kids to do and still not disturb the neighbors, we didn't spend as much time there. We did stay with them now and then and always had fun there too. Grandma was pretty neat.

My grandpa always greeted me enthusiastically with "Well Hello Honi!" And Grandma always had a big hug and kiss for us. She had beautiful African violets and other plants. My sister still has some of her violets and I have a wax plant (hoya) that she gave me years ago, that I enjoy everyday.

Grandma crocheted many beautiful doilies and afghans, and did lots of pretty embroidery work. I'm so glad I have things that she made as they're so special to me now.

Don't wait folks, start today to save things for you and your family that come from special people in your lives. The items may not mean much now, but they can become tomorrow's treasures.

The Visitor

After Karen's maternal grandfather passed away, Grandma stayed in their house alone for several years. Like most proud elderly folks living alone, she would accept help only when she really needed it, but was always very grateful. Because of some dependence on others, she would shop for groceries that would keep, and thus limit somewhat the frequency of trips to the store. Grandma didn't have a pantry so she would set things in the stairways to the basement and upstairs where it was a bit cooler and yet handy to get to. One evening, she was sitting all alone watching television and she thought she heard a noise from upstairs. It sounded like a footstep — then another — and another — methodic — deliberate, coming down the stairs.

Grandma sat there quiet, alone, helpless, and scared to death! Frozen in her chair, she listened to the "footsteps" coming closer and watched the closed white door that was all there was between her and her assailant.

Thump, thump, thump, and then the door flew open!

There, eye to eye, was a very shaken old lady and a sack of Kennebec potatoes.

***

Kidnapped

Bill and I were about to leave for a dance (our favorite Saturday night outing). Bill wasn't quite dressed yet; and I was all ready to go, so I strolled outside to find our twelve year old Kris and tell her that we were going to leave shortly. I hadn't seen her for the last half hour or so and figured she was probably just out somewhere petting her cats, as she loved to do.

I hollered cheerfully and unconcerned, "Kris, Kris, where are you?" I walked west of the house to the end of the sidewalk (toward the barn), and again I called, "Kris, Kris, where are you?"

Just as I was about to turn and come back to the house — assuming that she was off walking somewhere enjoying the nice summer day — I thought I heard a faint cry. It was not a happy or teasing "Mom" that I heard, but instead it was a pleading, frantic, "help-me-Mom!" cry that I heard.

Because of the buildings in the yard, I couldn't tell right away where the cries were coming from, so I wheeled around and hollered again, "Kris, Kris, where are you?"

Unable to understand her cried response, I hurried toward her voice and could finally understand her yelling, "I'm in the barn! I'm in a hole!"

I hurried west toward the barn querying my daughter all the way, "Kris, I can't find you! Tell me exactly where you are?"

"In the south end, in a hole," came her sobbed reply. "Get me out!" she pleaded.

I quickened my pace even more and rushed into the south door of the barn into a section that had a straw-covered dirt floor.

I knew of no hole in the barn floor, but there she was deep down in a dark hole in the ground, her out-stretched fingertips a good two feet below the edge of the hole.

Kneeling by the hole to quickly assess the situation, I asked, "Kris, are you alright?"

"Yes," she sobbed.

She seemed to be OK. I was relieved to have found her and to see that she didn't seem to be hurt, but I couldn't get her out by myself. "You'll be OK," I assured her. "We'll get you out. I'll go get Dad."

I dashed to the house to get Bill and he came and pulled her out, and she was safe again.

After Kris was rescued we looked with a flashlight into the hole that had held her captive, to discover a deep cavern that went back several feet under a cement platform in the barn. Evidently the cavern had formed because of dirt sinking away due to a leak in a hog waterer. We covered the hole with boards for the night and filled it with sand the next day.

The cavern had been gradually enlarging over possibly many weeks and Kris, innocently playing with her cats, had taken the one wrong step to cave the remaining dirt floor away and allow her to be kidnapped by the hidden cavern.

***

Figuring Income Taxes

Fresh and rested,
I gulp down a bowl of flakes.
Work on taxes starts:
Labor, feed, & fuel, & seed;
I'm really on a roll.
The figures fly from out my pen ...
Jan., Feb., Mar., & April;
May, it's dinner time.
A roast beef sandwich, I engulf,
Never even sitting down.
Back to my desk and on I go:
Pigs purchased, cattle sold,
A Check for 42.29.
This much principal,
That much interest.
Great Scott, the bus is here!
A little time to fix a snack,
And read a bit of mail.
Again back to the taxes ...
Numbers dance inside my brain.
Wow! It's time for bed.
Late news is already over ...
So tired I could sleep for days.

Another day and more taxes yet,
This time no breakfast at all.
Still tired, I force myself to start,
And the figures are progressing.
Catch the markets once or twice.
Next thing I know it's 1 p.m. and
I haven't stopped for dinner.
The calculator doesn't seem
To work right anymore:
9 and what are 17?
My brain seems to be going cold.
9 and what are 17?
I guess my brain's on hold.

I have to stop and take a break:
I dash to town to pay a bill,
Get some groceries,
Run some errands,
Time to pick Jerod up at school.
I fixed him some snacks and
Had my dinner about 4:49 p.m.
Then back to taxes once again,
Tomorrow is the deadline!
Bill comes to help with P.I.K.'s;
I read him my list of problems.
Was this ticket parts or feed?
Was this item bought or sold?
Finally, I fall asleep,
Oh, deep, deep sleep ...
And then all of a sudden
I'm driving my brown pickup
Across a muddy cattle lot!
I gunned it to make it through,
But halfway across I sank!
The pickup was being engulfed in manure,
And I was going under!
In seconds a little daylight was
Left to be seen
At the top of the driver's door window.
Thick, gritty, slushy manure folded
Slowly against the top of the window
And sealed out the last light.
Panic hit! Oh, I was doomed!!
My brain kicked in to save me,
And I shot straight up in bed!
Almost screaming, cold, and shaking,
For a moment I thought I was dead!
But there on the desk were the taxes,
All neatly done and in a stack.
I wasn't at the bottom of a mudhole,
So I could go back to sleep and relax.

Footprints

Grandpa and I were both named Bill,
And we have lived in the very same house
                        On the very same hill.

    100 Years have passed,
        But some things are still the same;
The old farmhouse still stands
        Just north of the lane.

The cobhouse still stands
        With its bin for cut wood,
Its jar room and small corner
        Where the separator stood.
And as I traverse the path
        From the house to the shed,
I know that here too,
        His bare feet have tread.

I know that he and his brothers
        Dug all of the holes,
Where they built the new barn,
        And set the red cedar poles.
The old schoolhouse floor
        Is the shed above the stalls,
And his Prince Albert cans
        Fill the squares in the walls.

As I drive across the fields,
    I can see in my mind,
Horses pulling a plow
    With Grandpa walking behind.
The check wire stretched tightly,
    Its buttons worn bright,
For the planter to follow
    And drop the seeds in just right.

I race back and forth
    Across the very same land,
That he walked, stooped over,
    As he did it by hand.
Our crops are the same,
    Only differ in scale;
And I feed with an auger,
    Not a shovel and pail.

I'm sure that it was never
    In his wildest dream
That he could pick 1000 bu. an hour
    With a shiny machine.
But he got it done
    And with far less expense,
For his cornpicker cost him
    Just fifteen cents.

Thur Apr 12

It had been a warm, sunny spring day in early April. We had a dozen calves on the ground, and they were all doing fine. The older ones were running around the trees and buildings of the empty farmstead with their tails in the air. Their mothers were running after them as if to make sure that "guy in the brown pickup" didn't pounce on them with another ear tag or a scour pill.

Those that were just a day or two old were lying off where Mom had placed them; and she would be eating hay with the rest of the herd until I got too close to her baby; and then she would come running.

Everyone looked like they would be all right until morning. A light rain started to fall, as I went back across the road to supper. The ten o'clock news said that the rain would turn to snow by morning, and the temperature would fall to freezing. I took the flashlight and checked the cows one more time before going to bed.

The next morning, we had had about an inch of rain, and it was snowing and blowing out of the northwest. The cows were all huddled up south of the old chicken house; their babies were standing among the entire herd, hunched up and shivering.

After I had accounted for all twelve calves, I noticed #51 cow heading off through the mud towards the old hay rake. I followed her, and just as I feared, her new baby was laying flat on his side in the cold mud. He had flopped in under the side delivery where she couldn't get to him, but was still alive. The low pressure area that had brought the rain and snow had also triggered his birth. I'm sure he didn't think much of his new home.

His mama would normally chase me away, but she just watched as if asking for help, as I pulled him from beneath the rake and lifted his head out of the mud. His body temperature had fallen, and he didn't have a lot of time. With his hair plastered full of mud, he was more than I could carry; so I propped him against the post pile and headed home for something.

I didn't think the pickup would make it through the mud so I took the 7000 Ford tractor back to where he was laying. Adrenaline was all that got his muddy limp body up onto the tractor and across my lap. I knew a bathtub full of warm water was all that would save this guy, so we headed for the house.

This wasn't the first time this had happened, so Karen had papers on the floor and the water running, as I wrestled my baby into the bathroom and into the tub (it sure was easier before we put those darned shower doors on). I held his head out of the warm water and rubbed the mud out of his hair with my other hand. It didn't take long until he shook his head and said something, I don't know what, but it was a welcome sign.

We got him warmed up and dried off, but now he needed some colostrum. I knew where there was some but that's a whole 'nother story. I got my lariat and pop bottle and headed back across the road.

Later that afternoon, I smiled to myself as I patted him on the head. Then I got the next ear tag out of the package and hung #13 in his right ear.

Our Wishbook

What happens shouldn't surprise us,
As we open up our shores.
Sears Roebuck just announced
That they'll close their catalog stores.

It wasn't just a catalog,
No, it was so much more.
Within its covers was contained
A whole new world to explore.

Mom and Dad would order some things,
But only if they were needed real bad.
Then we could thumb through the pages,
And see what the city folks had.

We could have whatever we wanted
Even if, but only in our heads.
New clothes - a doll - a rifle,
Bicycles or maybe shiny new sleds.

We would take our turns,
Cause we knew we had to share it.
Dad would get real mad,
If we would fight and pull and tear it.

There were no coupons, no rebates.
Nothing was on sale.
We simply filled out an order - check enclosed,
Then dropped it in the mail.

It was the center of attraction.
Then its popularity would wane,
But only if we were certain
That the shiny new one came.

Then it was retired
To the little house behind,
Where we re-read each page carefully,
For the very last time.

Saturday Nights At The Acova

The Acova Ballroom, I miss it so! Good music, good visits with friendly people, good food, and really good times! People from miles around would come to Avoca almost every Saturday night for a dance at The Acova (Avoca spelled backwards) from 9 p.m. to 1 a.m.

As you came in the west door of the big white wooden dance hall, you'd see the natural wood colored open rafters of the high arched ceiling, and walls of the same color all around. A coat room and lunch counter were on the right, down the west wall; a row of booths were straight ahead along the north wall. The band stand was across the dance floor, in the middle of the east wall; tables and chairs were all along the south. It wasn't fancy, no interior decorator's dream; but some dreams were born here, and many memories were made here, as "good times" came in the form of dancing, here at the Acova.

The "regulars" of the Acova would come as early as 7 or 7:30 p.m. to get their "favorite tables," especially on nights when a big crowd was expected for one of the most popular bands.

Some of these bands were "Eddie Skeets," "The Six Fat Dutchmen," "Whoopie John," "United," and "Earl Russell." The music ranged from polkas and waltzes, to modern like two-steps and jitterbugs, with a few more unusual thrown in now and then for fun, like "The Flying Dutchmen," shottish, or the "Chicken Dance."

Sometimes the fun loving crowds were so large that extra tables and chairs spewed onto the dance floor, ironically taking up the area that offered the best time to be had by all!

And everybody usually did have a good time, even the band, as they played their hearts out, enthused by the exuberance of the crowd. Why, Eddie Skeets even traditionally brought birthday cake for the whole crowd to celebrate his March birthday with the people. On a night when the people were in an especially good mood and the spirit of the band was mutual, the band could be cheered and cajoled into playing beyond their 1 a.m. quitting time, to prolong the fun for all.

At about 11 p.m. the band would take an intermission, and many people would head out to their cars ... to bring in their lunch stuff. Sandwiches, cookies and cake, crackers and chips, and nuts were set out and pooled among small groups who always sat together. If you'd come alone or hadn't brought lunch, someone would invite you to share theirs (or there was a lunch counter). The local news and gossip, and problems of national and world affairs were bantered about between mouthfuls, with jokes and laughs a plenty too.

After twenty minutes or so, the band leader would announce the next dance, the chairs would be pushed back from the tables, and once again people would pour onto the dance floor. He'd often start with a selection of a little slower pace until everyone's lunch got settled ... I can hear him yet, "First couple down center and there you divide; the gents to the left; the ladies to the other side; now honor your partners and don't be afraid; to spin your corner lady in the waltz promenade!"

After this waltz quadrille, there'd be more polkas and moderns, and then maybe a circle two-step: The band leader would call, "All join hands and form two big circles on the dance floor; ladies on the inside, gents on the outside." With the music the ladies would circle left and the gents right; and like musical chairs, when the leader gave the call, you danced with whoever grabbed you, or whoever you could grab, before someone else did ...

Or you might get left out (which I often did, and I'd feel like a rejected fool having to make my way through the dancers to my table to sit down. Other's got left out too, but it didn't make me feel any less a fool). You see, in a circle two there were often more men than women, because you could start this dance without a partner, and this was a man's chance to dance with someone other than his wife, and his chance to steel a hug or rub close to some big bazooms. The set usually lasted long enough so you could get back in and try again, and so that you could have at least three or four different partners (some were good dancers, and some were not). And a circle could be a woman's chance to get to dance with someone she had been dreaming about ... and that could lead to future "memories" at the Acova Ballroom.

***

Making Memories At The Acova

Since we were about ten or twelve years old, my sister and I had been coming with our folks to the Acova on Saturday nights. We'd sit in the booths with eight or ten young people our ages (who also came with their parents) and we'd talk and laugh, and watch people; and we learned how to dance.

It was here in these booths, one late summer evening in 1965, that I was sitting with friends when I saw a good looking guy come in the door ... after that night when I'd go to the dances with my folks, I'd still sit in the booth with my friends; but now, I spent more time concentrating on who came in the door.

I'm not sure he knew I was alive yet; but some Saturday nights later, the kids I was sitting with took it upon themselves to stand up when he came in the door, and all motion, and point at me until they got his attention; and then they hollered at him, "She wants to dance with you!"

It was so embarrassing! But eventually as I continued to come to the dances, he asked me to dance more and more; and then asked to take me home one night.

My dad said no; and at another dance he asked again, and Dad said, "NO" again. The third time Bill asked me, I went to ask my dad's permission, and he didn't answer me. I didn't give him much time to either — I just took it as a yes.

Well, I continued to see Bill at dances, and we had our first date the day after Christmas of 1965. After that I'd see him at dances; and once in a while he'd ask me out; and eventually we dated regularly. Our memories together started at the Acova where we met in 1965, and three years later we had our wedding dance there.

***

Section IV

Journal Journey

Journal Journey

For the twenty-four years we've been married, I've kept a journal. Usually, it's farm information that Bill invariably asks me about like: "When did we sell the calves last year?"; "When did we turn the bulls out to the cows?"; "What day did I plant corn on the cemetery field?"; "What year did we buy the chopper?" I also write what else of note has gone on for the day, be it news, or family affairs, or thoughts that have passed through my mind. Some days I've written a lot; some days only one or two words; and sometimes large blocks of days are blank (like when we've been busy and there's no time or inclination at day's end to write). For reasons unknown, I can't find my journals for the years 1968, 1969, and 1976.

Anyway, the journals are fun for us to look back through: to bring back memories, to see how our lives have progressed and to help us look ahead to the future.

I want to take you on a "Journal Journey" so you can see what it's like to look, listen, laugh, and survive on a farm in Iowa. (Or is this Heaven?)

The journal entries appear just as they were originally written, with some abbreviations & note-style incomplete sentences; and I've included added information in parenthesis. I won't bore you with every entry, just the indicative ones & best stories from 1968 to the present.

Abbreviations frequently used in the text:

    & . . . . . . and   lft. . . . . . . left
    A. . . . . . . acre   mtg. . . . . meeting
    B.D. . . . . birthday   N. . . . . . . north
    brd. . . . . . board   rt. . . . . . . right
    bu. . . . . . bushel   S. . . . . . . south
    ck. . . . . . . check   S.S. . . . . . Sunday School
    ck'd . . . . checked   sq. . . . . . . square
    E. . . . . . . east   W. . . . . . . west
    fert . . . . . fertilizer   wt. . . . . . weight
    hd. . . . . . head

1968

(I had quit at Iowa State University after spring of '67 & worked for a year in a feed company finance department. By then I knew I wanted to go back to college, & I went back to I.S.U. for summer sessions in June 1968. Later in June, Bill gave me an engagement ring, & we eventually set our wedding date for November 30th that same year. [We picked that date because Bill would be done with harvest by then.]

I didn't go back for fall quarter because I knew I was marrying a farmer, & thought a textiles and design degree wouldn't do me much good in western Iowa. [Not finishing college would become the biggest regret of my life. I'd still like to go back — there is just so much more I want to learn — so much more I feel I could do.]

Anyway, In late July of 1968 a farm house [owned by Leonard Peters] a half mile north of Bill's folks' came up for rent; & Bill rented it to hold it until when we'd be married. Throughout the fall, I worked as a waitress near my home at Atlantic; & in my spare time I painted rooms in our home-to-be, & cleaned & fixed. I also sewed my wedding dress, my three bridesmaids' dresses, & flower girl's dress.

We were married November 30,1968 at an afternoon church service in Atlantic, & had a wedding dance at the Acova Ballroom in Avoca, where Bill & I had met in 1965.)

Bill's friends intended to fill our car with ground corn cobs & coat the outside with molasses & more ground cobs, but we happened upon the stash prior to the dance & disposed of it. They resorted to stuffing our car with straw, coating the outside with syrup & straw, & dumping a whole can of black pepper down in the defroster.

After the dance & everyone had gone their merry ways, we changed out of our wedding clothes, cleaned the straw out of the car, & washed it; but we couldn't get at the pepper.

It was 4:30 a.m. before we left Avoca & headed south for our honeymoon. We were so tired we drove only as far as Carson & stayed our first night in a nice motel, for $6.

The next day we continued our cold trip through Missouri, Arkansas, Tennessee, Kentucky, & Illinois. You see, we couldn't turn on the heater or defroster because if we did, the pepper flew out & gagged us, made our eyes water, & caused us sneezing fits!

Finally we made it back to Iowa & reality & began our new life together in our white house on the farm.)

1969

(My journal for this year is missing but we sold hogs for $20 cwt in Jan. and $27 in Aug. In Dec. we bought a 1917 Model T Ford touring car from an elderly neighbor, John Dau.)

1970

Thu.1-01: Went to Gary & Betty's (Bill's sister's in Elk Horn for the annual Johnson family New Year's get together for dinner & supper).

Tue.1-20: Sorted hogs & sent load to Harlan, $28.50 cwt.

Wed.1-21: 20° Below Zero this a.m.

Thu.1-29: 3 sows got electrocuted in crib (a corn crib we converted to a twelve stall farrowing house).

Sat.1-31: My mom & dad had a 25th ann. dance in Avoca.

Mon.2-02: Went to Dr. weighed 135 lbs. (Started at 123.)

Thu.3-19: Got crib, mattress, & dresser. I was sewing curtains.

Fri.3-20: Dad called to say crocuses were up & blooming.

Tue.3-24: Had to pull the first calf (of the year) & he was dead.

Wed.3-25: Bill got up at 1 a.m. & 6:30 a.m. to ck. a cow. She had a heifer. We did chores & went to get a replacement calf (for 1st cow).

Thu.4-02: Went to Dr. Weighed 141 lbs.

Sun.4-05: Helen (Bill's mom) rode a sow & hurt her heel & knee. (We were chasing sows & one ran under her & she literally rode on its back with her feet in the air until she was cast off on the ground).

Wed.4-08: New tractor came (a model 8000 Ford).

Fri.4-11: Guys burnt off milo fields. ("The guys": Bill, his brother Duane, and their dad, Walter, used to do this to get rid of the trash on the field before it was time to disk the field for a new crop.)

Sat.4-11: I started to rake yard about 7 a.m. (About 11 a.m. I set fire to a pile of leaves in the road ditch east of our house yard. The fire immediately whooshed up the ditch toward the yard! I tried to stomp it out, but to no avail.

I ran to get the coaster wagon and a cream can full of water. Being seven months pregnant, I was hurrying as fast as I could, but I just wasn't moving as fast as the fire, & my can of water was no answer: I had to go get Bill!

I jumped in the car & raced to the field where Bill was putting on anhydrous, about a mile & a quarter away. Frantically I waved him down; & he jumped in the car to speed us home. As we approached the last hill that blocked the view of our place, smoke was everywhere! Bill thought surely I'd set the whole farm on fire!

He told me to call the fire department. Babbitts [neighbors] happened by & helped stomp, & spade dirt, & beat out the fire. It burned up toward the grove & up the back of a machine shed before we & the fire department got it all out ... Not a good experience at all!

Later I finished a baby quilt & took lunch to Bill in the field. Around 9 p.m. rain was coming, so I went to the field to find Bill & bring him home. We rounded up cows & calves, sorted off some who were closest to calving, & penned them in so they'd be out of the rain. It was 11 p.m. before we got in for supper ... Two of the cows did have calves between 3 and 4 a.m ... This was quite a day!)

Sun.4-12: Got up 8 a.m. I was kind of stiff.

Thu.4-16: Bill started plowing & plowed til after midnight.

Mon.4-20: Sewed baby gown. Varnished chest of drawers. Cut out yellow robe.

Tue.4-21: Guys in field. Bill came for supper about 2 a.m. Rained.

Sat.4-25: First 2 daffodils open this a.m.

Mon.5-04: Bill started planting (corn).

Tue.5-26: Finished painting ceiling in baby's room. Planted zinnias, marigolds, & petunias.

Thu.5-28: Saw Doctor. He said I could go anytime.

Sun.5-31: Went to Herman Woltmann's funeral. (Bill's best friend's dad.)

Thu.6-11: Went to doctor. He said I could go just anytime.

Sat.6-13: 4:30 a.m. my water broke. Spent day getting stuff ready for when I'd leave. 10:30 p.m. left for hospital.

Sun.6-14: Our first son, Alan William, was born at 8:48 a.m. (7 lbs. 3 oz. & 20" long.)

Wed.6-17: Rained all morning. Dr. said we could go home. Bill came to get us.

Sun.6-21: Father's Day. We went to Bill's folks' — first time Alan & I were out since we got home.

Tue.7-7: They oiled the road past here. Alan & I went to the doctor. Alan weighed 9 lbs. 6 oz. & Dr. said Alan could start cereal and cow's milk.

Sun.7-19: We drove our 1917 Model T Ford in the Shelby Centennial parade.

Mon.7-20: Bill shaved off his centennial beard.

Tue.7-28: Alan weighed 12 lbs. Dr. said he could start fruits, soups, & custards. Alan had his first DPT & first peaches.

Mon.8-17: Alan started vegetables: carrots.

Tue.8-25: Sold sows in Omaha $16.50/cwt. Went to state fair. Alan stayed with his Grandma Johnson.

Thu.9-03: Got my new Singer sewing machine: $211.20.

Tue.9-14: Bill helped John Dau ring hogs.

Sun.9-20: Went to my folks' for big family dinner for Calvin (my brother from San Diego, Calif.).

Sun.9-27: Bill combined first corn. I cleaned 6 stalls in the crib.

Mon.9-28: We sold 67 hogs for $19.50/cwt.

Tue.9-29: Helped Bill get cows out of the milo field.

Thu.10-01: Bill's combine transmission went out.

Mon.10-19: Alan got smallpox shot. Got him a walker.

Wed.10-28: Walt had surgery at Mercy in Council. (Had his gallbladder removed, I think.)

Wed.11-11: Snowing.

Sat.11-14: Alan's 5 mos. old, 19 lbs., 25 3/4" tall.

Thu.11-26: Went to Betty & Gary's for Johnson Thanksgiving. (Bob & Delores [Bill's sister in Atlantic] usually have it, but Bob's mom's funeral was yesterday [Pearl Bebensee].)

Tue.12-01: (Bill & Duane still combining: they do custom combining together, each with their own machines.) Alan's first two bottom teeth started to poke through. Went to folk's for Dad's birthday.

Wed.12-02: Bill sold hogs for $16/cwt.

Mon.12-07: Brought combines home. Bill & Duane went collecting (for custom combining bills).

Mon.12-14: Icy. Alan & I were going over home but ran (the car) off the road down by Andersen's ("T" intersection). (We weren't hurt, nor was the car, but we did tear out some of our fence as we drove through it. I called home from Andersen's; Bill came to drive the car out of the field [he was not happy]; & I was scared to drive anymore on the ice so stayed home and helped his mom clean for club.)

Fri.12-18: Icy. Bill drove us to Harlan & Alan got his first polio vaccine.

Wed.12-23: Calvin & Roseanna (from Calif.) here for dinner. Cal helped

Bill cut (castrate) a couple hundred pigs.

Fri.12-25: Went to Bill's folks' (for Christmas dinner, supper & gifts).

Sat.12-26: Cleaned & fixed. Had a party: Jo & Duane, Marlin & Darlene, Ronnie & Kay, Doug & Cheryl. Went to bed 2:30 a.m. or so.

Sun.12-27: Slept late. Cleaned 2 hog houses & platforms. Visited & played cards at (Bill's) folks'.

Mon.12-28: Chased cows & calves up & weaned calves. Alan had fever 101.4°

1971

Sat.1-02: Took Alan to Dr. He got a shot & medicine. Bill helped Jo & Duane move. (They moved from a home in Avoca to a farm on the next road east of us.) Started to snow at choretime.

Sun.1-03: Got over 10" of snow in the night. It snowed & blowed all day.

Mon.1-04: No milkman & no mail. Huge snowdrifts in the yard.

Tue.1-05: 10° Below (zero) this a.m. No school anywhere, even at U. of I. or I.S.U.

Mon.1-26: Sorted hogs. Sold 87 @ 226 lbs. @ $17/cwt.

Tue.2-02: I washed (did laundry). (Went to) club at Dorothy's. Had to help Bill clean crates & give pigs iron.

Sat.2-13: We sprayed cattleshed. Moved all the pigs from crib & 2 houses. Went to Valentines Dance.

Sun.2-14: Cleaned crib & little houses. Went to Duane's for Lori's birthday.

Tue.2-16: Alan got 2nd polio (vaccine).

Mon.3-15: Cut pigs in cattleshed. I washed. Went to Pork Producers Banquet.

Wed.3-24: First calf (of the season) black.

Fri.3-26: Bill sold calves at salebarn $34.10/cwt.

Wed.4-07: Walt disked. Bill put on dry fertilizer.

Thu.4-08: Vet came and sewed up #46: pro-lapse. Bill put on fert.

Fri.4-09: Pulled calf of #46.

Sat.4-10: Washed. I did chores. Bill plowed late.

Wed.4-27: Went to John Dau's funeral.

Sat.5-01: Rained some. Alan & I went to Mom's. I got my hair cut & set (in town) (which is very rare for me, as I have cut my own hair since I was in high school). Went to dance in Minden. Had fun.

Sun.5-02: Bill & Duane rung sows & vaccinated them. Went to Brix's for wiener roast.

Mon.5-03: 5 new red calves now in lot. Let sows in pasture. Mowed all the yard today. Bill moved barn & chicken house pigs to Bud's.

Wed.5-05: Bill planted corn at Bud's (Allen Scheel).

Mon.5-17: Bill finished planting all but 17 acres of milo. Broke another wheel bolt.

Tue.5-18: Sold hogs 79 @ 241 lbs @ $17.75/cwt.

Wed.5-19: Helped clean crib this a.m., washed after dinner, went to Avoca, went mushroom hunting with Al & Bill.

Wed.8-25: Went to (Iowa) state fair.

Fri.8-27: Bill burned trees by creek. Went to Squealer Feeds for dinner. Went shopping at new Gibsons store in Harlan. I started to paint Al's bedroom.

Mon.9-06: (Labor Day) Ned Paulsen came to cut silage.

Tue.9-07: (Worked filling silo.) Fixed 9 qts. pear butter (Bill loves it).

Wed.9-15: Bill went to get new combine.

Wed.9-29: Blew like crazy. Hog house flipped over out north.

Sun.10-03: Bill & Duane combining.

Mon.10-04: Fixed fence til noon. Cleaned house for club.

Tue.10-05: Happy Dozen Club here, 12 (ladies) & 4 kids.

Wed.10-06 Combined milo up home. I hauled in all day.

Tue.10-26: Helen had her gallbladder taken out.

Wed.10-27: Gina born (Bill's brother Charlie's girl).

Thu.10-28: Sis was home (from Ames), but I had to haul in milo. Alan was at La Vere's (baby-sitter/neighbor).

Sun.12-26: Bill & Walt chased cows home.

Mon.12-27: Weaned calves.

Fri.12-31: (Went to New Year's Eve) Party at Ronnie & Kay's.

1972

Sat.1-01: Dad called to wish us a Happy New Year. Dinner at Betty's.

Thu.1-06: Planted tomatoes & marigolds (inside in pots, of course ... must have cabin fever).

Mon.1-10: Al & I went to surprise come-as-you-are club at Connie Robinson's. (About noon, Alan & I were in the shower getting cleaned up to go to club. There was a knock at the front door [our front door is on a porch only about 3 ft. from our bathroom door]. Before I could even shut the shower off & collect my thoughts, Alan had slipped out of the tub, flung open the bathroom door, & answered the front door — in his birthday suit!

I didn't know how I was going to retrieve the child or talk to whoever was at the door, because I too was in my B.D. suit.

As I heard him open the outside door, a surprised female voice said, "Well, hello there ... Is your mommy home?"

Recognizing the voice, I answered her question, "Yes, I'm here, Connie, but I'm in the shower."

She broke out laughing and finally composed herself to reply, "Karen, You won't believe this but, I'm going around to surprise all the club ladies and tell you to come to club this afternoon dressed just as you are right now."

Well, it certainly was a "surprise"! ... and I couldn't hardly go to club "dressed" exactly as I was right then — but, I did go with my wet hair wrapped in a towel, & my bathrobe on.

Later, on my way home from club, in the cold & snow, I thought, "What would anyone have said if they'd have had to come help get me & my car out of a snowdrift.")

Thu.1-13: Got bedroom suite for Al for $75 (to prepare a new place for him so new baby could have his crib & room come June).

Fri.1-14: 14° Below Zero! Al onery as the dickens.

Sat.1-15: 12° Below Zero. Cold & windy. Two tomatoes up. Went to dance in Minden. Had fun.

Mon.1-17: Marigolds up. In 40's today. Painted upstairs.

Mon.1-24: Weather was terribly windy & cold — lots of schools closed. Helen & I both cancelled Drs. appointments.

Tues.1-25: Sorted hogs. $27.50/cwt. Bill & Helen took taxes to lawyer. Went to feed company supper in Harlan—delicious.

Wed.1-26: Washed. Went to Case fish fry at noon. Alan won a (toy Black Knight) Case tractor: first name called for door prizes. Went to Duane's to play cards. Took ice cream stuff & used our new (crank ice cream) freezer for the first time.

Sat.2-05: Bill went to Omaha to get Ford wheels. Went to Valentines Supper Dance in Avoca. Had swell time.

Wed.2-16: Waxed Al's room. Put (area size) carpet down. Painted wall in bathroom 2nd coat. Painted some woodwork upstairs.

Sat.2-19: (My sister) Sherry's shower. Got lovely gifts. We got her wedding dress material. I started to sew on it.

Sat.2-26: Sis's wedding. Got up 5:20 a.m. (to chore & get over to my folks' to pick them up & go to Iowa City for the wedding). Sis had nice wedding. (We got back to folks 8 p.m. & came on home to do chores).

Fri.3-10: Baked cookies for church bake sale. Went up to clean in the shop. Had late dinner & Bill went to salebarn. Finished putting wrenches & tools away in shop after dark.

Mon.3-20: (First day of spring.) Sorted hogs from barn & cattleshed. Sold 80.

Tue.3-21: First calves (born). One nice little black baby–black mom. One dead black/white face red mom.

Tue.3-28: Made jello for church deal. Painted Upstairs. Al painted too! ICK! Didn't go serve at church. Went to benefit supper for Everette (my Dad's brother who has cancer) in Marne. 500 + there.

Sun.4-02: (Easter) (Twin calves born) Johnson gang and my folks here for dinner & supper.

Wed.4-05: Fixed fence up home all day. Bill disked at Bud's until about 10 p.m.

Thu.4-06: Seeded oats

Mon.4-10: Vet came for little twin calf. Bill had to pull a cow out who was stuck in the creek, but she (later) died. He put on anhydrous.

Wed.4-12: Little twin died. Bill put on anhydrous & then put on the plow.

Thu.4-13: Bill ran over a fork & had a flat tire on the new Ford (tractor).

Sat.4-29: Rained. Moved cows with calves from here to pasture. Sold hogs. Went bowling in Atlantic with Brixs, Duanes, Marlins, and Garys. Had fun.

Tue.5-02: Went to Mom's surprise birthday supper. 34 there.

Fri.5-05: Lost one here today (calf died). 30 (calves) here now. Bill started planting corn. I planted sweet peas & geraniums.

Thu.5-18: 141 lbs. Dr. said it sounded like a boy. Bill finished planting beans at Bud's & two wet spots of corn — All Done!!

Fri.5-26: Bill bought 115 feeder pigs at salebarn. Got 3" of rain in afternoon & evening. Hailed a little too.

Sat.6-03: Bill sprayed (weeds). Replanted corn here at our place.

Thu.6-08: 139 1/2 lbs. Saw Dr. Said I should go by the 15th.

Wed.6-14: Folks came for dinner for Al's birthday.

Wed.6-21: Went to hospital about 12:30 a.m. Helen came to stay with Alan.

Thu.6-22: Bill went home (from the hospital) about 10 a.m. Betty came to get Alan. Pains (contractions) quit about 3 p.m. Nothing all night.

Fri.6-22: Bill came to get me about 10 a.m. & we went to Elk Horn to get Alan. I slept after dinner. Bill went to salebarn.

Sat.6-24: Washed. Stomach hurts awful this afternoon.

Sun.6-25: Went to Johnson picnic. Sure got tired.

Wed.6-28: 7:39 a.m. Kristin Kay was born (7 lbs. 9 oz. 20")

Thu.6-29: Bill had a bouquet of flowers sent to me (the first & only ones I'd ever gotten from him ... they made me cry).

Sat.7-01: Helen came up (to the hospital) to get Kristin & I about 2:30 p.m. Bill was making hay. Everything went O.K.

Sun.7-02: My folks came for dinner. Bill was cultivating. Alan came home shortly after 4 p.m.

Mon.7-03: Al took nap & woke up with a temperature.

Tue.7-04: Al still hot & sickly. It's his teeth. One top one trying to come through.

Sat.7-08: Washed. After dinner, I started hemorrhaging. Helen came down & we called the Dr. He ordered me some pills. Sis came to visit & stayed the night to help with the kids.

Sun.7-09: Plenty weak today. Helen & Jo were here, Jo brought dinner. My folks came & Dad helped Bill bale hay.

Mon.7-10: Better—just tired. Al went off to Bill's folks for the day. Bill mowed at Bud's. I added 1 oz. to Kristin's bottles to make 5 oz.

Tue.7-18: Kristin went for 3 wks. ck-up: 8 lbs. 12 oz.

Wed.7-19: Boys started combining.

Thu.7-27: First time I went to Harlan for groceries with both kids. Bill & Duane vaccinated pigs for erysipelas. Bill helped Duane put siding on.

Sat.7-29: I went over home. Mom kept kids & I went to Craze Daze (in Atlantic). Had swell time! Had sitter & went to tractor pull at Avoca fair.

Mon.7-31: Kris started cereal. She slept through the night all this week. Bill sorted old cows without calves.

Sat.8-05: Kris started fruit.

Sun.8-06: Bornholdt's came for picnic dinner. 20 here. Made ice cream. Raked a little hay & baled 3 racks. Came back from making hay 9:30 p.m. Kris started whole milk with evening bottle.

Tue.8-08: 6 wks. ck-up: Kris weighed 10 lbs. 6 oz. Bill went to Dunlap (salebarn) & got 20 sows & 20 black calves.

Wed.8-23: Sows started having pigs.

Sun.8-27: Loaded fat calves.

Sat.9-02: Bill came home with sales slip at noon for new color TV. It came about 5 p.m.

Sun.9-10: Rain

Mon.9-11: Flooding in Harlan & Avoca. Schools closed.

Tue.9-12: Rain. Flooding yet. We drove around in Avoca (to see the damage). Wind 5 p.m.

Sat.9-16: 3 or 3:30 a.m. Hailed. It broke open most of my watermelons. I cleaned all day for Sun.

Sun.9-17: Had Kristin baptized. Betty & Gary (her sponsors) and my folks were here for dinner.

Thu.9-21: Finished making hay. Served at church supper.

Fri.9-22: Bill & Duane started combining Manz's beans.

Sun.9-24: Cows in the corn. We fixed up silage wagons. Bill & Duane combined at Earl Sievers'.

Wed.9-27: Started cutting silage.

Tue.10-10: My folks came over & brought Bill an (antique) icebox (for his birthday). (Later, I refinished it.) Bill was combining at Sonny Weise's.

Sat.10-14: Bill & Duane combined at Keith Allen's. Went to fireman's dance in Avoca.

Thu.10-26: Bill & Duane doing corn by cemetery. Folks went to Belleville, Kan., to get cylinder bars. Bill decided to trade for new combine.

Tue.10-31: We took Alan trick or treating in Avoca & then over home. He had a swell time.

Thu.11-09: Boys were combining at Jerry's. Got combine stuck about noon. Broke a tie rod on a wagon so I went to Elk Horn for that.

Sat.11-11: Bill & Duane went to Fort Dodge & got new Bobcat loader.

Tue.11-14: Snow storm. Most schools got out at noon.

Thu.11-16: Weaned calves.

Sat.11-18: Left home at 6 a.m. to go over & go to Ames with my folks. Sis graduated from ISU. (Interior Design Degree.)

Tue.11-28: Kris got her first tooth.

Fri.12-01: Hauled in corn.

Sat.12-02: Had sitter — hauled in corn at Bud's.

Mon.12-12: Went to town & got (Christmas) tree.

Sat.12-23: Took kids to bank in Avoca for pictures with Santa Claus.

Sun.12-24: Christmas Eve at (my) folks'. Their new 'fridge was delivered.

Sun.12-31: Bill finished corn on Minnie's — all done at home now. New Year's Eve dance in Minden. Had fun.

1973

Tue.1-02: Bill went to (Herb) Rock's to combine.

Fri.1-12: Sis home & we opened Xmas gifts.

Sat.1-13: (Bill's) folks & Garys left on vacation.

Sun.1-14: Bill & Duane put up electric fence around John's. Lost black calf in barn. Dad called to say Everette was pretty bad.

Sat.1-20: Duane finished down to Rock's. He helped Bill fill wagons at Bud's. Fire at (Gary) Damgaard's. (Our neighbors were remodeling a house to move into and it burnt down.)

Sat.1-27: Went down toward Brix's to sleigh riding party & got (car) stuck (in snow).

Sun.1-28: Dad called to say Everette had passed away at 8:30 a.m. (He was just 38 years old and had a wife & 6 kids.)

Sun.2-04: Bill ushered at church. Went up home for supper & cards.

Fri.2-09: Spent a.m. thawing out the combine. Bill went to salebarn.

Sat.2-10: Bill combined 33 A. corn for Bernard Klindt. Went to Corley to Six Fat Dutchmen. Huge mob.

Tue.2-20: Bill combined. I did chores.

Wed.2-21: Bill finished up combining for Bernard Klindt.

Mon.2-26: Bill combined down to Leonard's.

Sun.3-04: Kris first stood up in her bed (crib).

Tue.3-13: Didn't go to club. Helped Bill all day. Ford was stuck. Wagon of corn stuck. Mixer stuck. Super muddy!

Wed.3-14: Moved 8 sows & pigs to Bud's. Moved gilts up home.

Thu.3-15: First calf, dusty red.

Wed.3-21: Kids & I went over home for Ford parts. Bill combined at Leonard's & Bud's. Duane in beans.

Fri.4-06: Bill combined at Bud Hamdorf's. Pulled calf about 2:30 p.m.

Sat.4-07: Started disking. Put on fertilizer.

Sun.4-08: Snowed all day. 2 new yellow calves. Pulled one.

Mon.4-09: Blizzard. No school most places.

Sat.4-14: Seeded oats out N. & on W. 80. Pulled a calf before dinner.

Mon.4-16: Snowed in night. Vet pulled huge calf. He died. Got 2 (replacement) calves.

Sun.4-22: (Easter) at Jo & Duane's. Walt & Bill plowed.

Mon.4-30: Sorted cows & calves & took 20 cows with calves to pasture.

Thu.5-03: Dad helped Bill cut 200+ pigs.

Fri.5-04: I washed, mowed etc. Walt got stuck plowing at Bud's. Bill stayed out til 3 a.m. plowing.

Sat.5-05: Rain. Sis was home so kids & I went to visit.

Mon.5-14: Kris walking pretty good this week.

Wed.5-16: Planted 20 tomatoes, broccoli, peppers, parsley, peas, & lettuce. Bill started on beans on Bud's.

Thu.5-17: Took Kris' bottle away.

Mon.5-28: Took kids to Betty's. Went to hospital.

Tue.5-29: (I had surgery to have a Baker's cyst removed behind my left knee.)

Thu.5-31: Helen came to hospital to get me.

Fri.6-01: Walt went to hospital (ulcer). Bill spraying corn.

Mon.6-04: Picked up kids & Julie (niece) came along to help with kids.

Wed.6-06: Brought pigs down & put out N. Duane here for dinner. Moved cows with calves from here to pasture. Washed.

Fri.6-08: Got the last of my stitches out.

Sat.6-09: Made hay after dinner. Walt came home. Went to dance in Minden. Julie went home.

Sun.6-10: Hay guys here for dinner. Finished by lunch time.

Thu.6-14: Bornholdt's here for Al's birthday.

Thu.6-28: Folks came for supper for Kris' birthday.

Mon.7-02: Rain. (My) folks came over & we went to the zoo.

Tue.7-17: Boars to sows. 26 sows here.

Thu.9-30: Leonard came up to tell us we have to move (his son will be moving here).

Mon.10-29: 14 Sows to boars at Bud's. Put corn head on. Put 148 pigs in cattleshed from cow barn & crib.

Sun.10-23: Took combine to fairgrounds shed at Avoca (to store it for winter). Over to folks' for Christmas gifts.

Tue.12-25: Jo's for Christmas dinner.

Sat.12-29: Jo & Duane helped us round up cows & calves & we weaned calves.

Mon.12-31: Had sitter after dinner & cleaned in crib. Picked up Jo & Duane & went to dance in Minden.

1974

Tue.1-01: Went to Betty & Gary's for dinner.

Wed.1-02: Radiator in pickup froze up. Burnt belts off grinder. While kids were napping, I finished cleaning farrowing house. Took Christmas tree down.

Thu.1-03: Went to see (Bill's) folks' new house & have a pizza with them. (Since we have to move, they decided to retire & move to Shelby; & we'll move to the home place.)

Sun.1-06: Auctioneers came to list folks' stuff (for household sale of items from their farm home). (They treated themselves to new furnishings for their new town home. You see, as it goes on the farm, machinery, livestock, & other expenses always come first; so Helen hadn't had new furniture or curtains & such for years. She was like a kid turned loose in a toy store, as she picked out items for their new home. I was so tickled for her, for both of them; & was glad they seemed happy with their new home, because I felt awkward & uneasy about moving in to a place that had been their family home for over thirty years.)

Wed.1-09: Cleaned out my big cupboard & started packing.

Sun.2-03: (My) folks came for dinner. Dad & Bill went to Elk Horn for wallboard & cupboards. (Gary & Betty own the lumberyard there.) Gary & Bill put up new (kitchen) ceiling (at our future home). (We did a little re-doing before we moved in — this really made me feel uneasy because Helen would have loved to do this while she lived here — She had been a good mother, & a hard working farmwife, & certainly would have deserved it. Helen did her best to make me feel at ease & wasn't the least bit resentful; for she was a dear, sweet person, & the best mother-in-law a girl could ask for.)

Mon.2-04: I plastered all day. Alan & Bill went to his folks' to figure taxes.

Tue.2-05: To Harlan for paint & wallpaper. Bill & Walt went to the lawyer. Kids & I went to club. We painted porch & plastered until 11:30 p.m.

Thu.2-28: We moved. (Family & friends helped.) (We only moved a half mile down the road, but everything still had to be boxed up & hauled & then wait to find its new spot in another home.)

Fri.3-01: Al was outside blowing bubbles (with a bubble maker & bubble soap) right after breakfast.

Sun.3-10: Greeters at church. Dinner at Bill's folks'.

Wed.3-13: Bill went to Harlan with his dad about land (We owned, or were buying, part of the farm that was a bare 120 acres & Walt & Helen owned the 80 with the house & buildings ... [Upon their retirement, we had split our farming partnership with them & bought their half of the livestock & machinery.] Now they had decided we should also switch deeds with them so we'd be free to fix & care for the house & buildings as we saw fit, & we'd rent their farm acres & continue to farm all the ground.) ... Got nine gilts. Fixed track on crawler. Pulled rest of fence out down home. Bill went to Rocky Mountain oyster fry.

Sun.3-17: First two new gilts had pigs. Painted bathroom ceiling & did sewing room ceiling.

Tue.3-19: Bill spread fertilizer at Bud's. I took out fence there all afternoon.

Wed.3-20: Snowing. Bill hurried to finish spreading load of dry fertilizer.

Thu.3-28: Foggy. Red cow had yellow baby die in creek. Had 2 cows cleaned by vet. Cylinder bars came. Kids & I went to Harlan.

Thu.4-11: Rained. Cattle out at Laubert's & up N. Ran in rain for couple hours after them.

Fri.4-12: Bought 16 cows & calves at salebarn.

Fri.4-19: Counted 120 cattle out west.

Sun.4-21: Finished plowing. Plowed garden. Took off plow. Went to see *The Way We Were* with Bec & Wayne (Jacobsen).

Sun.5-05: Had a picnic.

Sun.5-12: Went to Circus in Des Moines with Mom & Dad. Went to Bill's folks' in evening.

Fri.5-17: Took sows to Bud's. Brought 2 loads home. It hailed at chore time.

Fri.5-24: Got beagle puppy. Kids called him "Beagle."

Fri.6-21: We went to airport with Mom & Dad to get Cal & Roseanna.

Sun.6-23: 45 here for picnic dinner to see Calvin's & Sis'.

Sun.6-30: Johnson (family reunion) picnic.

Thu.7-04: Finished (making) haylage. Went to Bec & Wayne's for supper.

Sat.7-06: Neighbor lost the back wheel on his tractor (while going down the road). (The wheel ran off the road, bounced clean over the fence and out into a corn field so you couldn't even see where it landed. It really surprised him when his tractor came to a halt in a heap on the road, but he wasn't hurt.) Went to see *American Graffiti* (a movie).

Sun.7-07: Made hay — alfalfa.

Thu.7-11: Bill went to combine. I got Kris' room all sanded — put first coat (of paint) on ceiling.

Thu.8-01: Took 42 sows to boars on Bud's. Brought 9 home. Put 153 pigs in cattleshed from crib.

Tue.8-06: Making hay.

Sun.8-18: Got out old car (1917 Model T Ford) & drove around some. Went up to see Walter in hospital.

Sun.8-25: Took Kris to Harlan to emergency room to have a piece of corn taken out of her nose. (Kids!) (Dr. Markham had a special little tool for just this purpose: he got the kernel of corn out & we went on to a picnic at Prairie Rose.)

Wed.8-28: (My) folks & (Dad's brother) Arlin came to help pour cement for east porch/patio & tore shingles off E. side of washhouse roof.

Sat.9-21: Started chopping corn (to fill a pit silo).

Tue.9-24: Boys (Bill & Duane) started combining beans at Earl Sievers'.

Sat.10-19: Guys at Herb Rock's (combining). Started stove in dining room for first time (this season). (We have a free standing old oil burner stove for heating.) I planted daffodils, tulips, and crocuses.

Tue.11-18: Finished last of our corn (in Grandma's field) 60 bu./A.

Wed.12-4, 5, & 6: Poured cement: for corral waterer, S. end of barn, W. cattle waterer, & (feeding platform) E. of barn.

Thu.12-12: Put new cement tanks on platforms. Put up last of corral planks & hung gates.

Sun.12-22: Christmas over home with Sherry's & folks — really nice day. Dad shipped cattle.

Mon.12-23: Worked cows. Weaned calves.

Tue.12-24: Moved 90 cows to Minnie's.

Thu.12-26: Cleaned crib. Weaned pigs. Took 22 sows to boars. Ground cobs (for crate bedding). Shot sows for Lepto.

Tue.12-31: Went to New Years Eve Dance in Minden.

1975

Wed.1-01: Went to Betty & Gary's for turkey dinner.

Sat.1-04: Sows & pigs in crib are all sick: TGE (we weaned all pigs & got a pig nurser, but despite all our efforts a lot of pigs died.)

Mon.1-06: Bill ground for cattleshed (hogs). I ground for (hogs & sows) in barn & grove. Took corn to Bud's (for sows & pigs).

Fri.1-10: Hurried to get chores done before bad snow started about noon. Blizzard. Schools all let out about noon.

Sat.1-11: Zero. Blizzard. We're completely snowed in. Silage wagon frozen. Crawler under a big drift. Threw 30 bales out N. to fat cattle & put it in the green chop wagon. No mail.

Sun.1-12: 5° Below Zero. Sunshine.

Mon.1-13: Snow plow finally went by. Mailman did too. We dug crawler out of the snow. Bill took pickup load of hogs to Omaha for Duane.

Wed.1-15: I cut Krissy's hair. Snowed all afternoon.

Sat.1-18: 3 ins. of snow.

Sun.1-19: We ground feed. Cold!

Tue.1-21: Did laundry. Helped outside all afternoon. Bill slid crawler in ditch. Cleaned red hog house, crib, cattleshed. Spread manure. Broke a key. Hole in crawler radiator. MF tractor started spewing power steering oil as we tried to feed silage. We used Case tractor (for evening feeding). Got straw.

Wed.1-22: Cold & windy. Bill went to Harlan to get radiator fixed. Got crawler fixed again. Fat hog dead on S. platform. Grinder broke. I patched coveralls.

Thu.1-23: (Worked on income tax figures.)

Sun.1-26: We worked on books for taxes.

Mon.1-27: (More tax work) to lawyer.

Sun.2-02: Calves got out over the fence out north (because of deep snow).

Tue.2-04: Snowed 5 or 6 inches in the night.

Sat.2-08: Snowed & blowed. Worked outside all day. Ground 4 batches feed. Took mixer of corn & oats to Bud's. Fed cows hay. Went to Boysen's dinner-dance (in Avoca).

Mon.2-17: Loaded out cattle.

Tue.2-18: Went to Omaha to see 14 cattle sell. Ate dinner at Johnny's.

Tue.3-04: Sold 76 hogs @ 210 lbs. @ $38/cwt.

Wed.3-05: Snowing. (All of us have bad colds.)

Mon.3-17: I stained Al's bedroom woodwork. Painted after dinner. Bill went to a sale.

Tue.3-18: Wallpapered in Al's room.

Sun.3-23: Slept late. 70° windy.

Mon.3-24: 20°. Blowing like crazy. Snowed in the night. Miserable weather. Schools were closing.

Thu.3-27: Stormy. Rain, ice, sleet. Blew our TV aerial off. Ground few batches feed.

Sun.3-30: Kids dyed their Easter eggs after they found their baskets of treats. Went to Duane's for dinner & supper.

Fri.4-04: Helped outside. 2 extra guys for dinner. Poured cement (in farrowing house to make floor slope to center for easier cleaning). I worked with cows & fed hay. Kids played outside.

Tue.4-08: Went to Omaha with Bill to an eye doctor. Bill had a collusion (a kind of growth) taken off of his eye ball.

Fri.4-17: Disked & harrowed after we seeded oats. Did a mess of chores and didn't get in until 9:30 p.m.

Fri.4-25: Waxed kitchen floor. Scraped paint outside. Raked off garden. Planted potatoes. Worked outside until 8 p.m. Bill got 94 pigs at the salebarn & took beans to town to be cleaned. He hurt his thumb in a V-belt at Bud's.

Mon.4-28: Outside all day (doing chores, etc.).

Wed.4-30: Outside all day choring. I ground for cattleshed (got super stuck). Ground 3 other batches feed. Bill hauled manure.

Sat.5-03: (Bill) put on anhydrous.

Sun.5-04: I hauled manure — fixed dinner — disked — chored — fixed supper for Duanes (they helped us haul manure).

Mon.5-05: Hauled manure all day. Jo helped after work. Bill disked until 1 a.m.

Tue.5-06: Hauled manure — rained some — didn't go to club. Bill went after seed & chemicals. Chored early & came in & slept.

Wed.5-07: Disked until 9:30 p.m. Had sitter. Bill planted cemetery field (a 45 A. field on our farm that has an old graveyard fenced off in one corner: Olsen Cemetery).

Thu.5-08 & 5-09: Disked.

Sat.5-10: I Disked. Bill finished planting corn at Bud's at 11 p.m.

Sun.5-11: (Mother's Day) Mowed yard. Planted strawberries, tomatoes, peppers. To Bill's folks' for supper.

Tue.5-13: I worked in garden all day. (My garden happened to be in the path of trucks, etc. that were doing dirt work for the sight of our new finishing house. Bill had disked it several times to take out their tracks & it was a complete clod patch! ... After working feverishly with spade & hoe to pulverize the clods, I got totally disgusted & got my trusty 310 Case crawler [like a small Caterpillar].)

    I tipped its loader bucket down; drove onto the garden from one side, toward the other side near a fence; carefully lowered the bucket to get just the clods & no dirt; & backed up the crawler, pulling the clods off the garden with my crawler's bucket. After doing this the length of the garden, I pushed the disgusting clods entirely away from my garden & proceeded to plant onions, peanuts, lettuce, peas, beans, pumpkins, carrots, limas, and cucumbers.) Bill disked & springtoothed at Bud's.

Wed.5-14: I did dishes, chores, laundry, & helped get planter ready. Bill started planting beans at Bud's.

Mon.5-26: (Memorial Day) Bill sprayed corn. Sprayed hogs while waiting for sprayer to fill. I did chores, laundry, & sewed a suit.

Mon.6-02: (Making haylage) I chored, fixed dinner for 2 extra, ground 2 batches feed, went to Bud's to get baler, fed sows, put battery fencer on down N, fixed lunch for men.

Tue.6-03: Bill & I turned over hay. (Bill) Babbitt came to chop at 10:30 a.m. till 3 p.m. I fixed dinner, packed in pit (silo), went after baler parts, fixed lunch, did chores. We baled 540 bales (small squares) & ground feed.

Wed.6-04: Cut thistles in pasture. Bill put cement tiles in creek & made bridge for cows.

Sat.6-07: I painted rest of S. side of house.

Sat. 6-14: Al's 5th birthday. Chored. Went to Harlan for materials to build a picnic table. Got a (toy) crane for Al. We built a plank picnic table. I started to clean (house).

Sun.6-15: (Father's Day) Picnic here (my side of family). Went to Bill's folks' about 8 p.m.

Mon.6-16: Bill cultivated. I stepped on a nail & went to Harlan for a tetanus shot.

Tue.6-17: I cut thistles, ground feed. Bill cult. beans.

Wed.6-18: Rained 2". I was tired all day. Chored, ground feed, hooked up (electric) fence along pasture.

Thu.6-19: Sorted pigs & castrated pigs. (Neighbor) Terry Hamdorf helped. Moved & sorted sows. Sold sows & hogs to Omaha.

Fri.6-20: Builders dug out the pit (for finishing house). Alan was sick all day— too many mulberries. I hoed in garden. Cattle were out when I went to chore. Bill cultivated.

Sun.6-22: Went to Marne Centennial Parade. Johnson gang here for supper for kids' birthdays.

Wed.6-25, 26, & 27: We drove (straight) truck to Hortonville, Wisc. to get new electric grinder & feed center for the new finishing house.

Sun.6-29: Took cows & calves from corral to S. creek. **Turned bulls out.**

Thu.7-03: I did dishes, laundry, walked beans (1 1/2 hrs.), fixed dinner, pushed haylage (in the pit) (Babbitt's chopping hay here), fixed lunch, did chores, quit 7:30 p.m.

Fri.7-04: Made hay until about 6:30 p.m. Went to Minden to watch fireworks.

Sun.7-06: We drove our Model T Ford in Minden's Centennial Parade.

Mon.7-07: Bill & Duane combined Kenny Osbahr's wheat.

Tue.7-08: (Bill custom baled straw & hay.) I mowed yard, chored, walked beans a while.

Wed.7-09: Bill worked on combine & cut alfalfa. I fed sows, chopped weeds, walked beans, chored, & picked peas & beans.

Sat.7-26: I got up 6 a.m. & went to Craze Daze with Sis. Alan & Bill went to tractor pull. We went to Pott. Co. fair.

Tue.8-12: We moved first pigs into the new finishing house! (a modified open front building with 18 pens, each 8' wide with roof-covered 20'-long eating/laying areas; plus open 20' sloped aprons to drain manure to an opening in a covered pit; nipple waterers next to the pit opening; a feed center with overhead protein bins, to drop protein into an electric grinder; a corn bin set to auger corn directly into the grinder; & a flex-core auger to take the feed automatically from the grinder to all 9 feeders. All this at the touch of a few buttons, & the system will even shut itself off when it gets the last feeder full). (We moved pigs from all of our old buildings over the next few days ... Now we wouldn't have to grind mixers of feed every day for fat hogs & get stuck in the mud. We wouldn't have to bed hogs & fork out manure by hand, and clean out stinking hog waterers when they get plugged up.)

Mon.8-25: Alan got on the bus at 7:35 a.m. (for his very first day of school), got home 12:20 p.m.

Fri.8-29: (Walt's been in the hospital a week.) Today he went to surgery at Jenny Ed. to have a kidney removed.

Sun.9-07: Worked outside all day. Took out 2 fences, burned brush pile & old dilapidated granary. Bill put up yd. light.

Sun.9-14: Started on first field of corn.

Wed.9-17: Sent pot load of hogs to Fremont. Worked on combine all morning — put in all new snapping rolls. Bill went to Herb's after dinner to shell.

Tue.10-07: Postponed club as we were busy.

Mon.10-13: Cleaned all day for club. Worked until midnight.

Tue.10-14: I had club, 7 here.

Wed.10-15: Boys were at Leonard's and Clarence's. They did 120 acres today. I started to move big round bales.

Fri.10-17: Boys were at Hamdorf's & Keith Allen's. I chored, hauled last big round bales home from Laubert's. Painted some on house after dinner. Ran to bank. Helped shuffle the boys' pickup. Planted 5 tulips. Dug 2 begonias.

Mon.11-03: Sold 129 hogs to Fremont. Man hauled 90,000 gal.: 58 loads of liquid manure from the hog house pit.

Tue.11-04: I disked in liquid manure. Went to club. Bill & Duane finished on John's.

Wed.11-05: Leonard, Dennis, & Duane helped round up cows & calves. Vet came to work them. I did chores, fixed dinner for 5 extra guys, did dishes, fixed men lunch, ground feed. Duane & Bill finished our last corn on cemetery field.

Wed.11-12: First snow.

Sun.11-30: (Our anniversary) I cleaned the farrowing house. Bill & Duane got 500 bales at Elk Horn. I got silage wagon stuck (feeding cattle).

Sat.12-13: (Went with Mom to take Dad to Omaha airport & he flew to Calif. to visit Calvin's.)

Mon.12-29: Took 41 hogs to Fremont. Stopped at Omaha Stockyards to get check from 14 hd. cattle on today's market.

Tue.12-30: (Had to have vet out to do a cesarean on a sow. We put two sows in. Got back in the house after midnight.)

1976

(My journal for this year is missing ... but I know that in Feb. we sold hogs for $51/cwt and 966 lb. heifers for $36.50/cwt. This year we sold 1,579 hogs & 104 fat cattle.

I got a dishwasher & it is one of the joys of my life. One of the most soothing, satisfying sounds I know is the sound of my dishwasher doing my dishes after I've crawled into bed at night, dead tired from a hard day on the farm.

Tractor gasoline was 50 cents a gallon. In May we bought a '75 Pontiac Catalina for $3803. We set out a 1/4 mi.-long windbreak of Scotch pines & honeysuckles along the N. of our farmstead.

That summer we made a very important decision ... in 1976 not much was known about the long-term side effects of taking "The Pill" for the entire span of a woman's reproductive years. I did a lot of reading & research on the subject.

Although I had been pleased with the pill's effectiveness in enabling us to plan our family, my research left me quite concerned about those "unknown" long-term health risks. I decided not to continue taking the pill.

I further decided that the best alternative for me was a tubal. After much discussion with Bill on the matter, we decided that before I'd have a tubal, we'd have one more child ...)

1977

Sat.1-01: Slept late. Ate late dinner. Did nothing. (Bill says we did, of course, do chores.)

Sun.1-09: It was 15° below zero, so we didn't go off to S.S.

Mon.1-10: Bill threw out 35 dead pigs out north this A.M. They piled up because of the cold.

Wed.1-12: Bad! Bad! Day! Corn auger on little bin plugged. Pipes in finishing house boiler room broke (pipes ran under the floor of all pens to carry heated water from the boiler, to keep the pen's floors warm & keep ice & snow melted off the apron). Bill worked until 8 p.m. fixing. It was starting to mist, so he took 3 wagons of protein over to machine shed at John's (nearly 2 miles away).

Thu.1-13: Got hog house boiler running. Sorted fat cattle. Bill took 2 loads (28) to Denison. I went to (adult ed.) drawing class at Atlantic High School. Got home 11 p.m.

Sun.1-16: 24° below zero! Extremely cold so we didn't go to S. School. Did some drawings for class. Bill wanted to go to his folk's, but it's 18° below zero so we stayed home.

Mon.1-17: 13° Below Zero.

Tue.1-18: Kids made sugar cookies.

Tue.1-25: Bill discovered pipes under the floor along the pit in the hog house had never been hooked up right. That's why the pipes froze.

Wed.1-27: Class cancelled. Freezing rain, snow, & wind.

Fri.1-28: No school because of drifted roads. -14°.

Sat.1-29: No water. Basement pipes frozen. Bill left faucet on down there & when water thawed, basement was a foot & a half deep with water.

Sun.1-30: Boiler blew pipe off.

Mon.1-31: On the way to my folk's (for their anniversary), we hit a coyote on the interstate. (Since he was worth money for fur) we stopped & picked him up & put him in the trunk of the car. At my folk's, as we were going to open the trunk to show him to Dad, we heard low growling. We had just knocked him cold & he'd come to! Bill reached in with a bar to kill him & we left him for Dad to market. He got $40 for him.

Thu.2-10: I went to Dr. (137).

Fri.2-11: Cattle out. Alan missed the bus.

Wed.2-16: Grandpa Marxen died (my mom's Dad).

Thu.2-17: (My brother flew home from Calif., & my sister & her family came from Iowa City. They were here until 2-20.)

Mon.2-21: No School (President's Day). Alan was up early & had me fix waffles for breakfast. He and Bill took soybeans to Shelby ($7 a bushel).

Tue.2-22: Bill bought 270 little pigs. (We had quit farrowing, & now used the crib & barn for nurseries, to get 20 lb. pigs up to 40 lb. so they could go out to the finisher.)

Thu.2-24: Sold 100 cattle. My last drawing class.

Sun.3-06: Went to Sun. School & church, Bill ushered.

Thu.3-10: I went to doctor. Bill hauled manure. Pulled 4 calves today. I raked yard.

Wed.3-16: We went to Al's school Science Fair.

Fri.3-25: Bill got up 6 a.m. & seeded oats before wind came up. I did laundry, went after a water pump for big Ford. Got fabric for Al's curtains. Bill put on dry fertilizer.

Mon.4-04 & 5: I ripped porch siding off, painted ceiling, & Dad & Bill closed in a door & put up paneling.

Sun.4-10: (Easter) Bill put on anhydrous out N. There were 22 of us here for dinner & 17 here for supper. (After the company left, Bill put on anhydrous again until 2 a.m).

Mon.4-11: We got up at 5:15 a.m. Bill put on anhydrous, & I chored & went after tanks. Bill quit at lunch time to go haul manure, but injector on tractor was leaking, so we went to Harlan for parts & to price a new tractor.

Tue.4-12: Bill chored & left at 7 a.m. with Duane to price tractors in Atlantic. Duane will get our 8000 and we'll get a new 9700 Ford (135 h.p.) ($28,100). Bill went to Atlantic again after dinner for an injector. On his first load of manure he blew a tire, and then blew another one.

Wed.4-13: 1/2" rain. Bill went to the bank & to deliver some seed corn. Kris & I went after groceries. I framed a row of chickens embroidery piece I had finished, & hung it up.

Tue.4-19: Rained. Bill went to Harlan for parts. I went to Kindergarten roundup for Kris. Bill is working on crawler.

Wed.4-20: Bill took calf to vet but it died. Bill hauled manure from cow yard—got it done 7:30 p.m. after some rain. I cut out a dress. Went to help wash windows & clean at church. Mowed yard for 1st time this year.

Tue.4-26: Got (corn) planter ready. Bill started planting.

Wed.4-27: Bill finished planting out N. about 4 p.m. New 9700 Ford came about noon. Bill is spraying now (9 p.m.).

Fri.4-29: Bill finished planting cemetery field at noon. Went to S. place (100 A. we farm 12 mi. SE of us) to start spraying. I moved corn, ground, filled corn wagon, mulched strawberries, fed cattle. Dropped in bed about 9 P.M.

Thu.5-05: Sunny today after yesterday's wind, rain, & hail. I have laundry, dishes, & cleaning to do. Pit man hauled 18 loads of liquid manure on alfalfa field. Had Dr.'s appt. after dinner. All is fine. Bill & Kris filled ditches in alfalfa field. Bill plowed at Kenny's until midnight.

Sun.5-08: Mother's Day. Rained 15/100 ths. Didn't get up until 10 a.m. Fed silage. Gave hay to new cows.

Tue.5-10: Kris & Alan both got on the bus (today this fall's kindergartners go to school for a trial run). Kris was home by 11:45 a.m. Bill started planting beans. Got done 8 p.m. & went to disk. I fixed pasture fence. Ran after parts & 6 more bu. beans. Chored. Went to school art fair about 8 p.m. Bill went to Kenny's to disk.

Sat.5-14: Bill hurried to S. place to hoe. Got whole field done & was home about 8:30 p.m. I chored, did laundry, & turned over hay on well field (Shelby Co. Rural Water's well field: 5 mi. from our place). Mopped all floors. Helped Terry get to baling. Went to eat at Walnut with Jo & Duane.

Wed.5-18: We left at 7 a.m. for Clay Center, Kansas, to get our new dump wagon (for chopping hay & corn into). We pulled it home behind the pickup & got here about 9:30 p.m. The kids went along. Nice weather for a long drive.

Mon.5-23: Bill cut hay on Laubert's.

Tue.5-24: Alan's last day of school (for the summer). We got started chopping 4 p.m. Worked until 9:30 p.m.

Fri.5-27: Bill was up at 6 a.m. to mow. Started chopping at 10 a.m. I chored, fixed dinner for men, & mowed yard. To wet to chop so Bill mowed hay.

Sat.5-28: Made haylage all day by wells. Guys quit about 4 p.m. to go bale Duane's. I chored, fixed dinner & lunch, chored, sewed a white top. We went to Shelby Alumni Banquet & then to dance in Avoca.

Mon.5-30: Memorial Day. I cut thistles by creek in a.m. Bill sprayed thistle patches at S. place. We napped after he came home. Did chores & went over home for supper. Made some homemade ice cream.

Tue.5-31: I cut thistles for another 3 hrs. We picked some mulberries. Bill was going to spend the day helping Duane move big bales.

Thu.6-02: I cleaned out feed center. Moved 2 loads corn (we often move corn from other grain bins to the finishing house bin, for automatic grinding). I went to Dr. & He thought it was a boy & would be a big baby. Bill left to start cutting Bob Brown's wheat. Kids & I picked up loose hay on Laubert's & chored. Picked Bill up at 9:30 p.m.

Fri.6-03: Bill left about 7 a.m. for Bob Brown's to chop wheat. I chored & mowed by evergreens with bush hog. Helped Bill put cultivator on & he started N. of creek.

Sat.6-04: Sold 75 hogs @ $42.75. Went to Atlantic after the check. Dropped kids at folk's to stay.

Mon.6-06: Up at 6 a.m. Bill mowed red clover. I chored. Cows got out when I got a stalk bale. Had to go get Bill. Ground feed. Started chopping before 10 a.m. Finished about 6:30 p.m. Drove to check S. corn, 10 p.m. when we got home.

Thu.6-09: I stained sewing room doorway & kitchen door & mop board (I had been refinishing downstairs woodwork). Bill chopped 10 A. of red clover at Ronnie's. I put polyurethane on woodwork I'd stained, & bathroom door.

Fri.6-10: We chopped oats after dinner. Duane & Dave helped. I packed until Duane finished mowing. No water from deep well. Lost some hogs out N.

Sat.6-11: Tried to pull a calf: took cow to Shelby for a cesarean. Kirby came to put new pump in deep well & new pressure tank. We ate dinner about 1:30 p.m. I cleaned up & went (over to my folks) to get the kids.

Tue.6-14: Alan's 7th birthday. He got a watch & school desk. We chored & Bill helped Duane pour cement. Bill came home at 5:30 p.m. & cult. hill out N. I did woodwork & fixed window.

Thu.6-16: Went to Dr.— lost a pound. Bill moved corn out N. We went to Bec & Wayne's — went to Parkway for supper.

Sat.6-18: I finished my dining room woodwork. We went to Verda Dinesen's sale (neighbor on Duane's road).

Sun.6-19: Father's Day. I painted dining room ceiling molding white. We put up tetherball stake. Slept until chore time. Went to Bill's folk's for supper. Cranked ice cream.

Tue.6-21: We loaded 102 hogs for Fremont. Rain 15/100ths. Kids & I went over home, & I went to town & bought diapers.

Wed.6-22: I painted the dining room ceiling & molding. Plastered cracks etc. Bill finished cult. one bean field. He started cleaning the little pit. We didn't go to bed until 1:30 a.m. We were listening to it rain.

Thu.6-23: We got 7/10ths rain. I went to Dr. Bill cleaned out the pit (silo). I cut out nightgowns for Kris & I & finished mine this evening. Bill went golfing. Started to rain lightly at 11 p.m.

Fri.6-24: Chored. Chopped oats on Laubert's. I took hog ck. to bank, got robe & gown material. Bill went after parts & bought 155 twenty lb. pigs at salebarn. I chored & guys came in for supper when they finished chopping.

Sat.6-25: Duane mowed on Laubert's. We chored. Unloaded new pigs in cattleshed. The county oiled the road. Duane here for dinner. Started chopping 2 p.m. I fixed guys lunch & went to count cows & fix fence. Did chores. Sewed a little. Guys came in for supper about 11 p.m.

Sun.6-26: We went to Johnson picnic. Came home 5 p.m. & Bill went to cut hay on Gronborg's. I fixed sprinklers in hog house, fed cattle, moved load of corn out N., sanded plaster places in dining room, cleaned up mess, then cut my hair, showered, took kids up to bed.

Tue.6-28: Krissy got a red 16" bicycle for her 5th birthday.

Wed.6-29: I finished papering dining room. Vet was out for hogs. Bill combined oats at Rock's. Duane at Sonny's & Woody's. Terry baled Gronborg's. I went with lunch at 7 p.m.

Thu.6-30: Bill worked on bale poker for crawler. I did laundry, etc. I went to Dr. Kids went along. Bill & Duane combined. Brought 2 loads bales home from Gronborg's.

Fri.7-01: Bill & Duane hauled bales & combined Kenny's wheat. I hotted up bottom wire on John's. Feed truck got stuck in cow yard. I mowed. Cleaned up dining room, waxed floor, hung mirror. Fed cattle. Bill came home after 11 p.m.

Sat.7-02: Ground feed. Moved load of corn over. Bill went to check cows & finally found missing bull (purebred registered Angus from Montana). He was dead by the creek (we think he'd been struck by lightning). Took crawler to John's & bale for cows. Pulled bull out & buried him. I finished trim mowing. I pulled Krissy's bottom tooth: her first one to go.

Sun.7-03: Bill chored. He pushed down steep bank in our east houseyard & sloped it to the road. I took kids to S. School. Bill had left to mow, & we took his water jug & dinner to him. Nearly 100°. Turned on air conditioner. I fed cattle. Alan & I cleaned the sewing room & moved the crib in.

Mon.7-04: I did chores. Bill mowed hay & then went to Ernest Woltmann's to combine. I potted a fern & other house plants. Did 2 loads laundry. Put ruffle on Kris's nightgown. Fixed picnic stuff. We went to Avoca for an evening picnic & got home about midnight.

Tue.7-05: Bill left by 8 a.m. to mow hay. I took kids to swim lessons. Guy's & Jo baled straw on Kenny's. Dirty & hot! Kids & I took the big Ford & lunch down, & pulled wagon home. Then I didn't feel too good. Rested. Fed cattle. Sewed on robe. Bill was home about 7:30 p.m.

Fri.7-08: About 6 a.m. my water broke so I knew I'd be going to the hospital today. I tried to get everything in order. Mom & Dad came after the kids about 11 a.m. Bill was getting everything set up to chop hay after dinner. I had extra men for dinner. Duane, Hobus, Jerry, & Robert Andersen helped.

(Shortly after dinner I stopped the haylage truck driver, as he was coming through the yard from dumping his load in the pit silo out west; & I told him, "Bring Bill back from the field with the next load because it's time for him to take me to the hospital.")

We left for the hospital about 2 p.m. (but we had to swing by the hay field to see if they were doing all right running the chopper without Bill) ...

Everything advanced in a hurry & our son Jerod was born at 4:11 p.m. (7 lbs. 2 3/4 oz. & 19 1/2" tall) (Bill & I went down to the nursery to look at him.) I went to surgery & back to my room ... Bill went on home. The 9700 Ford had blown up (puffed black smoke & died) just as Duane finished chopping. Lindeman's brought an 8000 for Bill to use.

Sat.7-09: I was very, very tired. Bill chopped. No visitors until evening. Jerod is doing fine.

Sun.7-10: I felt much better. Mom, Dad, & kids came to see me. Bill moved corn etc., & came to visit in the evening.

Mon.7-11: Bill & Duane moved bales home from well field. Bill came up to the hospital this evening. He came in to hold Jerod & feed him a bottle.

Tue.7-12: Jerod & I came home. Kids & folks were here when we got home. Everything went well. I did get very tired. Bill started to walk beans in the evening.

Wed.7-13: Bill & Alan went to walk beans. Bill came back in time to feed cattle & take kids to swim lessons. After dinner I gave Jerod his bath & bottle, & Alan & Bill went to Kimballton salebarn. Picked the first tomatoes.

Sun.7-17: Rained 2". Slept late. Went to Grandma Marxen's. Went to my folk's & Alan had his duds along to stay a couple days. We sorted hogs. Betty & Gary & kids came to visit.

Mon.7-18: We got up at 5:15 a.m. & went out to load hogs. Bill took off for Harlan with 1st load & I fed Jerod. We loaded 2nd load & he was off to Harlan before 7 a.m. I did laundry & odd jobs all day.

Tue.7-19: We got up & went to walk beans from 8-10 a.m. Bill chored & went to Dunlap salebarn. I had cattle fed so he went to walk beans. We had chicken for supper. I did dishes, laundry, & misc. stuff. I started to mow lawn in evening.

Wed.7-20: Bill walked beans. I took Kris in to swim. Folks brought Al to swim & he came on home with us. I slept afternoon. Was very tired. Al & Bill went to Kimballton salebarn.

Fri.7-22: I went to Crazy Daze in Harlan after Jerod's 6 a.m. feeding. Bill & Alan went to salebarn. Bought 39 calves. We went to Shelby carnival. Got home 12:30 a.m.

Sun.7-24: Got 1.2" rain. I fixed a bug net for Jerod's basket (to protect him from annoying pests, while he was in the field with us, as we walked beans).

Tue.7-26: We slept past 8 a.m. Bill chored & ground feed. We moved some pigs out N. Bill did evening chores. I fed Jerod & we walked beans until 9:30 p.m. Kids walked home & were asleep when we got home. My eye is bad (allergy infection).

Thu.7-28: Bill hurried off to walk beans. I chored. Bill & Al walked beans all afternoon. Rest of us went to Dr. Jerod weighed 8 lbs. 2 1/2 oz. I got eye prescription. Had sitter this evening & went to funeral visitation & to Avoca fair.

Fri.7-29: Bill moved corn out N. & chored, and *finished walking beans!* I took kids to penny hunt at Avoca Craze Daze. Got neat bargains. Went to Hans Damgaard's funeral (Bill's great uncle). Bill took big kids to Avoca for Kid's Day games at 4 p.m. I washed diapers & fed cattle.

Sat.7-30: I went to Craze Daze In Atlantic. Al & Kris stayed with Bill, & Jerod stayed at Mom's. Later, Al & Bill went to tractor pull at fair. Kris, Jerod, & I went 7:30 p.m. to see Bill pull in 9,000 & 11,000 lb. class & Duane in 13,000 lb.

Tue.8-02: I won a pendant watch at the fair. A pink nightgown came from my brother & his family for my birthday.

Wed.8-03: I got a card & gift certificate from Bill & the kids for my birthday. Bill & Duane have spent today trying to get the haybine fixed. Bill mowed until 10 p.m.

Thu.8-04: We chopped; I had men for dinner; I ran after parts; I fixed men afternoon lunch; I chored, & fixed supper for men. A very exhausting day!

Fri.8-05: Rained so we sorted up fat hogs & Bill hurried them to Omaha. I sewed & chored. Bill went to salebarn and did evening chores. I grilled sirloin, did dishes, etc. Bill looked at my dryer: element was broke. He called for parts.

Sat.8-06: Harlan Builders man wrote up a contract for a machine shed for out N.

Sun.8-07: When I washed Jerod's head this a.m. the water in the sink was covered with tiny hairs. He was starting to loose his first hair — mostly in front & on top. Bill went to mow around creek fence, & cows were in John's; we fixed them up a new field. We went to Gary's for a fish supper.

Wed.8-10: I got up at 5 a.m. & fed Jerod, & we went to sort & load hogs for Harlan: 43 hd. grade & yield. Bill put my element in & dryer works!

Thu.8-11: We chored. Rhonda baby-sat & we went to horse races in

Lincoln with Bob Lockwood (a feed salesman friend). Duane fed silage for us. Had a really good time & was a nice day. We had a delicious supper at Johnny's in Omaha on way home.

Sat.8-13: I cleaned house & mowed lawn. Bill checked hay & then moved machinery for machine shed site out N. Pit man hauled 35 loads liquid manure on hay ground. Kris learned to tie her shoes.

Tue.8-16: Elvis Presley died today (43 yrs. old). Duane came to help Bill take crawler tracks apart. Kids & Bill went to Omaha for parts & ate at McDonalds. They stopped at his folk's on way home.

Thu.8-18: We loaded hogs 6:30 a.m. for Harlan. I Hung out laundry, showered & cut my hair. Kris, Jerod, & I went to Dr. Jerod weighed 10 lbs. 5 oz. Got first DPT. Kris got DPT & polio vaccine. Bill & Al worked on (machine shed) site.

Sun.8-21: We went to cast iron seat convention in Atlantic. Bill got a neat "IRON AGE" wrench.

Fri.8-26: Bill went to Harlan for new tires on the front of the car. Kids & I & Mom left for my sister's in Iowa City (we were to go to a baby shower for her there Sun.)

Mon.8-29: Jerod ate at 5 a.m. & then we went to sort & load 2 loads hogs. It was 7:10 a.m. when I came in to help the kids get ready for school. Bus came 7:50 a.m. so they made it just fine. Kris liked her first day of school.

Wed.8-31: 1.85" rain. Mom kept Jerod & rest of us went to see *Star Wars* in Atlantic.

Sat.9-10: Hauled bales. Went to Wanda Brown's wedding & dance (neighbor girl).

Mon.9-12: Rain. Had sitter & went to see *Smokey & the Bandit.* Pizza afterwards. Got groceries for silage help.

Tue.9-13: Chopped.

Wed.9-14: Chopped from 9 a.m. to 8 p.m. Super hectic day! Went to Avoca after dinner for belts for feed system out N.

Thu.9-15: Crew started on machine shed out N. We chopped from 9 a.m. to 7 p.m. I ground feed. Jerod got 2nd DPT & 1st polio at Dr. I fixed men lunch. We sorted up hogs & Bill took 42 to Omaha at 9 p.m. Had a terrible time loading them.

Sat.9-17: Men came 6 a.m. & set poles for the flat storage shed. Bill went to Babbitt's 3 p.m. to chop. Broke chopper.

Mon.9-19: Bill went to Babbitt's to chop for them. I chored.

Thu.9-22: Bill chopped hay for Babbitt. I stripped woodwork, mowed lawn, chored, got groceries. Crew put roof on shed out N. Guys came 5:30 p.m. & put trusses up for shed out W.

Sat.9-24: I went to Atlantic for an exhaust fan. Kids took duds & stayed at Grandpa & Grandma's.

Mon.9-26: Duane combining at Leonard's. We went to S. place to combine. Very busy day. I went to painting class.

Tue.9-27: Jessica was born 2:10 p.m. (my sister's daughter). We brought equipment home from S. place. Duane finished a jag on cemetery field. Terry got done mowing on Laubert's.

Sat.10-01: Jerod had his first meat dinner. Poured cement in flat storage shed. Two cement trucks were here before we were ready. My folks came ... Guys came in for dinner at 5 p.m., after having to work to cover tracks where the dog had walked all over in their fresh cement. Rainy.

Sun.10-02: Jerod turned over from his tummy to his back (for the first time).

Mon. 10-03: Bill's birthday. He was combining. I moved big bales. I went to my painting class — fun!

Tue.10-04: Bill combining. Kids & I went to club at Maye's.

Thu.10-06: Bill did yield contest corn by N. creek. & then combined at Woody's. Kids & I went after groceries.

Mon10-10: Got up 5:20 a.m. to sort hogs. Jerod was up at 6:30 a.m. Kris woke up with bubble gum all over herself, & her chin was stuck to her neck & chest. It rained. We worked on the combine & put some machinery in the new shed. Bill poked a hole in the combine radiator. Rita baby-sat & I went to painting class. Bill worked in the flat storage shed.

Wed.10-19: Got up 5:15 a.m. to sort hogs in W. side of barn & in finishing house. Sold them grade & yield. Terry came to help. He & Bill ate waffles before they took off to combine.

Thu.10-20: We started combining our beans and Bill worked until 2 a.m. (He was planning to quit at midnight but he didn't realize his watch had stopped at 11:30 p.m.)

Fri.10-21: Finished up our beans just before noon. Bill went to salebarn & then to Kenny Osbahr's. I went to Harlan after bin fan, chored, went after 50 pigs at salebarn. Rain.

Sun.10-23: Rainy all day. Jerod was up at 5:30 a.m. Bill worked on wiring new shed & we set the big poles. Had pizza for supper & Bill, Al, & Kris went to his folk's.

Mon.10-24: Rainy all day. I did a lot of laundry. Bill & Duane strung wire for flat storage shed & hooked up yard light. Bill kept the kids while I went to painting class.

Tue.10-25: Put cornhead on the combine & we headed to the S. place. Broke a bolt & had to take the feeder house off. Used the dump wagon as it was too wet in the field for the truck.

Wed.10-26: Jo helped haul from S. place. We finished there! Duane & Jo were here for dinner. I swept flat storage shed & put sealer on the floor.

Sun.10-30: We started to sort cattle 10 a.m. Jerod was awake at 10:30 a.m.— goofed up from the time change. I called Terry to help sort. Rained all day. After dinner we loaded cattle: 100 head to Oakland— what a muddy mess of clothes!

Mon.10-31: Chored. Bill went to Oakland for the cattle check. He then went to Duane's to haul in corn. I went to my art class. Bill took the kids trick or treating.

Tue.11-01: Chored. I took Alan to dentist to get a front tooth pulled (to make room for permanent ones). Dashed over to my folks' as Sherry's were home. Bill had been combining on John's and was home early because he had a bearing out.

Wed.11-02: Jerod to sitter 8:30 a.m. to 7:30 p.m. I moved corn to flat storage shed. Bill combining. Nice sunny day.

Thu.11-03: Jerod at sitter. I moved corn to flat storage shed. Motor went out on big bin.

Fri.11-04: I finished filling flat storage shed, & went to parent-teacher conferences. My dryer quit working.

Wed.11-09: Super yuk day! Kids out of school at 10:15 a.m. because of high winds and expected blizzard conditions. Half the electricity is off this evening: no TV picture, plug-ins won't work. All went to bed early.

Thu.11-10: Bill hauled manure. Bob (Hundt) brought my new dryer just before noon. I washed 2 loads of clothes and my washer's pump sprung a bad leak.

Fri.11-11: Bill hauled manure. I cleaned out kitchen closet in search of mice (disgusting little creatures always try to come in in the fall, until I catch a few and change their migration plans).

Sun.11-13: I talked to Mom & she told me that Calvin and Roseanna have a new baby boy, Clinton Wesley.

Mon.11-14: I polyurethaned woodwork, & hauled manure after dinner.

Wed.11-16: Went to open house at school & visited at Bill's folks'.

Thu.11-17: Took Jerod for his polio vaccine & got groceries. I hauled manure after dinner. Bill went to windrow milo stubble on Sonny's.

Fri.11-18: Took Jerod to sitter. Kris got off bus there after school. Bill & Duane combined. I hauled manure all day— finished the fat cattle yard. Just got home from the sitter's & had to take the truck to go after 60 pigs that Bill had gotten at salebarn.

Thu.11-24: Fat cattle out & old cows out. We didn't go to Delores' for Thanksgiving until nearly 4 p.m. We took the kids out to Grandma & Grandpa's about 9 p.m. and they had their duds along to stay overnight.

Sat.11-26: (Bill & Duane combined.) Bill broke feeder house bolts again. They got done & brought machines home. I went to folks' to pick up kids. Got new snow tires put on car. Went to dance in Avoca.

Sun.11-27: Snow flurries. Went to Bill's folks' for their birthdays.

Tue.11-29: Bill chored & we went to Betty & Gary's in Elk Horn to help them move.

Wed.11-30: No school. Kids at sitter's from 9 a.m. - 7 p.m. We brought milo bales home. Broke a wheel off the wagon on the first load. Bill hauled home & I moved bales to the gate all day. Miserable anniversary. Grandma Bornholdt called (to wish us happy anniversary).

Thu.12-01: Went to my folk's for supper for Dad's birthday.

Sat.12-03: Went to eat at Steak House, then went to dance.

Tue.12-06: Below zero. Got tree up. Had club here.

Fri.12-09: Bill bought 200 pigs at salebarn.

Sat.12-10: Hog waterers frozen out N. Bill thawed them out with heaters. We weaned calves.

Tue.12-13: Godfrey Andersen died. (Neighbor on Duane's road). Bill re-nailed tin on old machine shed roof.

Sun.12-18: Bill took kids to S.S. I wrote Christmas cards. Bill & Dennis

Brix went hunting. Went to S.S. Xmas program.

Wed.12-21: I finished Jerod's Christmas sock. (I had made each of the kids a big 2 ft. sock of green felt with pretty appliques, because it was our tradition to hang up socks for Christmas Eve for Santa to fill with goodies.)

Sat.12-24: Went to my folks' for chili supper.

Wed.12-28: We sorted hogs & Bill & big kids took them to Denison. Sorted fat cattle & Bill & Al took them to Omaha.

1978

Sun.1-01: Went to Betty & Gary's for dinner & supper.

Thu.1-12: I did laundry all day. Bill went to lawyer with tax stuff. I washed & cut Kris' hair after school. Went after groceries. Had sitter & we went to commodities mtg.

Mon.1-16: No school today. It was super cold. Sold soybeans.

Sat.1-21: Waterers frozen out N. Two pipes off in boiler room. Chored. Bill went to Duane's to work cattle. Went to see Grandma Marxen.

Mon.1-23: Al didn't go to school. He was sick & Kris started to get sick toward evening. I went to my pottery class.

Wed.1-25: Both kids (still) home sick. Jerod's temp. 102.6°. Called Doctor. Bill & Duane went after parts & got medicine. Bill has chills—very sick all night.

Thu.1-26: Bill felt awful all day. Kris was better.

Fri.1-27: Kris went to school. Al's temp. was normal.

Sat.1-28: Kids all went to Dr. Jerod got a shot.

Wed.2-01: Alan finally went to school. Jerod went to Dr. for another shot & new medicine.

Mon.2-13: No school. About 10" snow.

Tue.2-14: No school. Men came to lay new carpet in dining & living rooms, & our bedroom & Kris'. (I've never had anything but ugly linoleum floors, so carpet is a real treat!)

Wed.2-22: Bill & Duane went with a bus of men from Avoca Implement to Lexington, Nebr., to tour New Holland combine factory. I chored. Weather got blizzard-like. 30-40 m.p.h. winds. Guys got back to Duane's

& Bill stayed night there.

Thu.2-23: No school: snow drifts. Bill came home 10 a.m.

Tue.3-07: Chased cows from Laubert's so they could get at feed. Snow about a foot and a half deep everywhere.

Fri.3-17: Kids wore green so they wouldn't get pinched (at school on St. Patrick's Day). Loaded fat cattle for Oakland. Bill went to salebarn. We paneled bathroom wall.

Mon.3-20: Tulips & daffodils are up. 1st calf born. Bill checked on tiling & fertilizer. I went to pottery class.

Sun.3-26: (Easter) Jerod was baptized. Gary & Betty (his sponsors), Duanes, my folks, & Helen here for dinner.

Fri.3-31: Bill poured cement at Duane's. Went to salebarn. I pulled a calf. Another cow had a calf & wouldn't claim it.

Sun.4-02: Calf I pulled died. Bill took 13 cows to Omaha.

Mon.4-03: Black cow had twins. Young Hereford lost a calf. Bill went to Omaha to pick up cow check.

Fri.4-07: Superintendent called at noon for me to come get Alan. He'd gotten hit with a ball bat at recess. (I took him to the Dr.) he had to have 6 stitches above his left eyebrow. Bill got stuck with fertilizer spreader.

Sat.4-08: 2 1/8" rain. Lightning hit big pine tree by house & knocked out phone, water heater, TV, radio, & pressure switch in well. Went bowling & had a million laughs.

Mon.4-10: Kris, Bill, & I went to dentist. I had a wisdom tooth pulled. Went to Carol Andersen's (wedding) shower at Neva Manz's (neighbors).

Tue.4-11: Alan had stitches out. Bill had Ronnie, Marlin, Robert, Gary, Dennis, Wayne, & Duane here to play cards.

Mon.4-24: Planted marigolds & impatiens. We made forms out W. & poured 53 yds. concrete for fence-line (cattle) bunks. Terry and Duane helped.

Thu.5-04: Chores & disking non-stop 9 a.m. - 6 p.m.

Thu.5-11: Got planter ready & Bill planted out N. I fed silage, gave bales to cows, fixed dinner, delivered seed corn, mowed weeds in windbreak, fed silage—got stuck, mowed yard for 1st time (this yr.). Came in for supper 9:30 p.m.

Fri.5-12: Bill took hogs to Omaha, then finished planting corn out N. I went to Mother's Day plays (at school). Bill got 200+ pigs at salebarn.

Mon.5-15: Loaded hogs for Harlan. First fence-line bunks came. Planted 44 (replacement trees) in windbreak.

Mon.5-16: 8:30-11:45 a.m.: fed silage, chored & mulched new trees. (Fixed dinner & ate) Bill went to disk. 1:30-4 p.m.: I worked with fence-line bunks. 5:30-9 p.m.: I set posts, put in electric fence gate, fed cows, mulched more trees, fed silage, found shorts in electric fence. 9 p.m.-11p.m.: fed kids, put them to bed, emptied & loaded dishwasher, did load of diapers, took bath, turned on dishwasher, eased into bed, & listened with pleasure to running of the dishwasher.

Sat.5-27: Bill & Al got 12 calves at salebarn. Bill was M.C. at Shelby Alumni Banquet. Then we went to dance in Minden.

Sat.6-03: I finished texturing hall upstairs. We went to dance in Corley and to Duane's afterwards for breakfast.

Mon.6-05: Chopping. Supper about 11:30 p.m.

Tue.6-06: Jerod sick. Extra guys for dinner. Chopped hay. Guys came in for supper 10 p.m.

Thu.6-07: Chopping hay on well field.

Sat.6-10: Went to horse races (Omaha) with Wayne for his B.D. Bill won Daily Double. Went to dance at Sokol hall.

Wed.6-14: Al's 8th birthday. Kevin & Wade came to play. They had a swell time.

Fri.6-16: 105°. Bill cultivated at S. place.

Tue.6-20: Went to Omaha airport to pick up Calvin's.

Sat.6-24: 47 guests here for picnic for Calvin's & Sherry's.

Wed.6-28: Kris' B.D. She got a Barbie doll. Kaylee came to play. Dad took Calvins to plane. Took Jerod's bottles away.

Fri.6-30: Took Kris to emergency room (thought it was appendicitis) was an intestinal infection.

Wed.7-05: Walt had surgery for bladder cancer.

Sat.7-08: Jerod had flu. He was tired & not especially in a mood for his 1st birthday presents. We chopped on Laubert's.

Thu.7-20: Fed cattle for first time in new cement bunks.

Sat.7-22: (Kids stayed the night at my folk's) Duanes went with us to dog races in Sioux City, with Bob Lockwood. We stayed overnight in a motel.

Thu.7-27: We went to pickup pull at Avoca fair.

Wed.8-09: Sorted cattle. 181 fat yard. 100 middle yard. Paid Harlan Builders last on machine shed.

Thu.8-31: I was sick. Bill went to golf course (Thu. is men's night at the club house).

Fri.9-01: Bill helped Duane with sq. bales. Bill was sickly.

Sat.9-02: Bill in bed all day. We both had super headaches.

Thu.9-07: School out early, heat! Kids & I went over home. I visited both Grandmas in hospital. Bill went to golf night.

Sun.9-10: Bill, Alan, Duane, & Mike went to Spencer Fair.

Tue.9-12: Bill & Duane put brake linings on crawler & then went to Dunlap salebarn. I sewed & kids & I finished reading *Old Yeller.*

Wed.9-13: 4" rain. Bad wind damage on S. corn. River's up.

Mon.9-25: Had heifers on Omaha market. $50/cwt.

Fri.10-06: 8-11:30 a.m. sorted & loaded hogs, fed cattle, fed pigs in barn, unloaded wagon of corn. 1:30-3:30 p.m. book work & trip to bank. 4:15-4:45 p.m. chores. 6-7 p.m. fixed grinder. 7-9 p.m. dishes, laundry, supper.

Sat.10-07: 8 - noon chores, 3 men for dinner. 2:30-3:30 p.m. craft fair. 3:30-7 p.m. outside for chores. Then supper.

Sat.10-21: Boys finished (combining) beans.

Tue.10-24: While hauling corn from S. place, a man helping us upset our 9700 & two empty gravity wagons in ditch S. of Avoca, just before noon. (Thankfully he wasn't hurt too bad, & the tractor went to the repair shop.) ... Bill came home from combining 3:10 a.m.

Wed.11-08: Started combining this a.m. & got 33 loads done today. We finished our corn at 10:30 p.m.

Thu.11-09: Terry baled some stalk bales for us out N. Duane finished his corn.

Sat.11-11: Duane at Freddie Miller's. Bill on Leonard's. 8:04 p.m. Duane & Jo have a new baby boy, James Walter.

Thu.11-16: Snowed first time (of this season).

Thu.11-23: Worked outside all day. Sorted & loaded 40 cattle. Finished chores & went to Delores' for supper for Thanksgiving.

Fri.11-24: Went over home as Sis was home. She & I had a swell shopping trip. Bill got pigs at salebarn.

Sun.11-26: Snowed. Found dead cow by S. creek. Bill & I pulled auger out of grinding bin. It wasn't broken like we thought, but was plugged with ice.

Fri.12-01: Ice. No School. Bill went to bank & salebarn. We went to Dad's birthday supper.

Mon.12-04: Icy, no school. Worked all a.m. to ready fence for calves. Kids helped chase cows in from out W. We weaned calves. Vet came & vaccinated & poured the cows. Cows got out about 11:30 p.m. We fixed a calf waterer at that time.

Sun.12-10: 12°. Moved 4 loads of cows to Sonny's. Put up tree. Went to Bec & Wayne's for supper.

Sun.12-17: Christmas with the folks & Sis'. Kids' Sunday School program at church.

Mon.12-25: Sorted fat cattle. Went to Bill's folks' for dinner & supper. Loaded cattle for Omaha about 4 p.m.

1979

Mon.1-01: 10° Below Zero.

Sat.1-13: Blizzard conditions. Red twin died.

Sun.1-14: -15°.

Mon.1-15: Kids home from school 10 a.m. No water. I worked on income tax figures all day. Threw out a mess of pigs out N. — piled up.

Tue.1-16: -6°. We gathered up all the dead critters in a huge pile for the dead truck. Lost quite a few big hogs (180 lbs.); they piled up & smothered each other. I cleaned pens & Bill treated hogs. Worked on taxes. Bill went to lawyer at 4 p.m. Then to check on S. cows. Lost a newborn calf.

Sat.1-20: Kids had school (make-up day). Went to Bill Babbitt's 35th anniversary dance in Walnut. Breakfast at Brix's. Home at 3 a.m.

Mon.2-05: My folks came after Jerod. Pushed out (hog house) pens. Packed suitcases.

Tue.2-06: Duane came about 5 minutes after 6 a.m. to take us to Omaha for an early morning flight.

(He dropped us off at the airport & left ... Bill, Alan, Kris, & I were going on a trip to Orlando, Fla. with a group of Bill's fellow seed corn dealers. [This was our first vacation in over 10 yrs. of marriage, & it was so exciting to think we'd be flying away to sun, sights, & fun!]

We waited in line about an hour, kicking our suitcases ahead of us, as we slowly inched toward the ticket/baggage counter. As one agent tagged our bags, & we excitedly watched them glide away on a conveyor, the 2nd agent looked for our names on the ticket list, & then announced, "Why, you're booked on the 12:30 p.m. flight!"

I quickly showed them our letter from the travel agency, with instructions to pick up our tickets the day of our flight, & departure was plainly listed as 7:45 a.m. The agent checked further & replied, "I'm sorry, there's been a mistake: we have you on the 12:30 p.m. flight to Orlando."

Ohhh, we were disappointed ... they told us, however to wait; & if there were empty seats, they'd get us on this flight ... We waited until just before the doors to the plane were to close, "Sorry, there aren't enough seats. You'll have to wait for the 12:30 p.m. flight."

During our long four hour wait at the airport, the kids certainly got restless, & it dampened our spirits some; but we were soon climbing above the haze to bright blue sky, with nothing but flat white clouds below us.

Finally we were at Orlando airport; but to go along with our luck for the day, our bags were not! We were told that they had arrived on the earlier flight and someone had picked them up.

That evening, soon after our arrival in Orlando & drive to our motel, we were to go to a banquet. Although we had no dress clothes, we went anyway; & at the banquet, all of the ladies got a gift of a cosmetic bag. As I opened mine, I found it to be full of slimy yuk! A shampoo bottle in it was broken ... This made us laugh, as we decided that all that had happened to us today was funny.

After the banquet, most of the group enjoyed a relaxing swim in the elegant, dimly-lit motel pool. Since our swimsuits were in our "lost luggage," we sat & watched others having fun, while we thought about our vacation not going too well so far.

About midnight someone came up to us, by the pool, & said, "Aren't you Bill Johnsons? We've got your luggage in our room. It was going round & round on the airport baggage carousel; & we were told you were coming on a later flight; so we picked up your luggage & took it with us."

This was very nice of them, however, they had gone out on the town, forgoing the banquet, & we hadn't seen them until now, to find out that they had our suitcases. All this time we had been thinking that our luggage was lost, & pondering what we'd do in Florida, on our first "fun" vacation in ten years, with no change of underwear.

Wed.2-07: Up at 7 a.m. Went to Disney World. It was overcast & a little light drizzle was falling, so the crowds were down; & this was good, as we had no waiting in long lines & had fun on all rides. (We had a brand new instamatic camera with us to take "beautiful" pictures, but the shutter release wouldn't release ... I'd push hard & it wouldn't budge. Then I'd hold it down [at a height just above my knees] to push with all my might, because I thought if it was stuck, this might dislodge the shutter button. Well, this worked nearly every time, so we have many pictures of Mickey Mouse's feet, parade horses' hooves, & the bottom portion of many of the sights we saw.)

Thu.2-08: Went to Kennedy Space Center.

Fri.2-9: Went to Cypress Gardens. Cold enough I wore my winter coat. Toured Citrus World plant. Went to supper with a high school classmate of mine who lives in Orlando.

Sat.2-10: Went to Busch Gardens. Too much like Disney World & we were tired.

Sun.2-11: Back home. Duane picked us up at the airport. Folks brought Jerod home.

Mon.2-12: Bill & I had dental appointments. Got groceries.

Wed.2-21: I went to visit my Grandma Marxen & Aunt Lois (my great-great aunt). Bill moved some corn to grinding bin.

Sat.3-03: It snowed & blowed all day like a blizzard. Put black cow in barn & she had a calf. Many events cancelled due to the weather.

Sun.3-24: Bill got Case tractor stuck (feeding cattle) & it took the Ford & crawler to get it out. Got in after 9 p.m.

Sun.4-01: 5" snow.

Tue.4-17: Seeded oats.

Thu.4-18: I hauled manure from cattle yard. Bill put on dry fertilizer.

Sat.5-05: Bill disked til 11 p.m. I got a load of manure stuck in the field.

Sun.5-06: Duane came to pull my tractor out. I hauled manure & chored. Bill disked.

Tue.5-08: Jerod at sitter. Bill disked on S. place. I disked on cemetery field 9:30 a.m.- 3:30 p.m. Took Bill fuel, chored, & finished cemetery field at 11 p.m. Picked up Jerod, & did dishes & laundry til 1:30 a.m. Bill came home from disking at 3 a.m.

Wed.5-09: Bill disked all day. I went to Omaha with Bec, had a nice day. Chored & went to S. place to check on Bill.

Sat.5-12: Started first corn planting — on S. place.

Sun.5-27: Finished planting corn just before noon. Went to Shelby Alumni Banquet & to Bill's folks'.

Mon.5-28: Memorial Day. Went to Elk Horn. Bill was in a rope pull. Kids went swimming. Supper at Betty's.

Mon.6-11: Crew (from Kentucky) painted barn, old machine shed, old hog house, garage, & wash house. Bill mowed hay.

Tue.6-12, 13, 14: Chopped hay.

Sat.6-16 to 20: Cultivated.

Thu.6-21: Bill put on anhydrous. I went to hospital to see my Grandpa Bornholdt. Al & Kris stayed over home. Jerod & I chored. Bill came home 10 p.m. and went to club house.

Sun.6-24: Went to Johnson picnic.

Thu.7-05: Mom called to say Grandpa Bornholdt died at 7 p.m.

Fri.7-06: Picked Calvin up at airport.

Sun.7-08: Sis came home. All went to Grandma's for dinner. Came home & chored, & went back to funeral home gathering in Atlantic.

Mon.7-09: Chored & went to Grandpa's funeral. We got home at 1 p.m. & had to chop oats on Laubert's.

Sat.7-14: Bill pulled in rope pull at Shelby carnival. We all went.

Thu.7-19: Chopping on well field. County oiled Roads, so we couldn't haul haylage home, & Duane & Bill went to combine.

Tue.7-24: I took a casserole to Mable's — made bars to take to funeral. We went to Laubert's funeral. (Rogers' were neighbors — we farmed their ground). Bill was a pallbearer.

Mon.7-30: 2:20 a.m. juice (electricity) off — terrible wind— got kids out of bed & got them downstairs — 1.2" rain. Corn damaged. Ck'd cows, & corn at S. place. Bill went to tug-o'-war practice.

(This evening Bill went to Garvin Babbitt's [neighbor] to practice rope pulling with his team. After I'd gotten the kids up to bed, I shut off the lights & relaxed in front of the TV. I was watching Johnny Carson & *The Tonight Show* when the TV flickered and went off. As I looked toward the kitchen, I saw that the house was filled with an eerie orange glow coming from outside. Shivers waved through me as I hurried to the west kitchen window to look out.

FIRE! The shop was engulfed in a huge mass of orange flames!

Immediately, I called the fire department & Bill ...

My next instinct was to gather hoses! As I was trying to drag hoses, Bill & the tug-o'-war guys came & hurried to help me hook them up, but no water came! ... because the fire was lighting up the night, we hadn't stopped to consider that there was no power ... the fire had already burned the lines & blown the fuses.

Fearing that a fuel barrel near the garage/shop might blow up & catch the house on fire, I got the kids out of bed & took them to a safe distance out in the yard.

Outside, with the kids, we watched the fire trucks, with their flashing, spinning lights, come tearing into our yard. The men jumped out to plan their attack, however the shop was too far gone, & the decision was made to "let her burn."

The firemen kept an eye on adjoining areas & pushed a wall in toward the center now and then; but otherwise we all stood in the yard next to the big fire trucks, with their bright top lights still whirling, & watched our garage burn down.)

After the fire trucks left, the electrician (Lawrence Brown) worked until 3 a.m. to get our house electricity on. (We could still hear the oil in a 55 gal. drum crackling & boiling, & the fire still glowed & flared up the rest of the night.)

(Some days later, when our two year old, Jerod & I happened to see a fire truck on a road with lights flashing & whirling, he surprised me with this question: "Who's house are they gonna go burn down today, Mommy?")

Tue.7-31: This morning the shop was just a smoldering pile of burnt ruins. I called the insurance man & my folks. Picked some things out of the ashes & mess. Folks here for dinner. Bill finished oats on Leonard's.

Fri.8-03: Took kids to folks' to stay. Bill finished combining on Audrey's.

Sat.8-04: (Chored) Went to National Tug-o'-war Championships in Corning. Bill's team, The Clodbusters competed.

Tue.8-21: 1 7/10" rain. We loaded the pickup & went to Alter's (salvage co.) with our 1st load of iron (what was left from our shop fire). We were going to the zoo, but it was pouring, so we came home & got a 2nd load of junk & took it up to Council Bluffs.

Wed.8-22: Bill cut iron all morning.

Thu.8-23: I did chores & Bill cut up a bunch more iron. We took a load to Alter's again, & then went to the zoo.

Fri.8-24: Bill pushed the chicken house into a pile this afternoon (a worthless little building that sat next to the shop: the fireman had stopped it from burning). Bill & Al went to tug-o'-war practice.

Sat.8:25: Went to Julie's wedding (Betty & Gary's girl).

Sun.8-26: Cows out. Chored. Went to Iowa State Fair Tug-o'-war. Clodbusters got 6th place. Jerod & Kris stayed at my folks'.

Mon.8-27: Kids missed the bus — no clocks went off. Bill burnt the chicken house.

Mon.9-03: Labor Day. Bill mowed hay. I upset the silage/feed wagon in the pit. (Don't laugh, it was easy to do ... we had two dirt-walled, dirt-bottomed pit silos next to each other, separated by a 4' thick dirt wall. There was a huge mud hole across the mouth of the biggest, widest of the two pits, & we were currently feeding out of it. I usually backed my feed wagon into the pit, up close to the silage & used my crawler to load.

 Because I had to get back through the mud hole without getting stuck, I opted to stay close to the dividing wall to miss most of the mud; & then I gunned the tractor to back up the wagon. The problem was, my wagon gooshed sideways just enough to run the wagon's wheel up the slope of the dividing wall, & whoop!— my silage wagon fooped over on its side before I could say, "Oh no!"

 I went to get Bill & of course he said, "!☆✘✳✘☆!," & added, in total disgust, "I suppose you upset the tractor too!"

 I said, "No, the tractor's fine, & the wagon isn't hurt; it's just tipped over on its side [the wagon just happened to have a swivel tongue end which allowed the wagon to lay over on its side without even bending the tongue], so come & help me."

 He looked over the situation & told me to, " Go get a post." I didn't know what he wanted it for; but I didn't ask, I just went & got a post & handed it to him. Then he told me to bend over & put my hands on the tongue of the wagon, which I did. I didn't ask why, I was just trying not to disgust him any more. Soon I looked at him, & he had the post raised above his head like he was going to hit me with it!

 That quickly he burst out laughing, & I knew then that the whole post thing was supposed to be funny. I'm sure I said something like, "You lizard, you scared me!" and he just laughed ... he then helped me with the crawler & a chain to up-right the feeder wagon & I finished chores.)

Fri.9-07: Kids went to folks' for weekend. We had 21 here for a tug-o'-war team picnic.

Sat.9-08: Chopped.

Thu.9-20: Bill drove the combine to Red Oak & drove new one home. I went to art class. Bill went to legion to play cards.

Fri.9-21: Alan went to Kevin Goshorn's birthday party after school.

Wed.9-26: Started combining at Bill True's with new JD 7720 combine.

Tue.10-09: Filled silo.

Sun.10-13: Went to Iowa city to see Laura (our new niece).

Mon.10-22: First Snow of Season. Crawler wouldn't start — it was midafternoon when we got it started. No electricity 2:30 p.m. - 8 p.m. 2" rain overnight, then 4 to 5" snow.

Thu.10-25: Got two new gray & blue 300 bu. D.M.I. gravity wagons.

Mon.10-29: Picked end rows off N. field. Yield ck'd at 140 bu/acre.

Wed.11-21: Auger broke when I started to unload wagons. Duane put a new motor in our straight truck.

Thu.11-22: Thanksgiving. Duane & Bill fixed the auger after Duane brought the truck back. Went to Delores' for supper. Dropped kids out home to stay afterwards.

Fri.11 23: Moved 99 cows from out W. to Eggers' stalk field.

Sun.11-25: Bill finished up Duane's corn after midnight.

Thu.11-29: Finished corn on S. place. Bill finished at Keith Allen's.

Fri.11-30: Duane & Bill finished combining corn today.

Tue.12-04: Ag.F.S. started on the finishing house (we're extending the roof to cover the pen aprons & the pit lid, as snow in the pens & ice on the waterers has caused us grief).

Mon.12-10: Bill did 18 A. of beans for a guy. I hauled manure. We went to the kids' school Christmas program & then to Bill's folks'.

Sat.12-15: My folks, Sis & girls, & both Grandma's were here for Christmas supper & gifts.

Wed.12-19: Got new brown 1979 Ford 350 pickup.

Tue.12-25: Kids opened gifts about 7:30 a.m. All were pleased with Santa's goodies. Went to Bill's folks' for dinner, supper, & gifts.

Wed.12-26: In upper 50's. Spent all day outside (on chores).

(1979 was the beginning of a downturn in our financial situation. In Jan. we lost a number of hogs in our finishing building [to suffocation when they piled up in extreme cold weather]. In July we lost our garage/shop to fire & insurance didn't cover our total losses. In Dec. we took on the debt of extending our finishing house roof [we had to try to prevent future hog death losses, from bad weather.]

Another significant factor in our money situation was the price decline in our farm commodities. For example, hog prices took a sharp dive: in Jan. 1979 hogs started at $51 & fell to $37.50 by Dec., for a tremendous $13.50 cwt price drop for the year [that meant that a 240 lb. hog that brought us $122.40 at market that Jan. only brought us $90, for a similar hog by Dec. of 1979. That is $32.40 per hog less!] Cow & cattle prices were down as well & corn was less than $2 bushel.

Other factors were that the land, which we used for borrowing collateral for our farm operating money, was starting to drop in value; and interest rates were starting to rise.

Because we had bought 80 A. of ground in 1968 [after Bill's grandfather's death]; had bought Bill's folks' half of the livestock & machinery in 1974 [after his folks retired]; and had put a lot of money back into the farm in improvements in the 70's; we had accumulated a large debt. Consequently, when interest rates started to race upwards, we were negatively affected.

We had worked just as hard this year as any other year, but because of all the above factors we were losing ground [financially].

Although we ended 1979 with a net loss, and knew we were in financial trouble, we were still optimistic enough to think that we could work harder, that interest rates might come down, that farm prices might go up, & that we'd still be fine again [financially]).

1980

Tue.1-01: Went to Betty & Gary's for dinner & supper.

Tue.1-08: Harlan Builders came & started setting poles for new garage/shop.

Fri.1-18: Jerod & I went over home. (I went on to Atlantic & got some super buys for the kids.) (I love bargains & love shopping end of season sales.) Really nice warm day.

Wed.1-23: Went to a supper & wedding shower for Garvin & Judy Babbitt.

Fri.1-25: Sorted off little calves. 139 in W. yard. Put 64 Bill bought in with them to make 203. Put 71 in E. yard.

Mon.2-04: Bill went to first evening exercise class in Avoca. (A group of guys get together to play basketball once a week until spring field work starts.)

Wed.2-20: Bill hauled pit manure. We struggled to get nine new replacement feeders moved in (to the finishing house — hogs are very hard on equipment & facilities).

Fri.2-22: Bill went to salebarn. We went to Aunt Jennie's 90th birthday party.

Sat.2-23: I took Al & Kris skating in Harlan. Bill & kids worked in hog house all afternoon. Went to dance in Minden.

Tue.3-04: Snowed & blowed. Kids got out early. I went to club at Jackie's. Bill finally got waterers working out N.

Wed.3-05: Bill got 53 pigs at salebarn. Alan went to 4-H.

Thu.3-06: Two great big hogs dead in barn; Vet posted one. They have hot salmonella. Alan was sick — upset stomach.

Fri.3-07: I threw up & was sick all day. We sorted hogs in W. side barn. Duane took two jags to Harlan: 70 hd. $35.25. Bill bought 98 pigs at salebarn.

Sat.3-08: Kids & I went to my folks'. I went to see my Grandmas. Bill got 288 mixed hogs at Denison salebarn.

Wed.3-12: Snow. Bec & Wayne, & Jo & Duane, & us went to Omaha. We gals shopped at the mall & guys went to Farm Show.

Fri.3-14: Kris broke out with chicken pox.

Sat.3-15: Bill went to the Dr.— has hives. Got medicine for Kris' itches. Bill & Al went to Denison & got pigs.

Sun.3-16: Bill & Al went to Kelly's (Bill's brother Charlie's boy) birthday deal. I showed Kris how to sew.

Tue.3-25: I served breakfast at school to teachers at 7:15 a.m. for Porkettes promo. Bill moved corn to drying bin.

Fri.3-28: Outside all day making corral out W. & putting in fence. Never even came in for dinner. Jerod played pretty good by us until 4 p.m. when he came in to sleep. Bill & I chored & came in at 7:30 p.m.

Sat.3-29: Bill & kids ck'd cows & took a fert. spreader back. I sewed after dinner. They worked out N. in bin. Went to Shelby Fireman's dance. Alan came down with chicken pox.

Tue.4-01: Bill went to PCA. I went to club. Bill played in Farmers vs. Businessmen Benefit Basketball game at Shelby school. Jerod got chicken pox.

Sun.4-06: Bill & Kris went to Duane's for Easter. Alan, Jerod, & I (and their chicken pox) hunted Easter eggs here.

Tue.4:15, 16, & 18: I hauled manure all day.

Sat.4:19: For 12 hrs., I hauled manure & disked.

Sun.4-20: Bill went to S. place to disk. I hauled manure 8 to 5 p.m. Went to Harlan for food (groceries). Picked Bill up 8 p.m. Ck'd cows.

Mon.4-21: Bill disked. I chored & disked 8 a.m. - 8:30 p.m.

Sun.4-27: Took out fence, dozed out tress, & drug them to S. end along Andersen's. Almost dark when we went to chore.

Tue.4-29: Chored. Bill disked & put on anhydrous.

Thu.5-01: I cut out Mom's suit. Alan mowed lawn (for first time this spring).

Fri.5-02: Bill put on herbicide. Kids & I went over home for supper for Mom's birthday.

Sat.5-03: Chored. Worked on planter. He planted N. of creek.

Sat.5-10: Bill finished planting about 7:30 p.m. We went to Corley (dance) & to Colonial Inn to eat.

Fri.5-23: Kids' LAST DAY OF SCHOOL. I knocked old plaster off in Jerod's room (to re-do the walls with paneling).

Thu.5-29: Made 1st homemade ice cream, had 1st strawberries, during 1st tornado warning (of the season).

Sun.6-01: Kids went to S.S. We went to Bornholdt picnic.

Mon.6-02: Charolais calf got struck by lightning. Vet posted him. Bill took crawler apart. Kids went to Bible School.

Sun.6-08: Bible School program. Went to 1st tug-o'-war in Kimballton.

Won 1st place. Kids all stayed at folks'.

Sat.6-14: Alan's 10th B.D. Went out to eat & storm came up.

Wed.6-25: Chopped hay.

Fri.7-04: Went to parade in Avoca, then tug-o'-war in Walnut, & Anything Goes Contest at Avoca. Home to chore & back to ball game & fireworks. Terrible storm came up about 10:30 p.m. Trees, buildings, houses by Avoca damaged.

Sun.7-06: Took bulls to cows. Very, very hot. Bill went to tug-o'-war practice. I started to cut out & sew jeans.

Wed.7-30: Mom, kids, & I left for Iowa City & visited at my sister's until Sat.

Sun.8-03: Went to National Tug-o'-war in Corning. Bill's team got fourth.

Sat.8-09: Chored & went to Westfair. Clodbusters won 1st in four weight classes.

Mon.8-11: Went to sort hogs before 6 a.m. 231 hd. @ $48.99. 73.8% yield. Cleaned in hog house, dinner at 2:30 p.m. Took 9 boars & 6 cows to Omaha.

Sun.8-17: Kris & Jerod stayed over home. We went to State Fair. Clodbusters won 1st in tug-o'-war.

Fri.8-22: Bill got 100+ pigs at salebarn.

Sat.8-23: Bill & Alan got 144 pigs at Denison salebarn.

Mon.8-25: Sorted hogs 6 a.m. I got kids up for 1st Day Of School. Took 134 hogs to Harlan (to Western Ia. Pork)

Sat.9-06: 165 cows. 205 fats (cattle). We counted them.

Sun.9-07: Bill was replacing the chopper knives & sliced his hand. I took him to emergency room for stitches.

Thu.9-11: Went to Monster arm wrestling tournament in Walnut. Bill won a medal for right handed medium weight.

Fri.9-12: Went to Monster arm wrestling at Harlan. I got 1st place, light weight; Bill got 1st rt. & lft. med. weight.

Tue.9-23 to 29: Chopped, I packed.

Tue.9-30: Bill started custom combining.

Thu.10-03: I had a surprise party for Bill for his birthday. (He was late coming home from combining & when he did get home he didn't feel very good. He'd had an upset stomach and diarrhea all day, & was ready to hit the bed; but — there were 15 guests here for a surprise party, and it was 2 a.m. when they all left.) (He was surprised all right!)

Sat.10-04: Bill sick. He did combine after dinner. (I served samples at Fareway for Porkettes to promote pork.)

Sat.10-18: I worked at Fareway (for an Oct. Pork Promotion).

Wed.10-22: We yield ck'd at S. place — only 99 bu/A. Bill had a school board mtg. so we quit with only 2 rounds left.

Fri.10-24: After dinner, we did our LAST corn, N. of creek.

Sun.10-26: Kids to Sun. School. Roasted wieners in the grove. Ck'd out beaver dams. Rain started about 8:30 p.m.

Mon.10-27: Snow: First of Season. Bill went to Co-op supper.

Thu.11-20: Chased 100 cows to Eggers'. Trucked 57 to S. place to corn stalk fields.

Thu.11-27: Thanksgiving at Delores'.

Thu.12-04: I went to a farrowing school in Harlan. Very interesting (learned how to vaccinate a pig by practicing on and orange).

Sat.12-13: Al went to weekend 4-H deal in Atlantic. Waynes, Duanes, Garys, Dennises, & Terry & friend were here for Christmas turkey. Had a nice evening.

Sat.12-20: Sherry & folks were here for Christmas & gifts.

Thu.12-25: Opened gifts. Went to Jo's for dinner, gifts, & supper. A water pipe was broken in the bathroom when we got home.

Wed.12-31: Bill put on fert. at S. place. Went to Minden (dance) with gang.

(1980 was not a truly exciting year. We sold 1303 hogs & 158 cattle & did a lot of work, as is usual on a farm. What was unusual about this year is that interest rates continued to skyrocket toward an extraordinary 20%! Our finances were squeaking, and we were sinking into BIG TROUBLE!

This year of 1980 we paid $81,985 interest on our farm operating debt. That being by far more than we made, we ended 1980 with a net loss: a negative $117,120. We knew we were in a world of hurt now, &

everyday we felt the super stress that comes with overwhelming debt ... This was very depressing and would wear on us hard for the whole decade of the 80's.)

1981

Thu.1-01: I went to Barb Brown's fabric sale (at the Stitch Shoppe in Avoca). (In 1991 it became one more business that closed its doors on small town mainstreet.)

Mon.1-12: I went to Porkettes. Bill & Duane went to hedging meeting in Avoca.

Tue.1-20: Watched inauguration of Ronald Reagan. Cut hogs out North.

Wed.1-21: I picked up calf brain at locker & took it to school for Alan's class to study. Also took pork material to Home Ec Teacher.

Mon.2-02: Bus was 2 hrs. late. Co-op truck was stuck N. of us. We sorted load of hogs for Harlan. I cleaned like mad. We went to Pork Producers Banquet.

Tue.2-03: I cleaned & hurried like crazy. (I went to) my first oil painting class from 9 a.m. - noon. Bill was working on shelves in the shop. (I had) club here (after dinner).

Sat.2-07: Alan & I went to music contest at school; he played his sax; I timed from 8-12:15 p.m. Bill went to Boysen's supper-dance-breakfast. I had no baby-sitter.

Mon.2-09: I was installed as Shelby County Porkettes treasurer. Bill went to first exercise class.

Tue.2-10: No School — Blizzard conditions. Bill was covered with ice when he came in from chores. I planted tomatoes, flowers, & pumpkins in pots. Went out about 4 p.m. & chased middle yard calves in by old hog house for protection.

Wed.2-11: 20° Below Zero. No school. Bill & boys ck'd cows etc., We sorted out 7 cows & Bill took them to Omaha & went to a school board mtg.

Thu.2-12: Sorted & took hogs to Harlan. Cows were out. Bill got the pickup stuck & the tire came off the wheel. Feed truck came & our auger broke. Had meat on grill for supper — kids played with sparklers.

Sat.2-14: Lost a couple wheel bolts & cracked rim on honey wagon tire. Fixed it. Bill pumped the pit. I fed cattle. Bill changed oil in car. We dropped kids at my folks' 3 p.m. & went to Ames to National Arm Wrestling Championships. Bill got 4th lft. handed lt. wt. Made semi-finals in rt. handed lt. wt. I competed in women's fly wt. division, but lost.

Sun.2-15: got home from Ames 5:15 a.m. Slept until almost noon. Bill fed cattle — we snoozed — loaded last 87 fat cattle on two pots at 4 p.m.

Wed.2-18: Chored. Took a bunk to Al's 4-H calves. Bill finished pumping the pit. I cut out, stained walnut, & polyurethaned a circular wooden lid (for my Grandma's 30 gal. crock). (I use it for my kitchen wastebasket.) I cleaned & plastered Jerod's closet. Bill went to exercise class.

Tue.3-03: Al & Kris were home with the flu. I went to my oil painting class. Calf born in N. creek. Bill brought him in to put him in the bath tub (to warm him up) & took him back out [to his mom] at chore time.

Sun.3-08: Took kids to S.S. Bill felt dumpy — slept until 11 a.m. Kids were (roller) skating (in the garage) & Alan threw a broom at Kris. I took her to Harlan for three stitches in her head.

Mon.3-23: Jerod & Bill disked. Al, Kris, & I went to a concert Al was in at school.

Mon.3-30: Bill chored while I straightened up the house. We sorted & took 43 hogs to Harlan. Our PCA man came after dinner (to look at farm figures). Bill & I raked (leaves & sticks) in the grove, moved pigs, cleaned pens out N. Bill went to class.

Thu.4-16: .1" rain. Got up 5:20 a.m. to load calves. Bill & Duane each took a load up & were back at 7:30 a.m. Barrett came with two pots at 8 a.m. & boys each took a second load. Jerod & I went to Dunlap at noon to see our calves sell. Then I went to PCA, & got groceries. Had a pizza (at home).

Sat.4-18: Bill chored & ck'd cows. I did laundry, etc. Mowed lawn for 1st time. Had vet to pull a calf. Worked on Ford's air conditioning. Stayed home (tonight). Kids dyed eggs & I made a tiger kitty pillow for Christopher South (new grand nephew).

Sun.4-19: Bill helped serve Easter breakfast at church at 6 a.m. Chored. Betty's for dinner & supper.

Thu.4-23: Dad & Bill went to sale of John Dau's ground.

Fri.5-01: Bill started to plant corn on cemetery field.

Tue.5-05: Chored. Took seed beans to Wayne's. I went to club at Maye's.

Bill worked on planter shaft. We chored. Twins (calves) born today.

Thu.5-14: Ck'd cows. Bill went to plant on Louie's & I fed cows. Bill finished planting at dark.

Wed.5-27: Went out 6 a.m. to load hogs. I did chores between loads. Bill took last load at 11:30 a.m. Took 170. Did a few odd jobs. Went to Harlan for hog ck. & groceries. Loaded hogs for Omaha, Bill took them, & went to a school board mtg. I came in 9 p.m.

Wed.5-28: School's out. Bec called to say Wayne was in the hospital: upset his truck. Bill went down to Wayne's (to help with chores) while I did chores (here). We loaded hogs for Harlan. Cleaned the truck & Bill worked on haybine. I chored. Bill & Al ground for his calves.

Sun.5-31: Started to chop (hay).

Tue.6-02: Chopping. Bottom broke out of truck cylinder, box crashed down, & cylinder ram bent & went into drive shaft. Got Duane's truck to finish (haylage). Chored quick. Fixed supper.

Sat.6-06: I chored. Bill sprayed. Went to Centennial Parade at Irwin. It was good. Came home about 6 p.m. Went to dance at Legion & to Walnut for breakfast.

Sun.6-07: Didn't get up until 9:30 a.m. We went to 4-H picnic & (club member project) tour.

Sun.6-14: Al's 4-H calves were out. Chored. Folks brought Jerod & Kris home (they went Fri. to stay).

Fri.6-19: Kids & I went over home. Got Alan a 10 speed bike for his birthday. When we got home, we cleaned out the W. side of the barn, & Bill got 156 pigs (at salebarn). I fed cows while he went after pigs.

Wed.6-24: Went to Harlan after dinner to PCA (still trying to work out a farm plan they'll go with).

Sun.6-28: Went to picnic at Elk Horn park (with my side). Kris' 9th B.D. Bill went to Johnson picnic.

Sat.7-04: Got our 1917 Model T running, drove it to Avoca, & drove in tail end of 4th of July parade. Bill played in the town vs. country softball game. I went to my class reunion.

Tue.7-07: We chopped. Guys went to combine. We chopped again from 8:50 p.m. to 12:30 a.m.

Wed.7-08: Started chopping 9 a.m. Chopper broke just at dinner time.

Rained.

Thu.7-09: Chopping.

Sat.7-11: 100°. Bill combined. Quit to go to Shelby (Fun Days) pull. He went back to combine. Kids & I went to carnival. I worked in Community building (food stand) until midnight.

Sun.7-12: 100°. Bill chored. We went to tug-o'-war in Deadham. Did chores by moonlight about 10:30 p.m.

Mon.7-13: 100°. I fed cows. Bill & Al moved 1 load corn out N. Bill went to combine. I did chores.

Tue.7-14: Rain. Bill fed cows. We tied Al's calves to loosen their halters & spray them. Had meat on grill for dinner. I sewed after noon. Al & Bill went to (livestock) judging contest. I chored.

Sat.7-18: Sprinkler got left on all night in tomato patch & the iron (in our deep well) turned the (white metal) shed (rusty) brown. I scrubbed from 8 a.m. to 4 p.m. with cleanser. Went to dance at Legion & to Walnut for eats.

Sun.7-19: Took kids to S.S. Worked on short in electric fence. All scrubbed for 2 1/2 hrs. to finish the shed. Ate dinner at 2:30 p.m. Went to Bill's folks' & made ice cream.

Fri.7-24: Bill chored & went to see beef judging (at Avoca fair). Jerod got 71 pennies in the penny scramble. Kids were in athletic contests by fair grandstand & all won a couple dollars. Bill, Al, & Kris went to Chitwood Thrill Show.

Wed.7-29: Chored & hurried to (Shelby Co.) fair. Alan showed his 3 calves. He was done at 3 p.m. Then I worked in food booth until 7 p.m. Came home about 9 p.m. & chored.

Fri.7-31: Chored & went to calf auction at fair. Al got $66.50 & $66 for his 1195 and 1145 lb. calves. Went to Oakland to view carcasses (on the rail) at 4 p.m. Came home about 7 p.m. & cows were in Schuster's corn. Fixed fence for 2 hrs.

Sat.8-01: Bill chored & went to pull shattercane until dinner. I did dishes, laundry, polyurethaned sewing room woodwork, & stained my printer's (old newspaper type) box. Bill went to do some collecting. I was choring when he came home. We shucked sweet corn from Herb Rock's & had some for supper. Rain at news time (10 p.m.).

Mon.8-03: Went to PCA at 1:30 p.m. They said they could only finance us until the end of the year. (What a birthday present!) Calvin called about 8 p.m. (for my B.D.).

Sat.8-08: Took sick calf to vet about 8:30 p.m. He died.

Wed.8-19: I did laundry all day. Cleaned shelves & put them in my sewing room & reorganized patterns, etc. Bill went to Oakland ASCS to certify acres, & ck'd cows on S. place.

Sat.8-22: Took Al to orthodontist in Council Bluffs. Went to Lewis & Clark Park before coming home. Went to Bob & Barb Brown's 25th anniversary barbecue.

Sun.8-23: Got up 6 a.m. Went to State Fair with Duanes. Kids stayed at folks'. Bill got 2nd in rt. handed arm wrestling.

Mon.8-24: First day of school. Very foggy.

Tue.8-25: Bill went to talk to Avoca banker.

Fri.8-28: (Mom, kids, & I went to Sis' for the weekend.)

Tue.9-01: Sorted calves & worked 88. Moved 118 pigs out N.

Tue.9-03: Went to PCA 9:30 a.m. to discuss line of credit.

Tue.9-08: Chored. Went to help Mable Rogers for her sale. Bill sat at poles for school board election noon - 3 p.m. He went on helicopter ride with Cox. Mable's sale was at 5 p.m. Fed cows in dark.

Sat.9-12: Bill started chopping on Raleigh Woltmann's — ran a gathering chain in right away. Had trouble all afternoon.

Sun.9-13: I fed cows. Bill left just after 8 a.m. to put on a sprocket & chop on Woltmann's. I took kids to S.S. & visited folks. Did nothing neat. I fed cows. New blk wf hfr.

Sun.9-20: (Started chopping here).

Sat.10-03: 2.2" rain. Willy's 40th B.D. We finished chopping out N. about 11 a.m. Chili for dinner. I went to craft fair in Avoca 3 p.m. Bill was working in shop when I came home. It just poured. We went to Walnut Legion (dance) with Duanes & Waynes.

Mon.10-05: Chopped hay on Laubet's.

Tue.10-06: Bill combined. Kris washed store windows in Shelby with 4-H bunch after school.

Fri.10-16: Combining on S. place. Bill came home 2:30 a.m.

Sun.10-18: 9 a.m. Drying bin caught on fire. Fire trucks & neighbors came. Men here for dinner. (With the help of neighbors & their trucks & wagons we emptied all the corn out of the bin by 2 p.m. and got the fire out.) ... We then headed to S. place about 4 p.m. & Finished! (corn there).

Tue.10-27: Sold 52 cows in Dunlap. Bill combined.

Mon.11-09: (Combining here) Poked hole in back wagon tire & went to Harlan for new one ($203). Jerod at sitter all day.

Mon.11-16: Finished combining.

Thu.11-19: A little snow & cold. Went over home (evening). Very slick. 5 semis off interstate. Did books from 11 p.m. to 1:30 a.m.

Fri.11-20: Worked with Bill on figures for 9:30 a.m. appt. with Federal Land Bank. Cows & bulls were out & I chased for and hour or so. Had to hurry to school by 11 a.m. for lunch with the kids. Bill & Duane went collecting. Kris had eye exam in Harlan 3:30 p.m. I fed calves.

Sat.11-21: I was exhausted. Had to hurry to clean house as a Wilson Seeds man came at 9 a.m. to sign Bill up as a seed corn dealer. Laurie Bornholdt was killed (She was my cousin. My Dad's brother Ross' daughter.) (She died tragically in a car accident when the car she was a passenger in overturned near Elk Horn. She was a Walnut High School senior.) Such a terrible sad thing.

Mon.11-23: Went to PCA.

Tue.11-24: Sherry came home. Bill went to Land Bank 3:30 p.m. Went to folks' & then to Atlantic for visitation for Laurie's funeral.

Wed.11-25: Went to Laurie's funeral. My folks & Sis went with us to Atlantic cemetery, & back to Walnut for fellowship. Folks came over for supper with Sherry & her girls.

Thu.11-26: Thanksgiving Day. Started to snow. Went to Delores' for supper.

Fri.11-27: Bill went to Avoca salebarn. Al picked up field corn with 4-H kids (a money making project for his club). I took Kris to pick out frames (for her new glasses).

Sun.11-29: Sorted off 60 cows to take to S. place. Chased 101 over to Louie's. Went to Bill's folks' for their B.D.'s.

Mon.11-30: Raining. Snow after dinner. Kids out early. Had to take kids to school 'cause we didn't wake up until 7:50 a.m. Chased in cows & took 3 loads to S. place. Figured & went to Land Bank at 3 p.m. (no definite answer yet on financing us). (Today's our 13th anniversary.)

Tue.12-01: Snow. No school. Took 2 loads of hogs to Harlan. Went to PCA. — nothing definite — nothing promising. Went to my folks' for Dad's B.D.

Wed.12-02: Bill had school brd. mtg. I cut out & made Alan's shepherd outfit for S.S. program. & mended. Al had 4-H.

Sat.12-05: Kids & I went over home. Bill went to Denison salebarn. I sold Jerod's wonder horse for $25 & did some Christmas shopping — or looking.

Tue.12-08: Alan & I vaccinated 50 pigs & put them in their pens. Bill was sick — terrible stomach ache.

Wed.12-09: Took information to bank. Went to PCA at 10 a.m. Bill had Dr.'s appt. at 11:15 a.m. Bill had school brd. mtg.

Thu.12-10: Bill had his stomach x-rayed. We came home & figured some. Went to see man at Avoca bank. Went to ASC, to Shelby Co. Mutual on grain bin fire, to PCA. Home to chore.

Sat.12-12: Took Kris to get her new glasses. Got Bill's medicine (for an ulcer). Kris & I went to 4-H dinner. Took kids to S.S. (program) practice. Duane took Walter to hospital. Sorted calves & treated some. Went to F.S. dinner dance.

Sun.12-13: Went to S.S. Christmas program.

Mon.12-14: Porkettes 9:30 a.m. PCA after dinner. Appt. at FHA. Bill stopped (at hospital) to see his dad. We fed & treated a few calves. Bill went to chemical school.

Tue.12-15: Bill chored & left 10 a.m. to sell seed corn. I cleaned house most all day. Made an apple pie after dinner (a rarity, because I usually don't do pies).

Mon.12-21: We went to hospital as Walter had a tumor taken out of his bladder.

Thu.12-24: Got a new calf over to Louie's. I went to Harlan after dinner for some gifts, etc. Went to see Walter & then had chili at Duane's.

Fri.12-25: Opened packages shortly after 7 a.m. To Betty's.

Sat.12-26: Went over home for Christmas with Sherry's. Went to see both Grandma's. Jerod & Al both got sick as we were ready to come home. Both were up in the night with vomiting & diarrhea.

Mon.12-28: Sold hogs to Harlan in the meat, $41.19 @ 229 lbs. Went to talk to Dad (about money problems). He had flu & I was getting sick.

Tue.12-29: I was sick all day. Al & Bill took 4-H calves to weigh-in at Avoca. Walter was released.

Thu.12-31: Went to New Year's Eve dance in Minden & to Becky's for breakfast. Home about 3:15 a.m.

(1981 had been a devastating, depressing year for us. With interest rates on our farm debt at nearly 20%, our interest costs in 1981 mounted to $90,618. Such high rates also caused a further drop in demand for land purchases, which in turn caused land prices to fall more, & hence eroded the value of our farm assets even further. [For example, our land plunged from a value of $2400 an acre to $1200 an acre during this farm financial crisis.]

With our fixed costs still going up, our farm prices still too low, & our net worth down, we slipped deeper & deeper into severe financial trouble.

We were down and being kicked hard! But we hung in there — some days with tears in our eyes & pain in our souls — but we went on with our farming and worked hard, as usual.

We figured day & night: plans to sell down, to get out of hogs or cows, or plans to diversify our farming operation. [We started to liquidate our cow herd & to sell our calves as feeders instead of finishing them.] We'd push the pencils, & talk, & discuss, & come up with a new cash flow plan: our hearts would quicken with a new glimmer of hope.

We'd go to our prospective lenders with papers & figures in hand, & lay out yet another new plan, only to be told, "No, we can't do it." "We can't back you."

Our lenders told us we should sell out — sell all of our machinery & livestock, & get jobs in town. We could keep our house to live in, but otherwise, we were told to give up our life as we knew it.

They couldn't possibly know how we felt at the thought of this, and of watching someone else farm our land. They couldn't know the gut wrenching pain we felt, the helplessness, the fear!)

(... It's 1992 now, as I'm writing the above segment to help explain my 1981 journal, but the memories come rushing back so hauntingly real & vivid, that I have tears in my eyes, & they're falling on my notes now ...

To this day, I hate to see farm sale adds! My heart aches for any families who loose their farms or are forced to sell out. "Mis-management" was the cry of unknowing non-farm people in the 1980's, but severe income & net worth drops and 20% interest costs on farm operating loans were hard to buck — impossible to buck — and thousands of farm families in this country were forced out of, or gave up, farming in the 80's.

[According to the *Farm & Food Facts* pamphlet of 1990, by the editors of the *Kiplinger Agriculture Letter,* the number of U.S. farms dropped from 2,437,000 in 1979 to 2,171,000 in 1989, & the U.S. farm population dropped from 6,241,000 in 1979 to 4,951,000 in 1988.]

A sad, sad time, because too many in this nation thought it was all our [the farmer's] fault ... they didn't stop to consider that the "cheap food policy" of our government was all coming at the farmers' expense: our exports were down, & hence our farm commodity prices were down; yet our fixed costs of machinery, fertilizer, & especially interest, were higher than we had ever seen! And this was all do to gov't manipulation of farm product prices to provide "cheap food" to this country & to the world.)

1982

Fri.1-01: Slept late. Took tree & all Christmas decorations down. Al & Bill chored. Read, & watched Rose bowl.

Sat.1-02: (Evening) played Scrabble until 2 a.m. with kids.

Sun.1-03: Snowed. Bill & kids ck'd cows at S. place. Stopped at Wayne's & rode in his (horse drawn) sleigh.

Sun.1-10: 20° Below Zero.

Mon.1-11: No school. No water. We figured again & Bill went to see Avoca banker & FHA. Roads were drifted bad. Hog waterers frozen again, grain bin auger frozen. Water came by bedtime (well pipes were frozen).

Thu.1-14: We went to Dunlap to watch our cows & bulls sell. (We sold 156 cows & 5 bulls.)

Fri.1-15: I worked on book work. Bill tightened up things outdoors for forecasted storm. Bad wind & cold.

Sat.1-16: I did income tax work & finished gray blazer & skirt. Bill went to talk to banker. Went to Michelle Larsen's wedding (neighbor girl), & to dance at legion.

Tue.1-19: Bill did some figuring & we went to PCA to give them new figures to stay with us. Guys went to ball game.

Fri.1-22: Raining — even thundering & lightning. No school. We had to go to PCA at 9:30 a.m. Visibility very poor. We got a few groceries & came home. PCA said no go. We went sleigh riding just at dark on

Louie's.

Sun.1-24: Jo, Duane, & kids came for dinner. Kids went sleigh riding. We played Scrabble.

Wed.1-27: Bill moved snow to prepare to pump the pit. We went to PCA at 1 p.m. <u>Finally</u>! they said they'd finance us this year. (Finally, with yet another new plan, & help from a couple private lenders, PCA said they'd finance us this year, with no promise beyond a review of our situation at the end of 1982.) We got a few groceries & came home.

Mon.2-08: <u>Finally</u> got new loan signed at PCA. Cleaned crib & ground feed. Went to Pork Producers Banquet with Duane's.

Thu.2-18: I went to Harlan for a job interview. (I would take a town job to help provide some grocery money).

Mon.2-22: (I was hired as 4-H program aide at Shelby County Extension in Harlan. I'd work a 30 hr. week with the county 4-H program. My work schedule was flexible so I could try to help chore, & sort hogs before I had to be to work, & I could have days off when I needed to help make hay or haul in grain.)

Tue.2-23: I worked 9 — 5. (My family were going to try to help me out with chores at home while I worked: well today, Jerod, only 4 1/2 years old, fixed Bill hot dogs & hollered at him to come to dinner, at 10 a.m.)

Fri.2-26: I was done at work at 11:15 a.m. Picked Jerod up at sitter & came home & cleaned. (There were) 30 of us here for pot luck (neighborhood club) supper — was fun evening.

Mon.3-08: Bill went to first exercise class in Avoca.

Mon.4-05: Kids had chili ready (when I got home from work: a nice surprise because I had a headache).

Tue.4-27: Bill took Alan to Al's woodcarving class.

Wed.4-28: When I came home from work, I discovered the bathroom stool had run over & no one had cleaned it up.

Wed.6-02: I taught Alan to harrow on S. creek field. Bill was disking. I went to work after 10 a.m. & stayed through a 7 p.m. 4-H Council meeting.

Sat.6-19: We unloaded 5 racks (of hay bales) before dinner; ate quick & started baling. About 3451 on (baler) counter. Got in 10 p.m. Cleaned up & went to Rita Peters' reception (neighbor girl & kids' baby-sitter).

(We made lots of acres of alfalfa into small square & big round hay bales all season. Some of what we used to chop for all of our cows, we now baled to sell each year.)

Fri.7-09: Kids helped Bill get combine ready to go. He started wheat at Herb Rock's. It started to rain about 8 p.m. & rained all night. We cranked our first homemade ice cream (of this summer).

Wed.7-21: Made hay until 11:30 p.m.

Sat.7-24: Went to arm wrestling at Avoca Fair. Finished combining our oats & went to help Jo & Duane with hay on Godfrey's. Had supper there.

Sun.7-25: We baled straw. Bill & Alan went to tug-o'-war (at Avoca's Fair). We baled straw until nearly dark & put loads in shed. 605 bales.

Mon.7-26: Bill raked hay. Duane baled 20 big round bales. They also baled little sq. bales. I got home 6 p.m. Mowed with bush hog (tractor rotary mower) until 9 p.m.

Fri.7-30: (I cleaned house). Bill & Duane combined on Leonard's. Mike & Alan baled on Jack's. My folks, Sherry's, & Duanes here for supper.

Sat.7-31: Al, Sis, & I went to (Atlantic) Krazy Daze.

Tue.8-03: The gang at work had cookies etc. for my birthday at coffee break. Went to 4-H carcass calf supper/slide show.

Tue.8-10: We all went to Council Bluffs with Alan where he got his palatal expander (at the orthodontist). Ate at Mc Donalds & went to see *E.T.* (movie).

Sat.8-14: Bill went to Denison salebarn & got 160+ pigs. Went to Julie's wedding (Gary & Betty's daughter). Jerod & Kris went to stay at my folks'.

Sun.8-15: Went to State Fair with Duane's. Bill got 5th in both right & left handed arm wrestling.

Sat.8-21: From 8:30 a.m. to 6:30 p.m. we put tin on the W. side of barn roof (N. half).

Sun.8-22: (Bill & team pulled in State Fair tug-o'-war.)

Mon.8-23: Bill, Duane, Mike, & our kids loaded our truck & a semi with hay for the (Omaha) zoo. Kids looked around at the zoo while Bill was unloading bales in the elephant house. Loaded up a load this evening & then had supper.

Wed.8-25: Kids started school.

Mon.8-30: Bill took a load (of hay) to the zoo — I helped him load before

I went to work. Bill took Doc (his dad) to hospital just before midnight.

Thu.9-02: I came home early (3 p.m.) & we nearly finished baling out N. — filled racks. Took Al to confirmation mtg.

Fri.9-03: Finished hay. Bill went to salebarn & brought home a pony. (The kids named him Silver.)

Thu.9-09: I worked. Bill made fence between us & Minnie's.

Sat.9-11: Bill went to Spencer Fair with Wayne & Terry. I took Al to Dr. for his football physical & Kris to 4-H.

Wed.9-15: I left work at 3 p.m., got groceries, came home & hurried to get ready for school board barbecue here. There were 23 of us here. Had a nice supper.

Sat.9-25: Took Al to dentist. I went with 4-H group to Omaha on awards tour. Got home midnight.

Mon.10-04: I helped get combine ready. Got to work 1:15 p.m. Bill & Duane combined at Herb Rock's. (Work) 4-H awards mtg. lasted until 1:30 a.m.

Tue.10-05: Rained lightly. Bill & I went to hospital to talk to Walt's Doctor. Walter had his 1st radiation treatment.

Sun.10-10: Took kids to S.S. & church. Alan lit candles.

Tue.10-12: Bill went to hospital to see his dad. I drained oil out of combine & fueled it up. Went to see Al's last football game & hurried to carcass mtg. Home midnight.

Thu.10-14: (Walt got brought home to Harlan hospital.) Bill was to open up corn fields for Bill True.

Sun.10-31: Bill left for hospital early (to visit his Dad). I took kids to S.S. & visited Helen. Bill started combining our beans. I took kids trick or treating. Bill didn't feel good.

Mon.11-01: Went to hospital about 6:30 a.m. I worked at office until 9 a.m. Then got Bill at hospital. I went to parent-teacher conferences. Bill tried beans. We unloaded truck in light rain & unloaded hay rack (into Louie's barn). To bed at 8 p.m.

Tue.11-02: Bill & I went to hospital 7:30 a.m. Dr. said Walter was stabilizing & could soon go to a home. Beans wouldn't go, so Bill put cornhead on & left. I had club. Went to vote.

Fri.11-05: Walter was moved from Harlan hospital to the Baptist Nursing Home in Harlan.

Sun.11-07: Lovely warm day. Finished our beans & moved to S. place about 4 p.m. to start corn.

Mon.11-08: We worked on corn at S. place. Bill's mom called shortly after 11 p.m. to say that Walter had passed away. I found Bill & Duane & Jo, & we went in (to Shelby) to Bill's mom's until 3:30 a.m.

Tue.11-09: Got kids off to school & we went to Helen's. Bettys, Duanes, Delores, Charlies, & us went to the Avoca funeral home to make funeral arrangements.

Wed.11-10: We worked on corn at S. place. Quit at 4 p.m. to chore & clean up to go to visitation at the funeral home. Bill went on to a school board mtg. after he dropped us at home at 9:30 p.m.

Thu.11-11: Rained (I said Walter had it rain 'cause he knew the boys wouldn't have to combine today). We went to Shelby church at 10 a.m. for Bill's dad's funeral. Many friends & relatives there. Spent rest of day at Bill's mom's.

(This evening I wrote a poem for Bill's dad; it's in Section VIII of this book.)

Fri.11-12: (I worked: an all day area wide extension staff mtg. in Council Bluffs. Bill was combining corn. I started driving truck about 5 p.m. to help haul corn home from the combine at the S. place. About 9 p.m., when I came back home with a load of corn, the drying bin was on fire!

I called the fire dept., got word to Bill at the south place, & called Duane's, & Babbitt.

[Duane has always been the first family member we call in an emergency because he lives close, & because <u>we can always count on him</u> to help us out.]

[Bill Babbitt is <u>a very valued & trusted neighbor & friend</u>: for years, he's been the person we consult for a knowledgeable opinion of farm business matters; & he's the one we call when we're in serious trouble because he's close, & he comes. He's been our safety net and rescue squad on several occasions, as has Duane.]

Babbitt, Rich Robinson, & Garvin came, & Bill, Duane, Kenny Osbahr [he was driving truck for us that day], & 6 fireman. We knew we had to get the corn out of the bin to stop the fire, but the floor auger wouldn't work. Babbitt got his big payloader & took corn out of a door slat in the bin. They filled the payloader's big bucket & dumped piles of hot corn out into a row on the ground.

It was very cold that night, but the corn stayed hot for a long time after it had been outside on the ground. Some of us stood in the hot corn to warm our feet. I kept the workers supplied with coffee, hot chocolate & sandwiches through the night.

When the corn stopped running out the door, the men got in the bin & scooped, working in thick smoke & burning hot corn, right on through until 6:30 a.m. the next morning, when the 4500 bu. bin was finally emptied — with only the last couple feet of completely burnt black solid mass remaining.

[We think the fire started when a bearing in the circu-flow in the center of the bin went out & got hot. While last year's drying bin fire was from fines under the floor.])

After everyone went home, Bill slept for 2 hrs. & went to combine. I had to fill feeders. Went to bed early.

(We were tired before this grain bin fire ordeal, as this had been a sad, trying week due to Bill's dad's death. Bill had just commented to someone at his dad's funeral that we had been so busy with harvest, but "at least we shouldn't have to worry about having a drying bin fire this year." ... That statement sure turned out to be wrong! ... but all the good people who showed up to help us through the long night of the fire helped to lift our spirits again.)

Sun.11-14: Clarence (Johnson) brought up his batch corn dryer & set it up. Bill & Clarence stayed up all night (to watch the dryer & keep it full, etc. to get the piles of corn up off the ground & dried, & into another bin).

Mon.11-15: Bill came in at 7 a.m. for breakfast.

Wed.11-24: Horrible hectic day at the office.

Thu.11-25: Went to my folks' for Thanksgiving with all the Bornholdt's. Went to Delores' for supper.

Sun.11-28: Went to Helen's for her B.D. Took great aunts Edna & Jenny along.

Wed.12-01: Rain. (I worked). Went to Dad's for B.D. supper.

Mon.12-06: We started combining on the tie pile field at 8 a.m. & ran clear til 2:15 a.m. when we finished the field.

Tue.12-07: A skift of snow to make it slick. We combined 8 a.m. til 10:30 p.m. when Bill finished the cemetery field.

Fri.12-10: I went to work. <u>Bill finished combining our corn</u> N. of the creek. All trucks & wagons were full.

Sat.12-11: (A man from Elk Horn, who'd heard about our bin fires, called this a.m. to ask questions about a grain bin of his he thought was on fire.) Bill & kids took a load of hay to the zoo. We went to my office Christmas Party (& at the party we got another call from the same man: he was sure now that his 10,000 bu. bin was on fire & he asked lots more questions to learn how we had handled our bin fires).

Sat.12-18: Bill took load of hay to zoo. I cleaned & did laundry all day. Kris & I went down by the creek & cut our Christmas tree (a cedar). It almost touches the ceiling, & is 5 ft. across, at least.

Sun.12-19: (My folks & Sherry's were here for Christmas dinner. We went to kids' S.S. Christmas program.

Mon.12-20: I worked. Bill was pallbearer at Minnie Peters' funeral. Went to Jr. High/High School Christmas Concert.

Wed.12-29: Weighed in 4-H calves in Avoca. Bill & Duane went collecting.

Fri.12-31: I went over home & the kids stayed there. Bill got 17 cows at salebarn. Went to New Year's Eve dance in Minden. Stopped at legion in Avoca for breakfast. (We had some good laughs & last moments with Ronnie Woltmann.)

1983

Sat.1-01: I did dishes, laundry, etc. Started to cut out a skirt & blouse. We went to S. place to ck. the field to see about taking cows down. Watered cows. We had just gotten home when Jo called to say Ronnie had been out snow mobiling with his kids & had had a heart attack ... she added, that he was gone. (Ronnie was Bill's best friend, and had been a groomsmen in our wedding. He was only 42 years old.)

(Bill wrote a poem about Ronnie & it's in Section VIII.)

Sun.1-02: A sad day. I cried as I made apple crisp to take to Kay's. Also took a casserole to her on our way over to dinner at my folks', to pick up the kids. We went to funeral home to see Ronnie.

Tue.1-04: Kids off to school. We hurried to Duane's & went to Ronnie's funeral. So many flowers. So many people there. A very nice service. (A special friend gone, but never forgotten.)

Wed.1-05: I went to work, after helping sort & load hogs. Had a very busy day at the office, & then mtgs. from 5 - 11.

Fri.1-07: We went to all day PCA Cash Flow Meeting.

Sat.1-15: We took Alan to orthodontist & went to the zoo with hay for the giraffes. Bill & Al went to Denison. Got 22 cows & 200+ pigs.

Thu.1-20: Alan got his top braces.

Sat.1-22: I had mtg. in Atlantic for work. Al went to a gun safety deal in Shelby. Bill & other two kids took load of hay to the zoo.

Sun.1-23: Bill took kids to S.S. I cleaned, etc. Re-potted several house plants. Bill went to his mom's to sort out Walter's clothes.

Wed.2-02: SNOW DRIFTS. No School. Jerod lost his 1st tooth.

Thu.2-03: No School.

Fri.2-04: Went to PCA & got our loan set up for 1983.

Tue.2-08: Bill loaded hay, by himself, & went to zoo. (We get 200 square bales on our truck.)

Fri.2-11: Loaded hay & took it to the elephants.

Tue.2-15: I got yellow daises at work from Bill (the only other time I had gotten flowers from him was when Kris was born, so they were really a special Valentine surprise).

Feb.2-22: Alan had an eye doctor appointment: 20-50 vision. Ordered glasses.

Tue.3-02: John Rosmann & I went to Omaha (to Channel 3 TV) to tape 4-H TV Spotlight. We ate at Johnny's Cafe. (John was one of my Shelby County 4-H Council kids.)

Sat.3-05: Al went to music contest. Kris played basketball. Jerod & I visited at Helen's. Bill went to Mez's sale.

Sat.3-26: Snowed & blowed all day. Electricity went out 3:15 p.m. Phone too.

Sun.3-27: Electricity came on at 3 p.m.

Mon.3-28: No School. Sorted & loaded hogs til 1 p.m. Took 3 loads. I went to work 2-5 p.m. The gang sorted & moved hogs out N. I was home by 6 p.m. & we moved crib pigs out N. Kids & I cleaned the crib. Bill went to basketball practice.

Sun.4-03: Easter. I cut my hair & Kris'. Kids went to S.S. We went to Jo & Duane's for dinner & supper.

Thu.4-14: Snowing & blowing. Bus ran 2 hrs. late. Kids were messing around & missed it. I made them start walking to school.

Thu.5-12: Bill finished planting on Louie's (that's the farm across the road from us. Louie Johnson, Bill's great uncle owned it, and before him John Johnson, Bill's great grandfather homesteaded there).

Mon.5-30: We went to my folks' after dinner, & Jerod took his duds along & stayed.

Fri.6-03: We went to Kris' softball game in Walnut. Folks were there, & Jerod came home with us.

Sat.6-04: We went to centennial parade in Kimballton.

Tue.7-05: (Bill & I [along with Margaret Plumb, Harlan] chaperoned a van of 12 Shelby County 4-H'ers to Green County Wisconsin, for a 4-H Interstate Exchange. [Green county, in south-central Wisc., is known for its dairying & cheese. Basic crops in the area are corn & alfalfa, with considerable strip cropping on steep hills. Southern parts of the county have some flat fields & rolling hills like around here.]

Host family for Bill & I were John, Joan, Cindy, & Aaron Salesman who live near Argyle, Wisc. on a dairy & hog farm, & have an on-farm feed store.)

Wed.7-06: (Our group & their hosts toured a Swiss Historical Village at New Glarus, which was named for a canton [state] in Switzerland, where settlers came from in the early 1800's to settle in Green County. Later, we had a fun walk through a 1/4-mi. long railroad tunnel on the Felix Statz farm [one of the host families] near New Glarus.)

Fri.7-08: (Our group toured a cheese factory that made Muenster & Swiss cheese [I love Wisc.'s cheeses, especially the aged Swiss!]. We had a picnic at the Sam Kaderly farm near Juda, & the 4-H'ers swam in their pool.)

Sun.7-10: (All of our group & our host families attended a farewell potluck supper in Monroe.)

(Bill & I really enjoyed visiting with John & Joan, & seeing their hog operation & Holstein dairy set up. Joan also took me to see a fascinating embroidery factory where eyelet & embroidered border fabrics were made. She took me to a fabric store with <u>4 floors</u> of beautiful fabric that was heaven for me to browse in! We also toured The House On The Rock which is something to see, with its huge collection of unusual antiques & fascinating displays [such as musical instruments like violins & full orchestras that play all automatically & mechanically, with no people].)

Mon.7-11: (We headed home with lots of good memories of a fun step into the lives or our warm, friendly hosts in Green County Wisconsin.)

Tue.9-06: Went to open house at school. Helen went along.

Sun.9-11: I painted a gallon of primer on the S. side of the house. Bill mowed hay. He took his combine to Herb's for first corn of the season.

Mon.9-12: My first drawing class (a 3 credit class through Iowa Western, at Harlan).

Tue.9-13: Bill mowing hay. He won re-election to school brd.

Fri.9-30: Took supper to Helen. Al & Kris went to homecoming.

Mon.10-03: Rain. Bill & Jerod went to dentist. Jerod got 2 front teeth pulled (to make room for new ones), & Bill got 2 fillings replaced. Bill took it easy today (his birthday, you know). Pola Peters picked me up & we went to Drawing class.

Fri.10-07: I painted primer on the E. peak (of the house). Yield tested beans: 54 bu/A. Misty. Tough — we quit at dark.

Sat.10-8: We finished beans! & Bill went to Raleigh Woltmann's & finished the last of the custom beans. I had 4-H awards banquet to go to.

Tue.10-11: We loaded a semi of hay. It's going to Kentucky.

Thu.10-13: We finished corn on Christian Home farm (or Doctor's farm: about 5 mi. S. of us) before noon. Shelled on Louie's — put in drying bin. I came in at 1:15 a.m. & Bill later. We finished our corn!

Fri.10-14: Bill changed oil in the combine & changed heads (our corn is in 30" rows, our custom people have 38" rows) & took off for Herb's. I unloaded 3 trucks & 2 wagons, & painted primer on S. of house.

(This is the last journal entry for 1983 — all summer, there were no entries either.)

1984

Sun.1-01: Sherry & Ken & my folks were here for our Christmas gathering.

Wed.1-04: I went to Omaha with 4-H'er Alex Fairlie & his father to tape TV 4-H Spotlight at Channel 3.

Fri.1-13: Bill got his bean yield trophy (for 1st place, conservation tillage division, 54.23 bu/A., Shelby County).

Tue.1-17: We did book work. Had pancakes for supper.

Sat.1-21: Went to Betty's to play cards. Home 3 a.m.

Mon.1-23: Bill had school board. mtg. at 9:30 a.m. We went to PCA at 11 a.m. to go over figures. Went to Red Lion at noon for my office farewell. Bill moved snow & set up auger across the road.

Tue.1-24: I went to work. Bill move 17 loads corn from bin across the road to hog house bin.

Wed.1-25: I went to work at 2 p.m. till 11 p.m. Bill went to community club mtg. for school board. He picked up Kris from her ball game.

Thu.1-26: Bill Helped Duane work calves most of the day. Duanes & us went to F.S. supper/dance.

Fri.1-27: Went to PCA at 8:30 a.m. to sign papers to set up new loan — no cosigners needed! I worked until noon. Cleaned up my stuff & was done! The last day of my extension job. Hurray! (I did love working with the people at my office & all the 4-H'ers & families from all over the county. I miss them all. But, the night & weekend meetings made me miss my kid's school functions; & I often made hay or hauled in corn until the wee hours, after I got home from work. It was like holding down two jobs, & my house always looked like a pit!)

Sat.1-28: We pushed out (cleaned) pens, lightened up pens, & cut a few pigs.

Sun.1-29: Alan & Bill went to a 4-H bowling deal in Harlan. High winds (40 m.p.h., gusts to 60 m.p.h.) blew them off the highway by Ted Allen's. A Harlan cop brought them home.

Wed.2-01: Kris' last basketball game. First sow had pigs. Bill pulled 1st one. Jerod pulled the 9th one.

Sat.2-04: Bill & I went to SCO Banquet, drove to Avoca afterwards. It started to snow like crazy, so we drove home by Duane's. We got caught in a ground blizzard & couldn't see the road at all. It was really a pip!

Sun.2-05: No water, & wind blowing like crazy. Pipes frozen.

Wed.2-08: I went to see Jerod's class sing for Band Mothers.

Fri.2-10: I chaperoned a bus, with Alan's class, to see the play *Huck Finn* in Omaha.

Fri.2-17: Bill had board mtg. 8:15 a.m. I spent all day in Harlan High School doing pork presentations (giving pork info & recipes to home economics classes on behalf of Shelby Co. Pork Producers & Porkettes). Bill went to salebarn.

Sat.2-25: We cleaned up the joint & did laundry. We all went to Betty & Gary's 25th anniversary dance in Minden.

Mon.3-05: When Alan chored, he found a sow in between the crates & she had torn her belly open by jumping where she wasn't supposed to be. We had the vet out for her & he suggested we take her to the locker.

Thu. 3-08: 1st calf of the season, a red bull.

Mon.3-12: (Duane helped Bill work our cows.)

Tue.3-13: Bill helped Duane work his cows.

Wed.3-14: Bill & Duane went to Machinery show in Omaha. Went to school spring concert.

Sat.3-17: Kris & I went to 4-H. Bill & boys went to a sale. We went to Shelby Fireman's dance in Minden.

Wed.3-21: We loaded a semi with hay. (Duane's & us both sold a lot of small square bales this year & usually helped each other load hay: we loaded hay semis on 3-31, 4-2, 4-4, & 4-5, for example, & many other days this winter.) (The semis hold from 550 to about 600 small square bales.)

Thu.3-22: Loaded a semi of hay. Bill was late for ball practice 'cause we had to tie up a cow & get her calf to nurse. Alan went to tractor safety class.

Thu.4-19: Alan & I went to Living History Farms & the Capitol in Des Moines, with his History class. Bill put on lime. Al & I chored. We went to Maundy Thursday services & Kris' first communion. Bill's mom got lost coming home from Betty's.

   (Alzheimer's disease was creeping up on Helen: today she'd driven to Elk Horn to Betty's, but on the way home, she had a memory lapse & got lost. When she hadn't come home by the time we expected her, we called Betty. Helen had left Elk Horn a lot earlier. We were concerned. Duane's & us made some phone calls & started to search for her.

   The boys first drove the roads we thought she'd have taken. We called Bill's sister in Atlantic & she contacted the police there. They'd seen a car like Helen's earlier, but she was no longer there ... the search continued ... Duane found out she'd been in Avoca that night; & finally, well after midnight, she made her way home. She tried to make us believe that nothing unusual had happened, but she couldn't tell us where she'd been. [Duane knew she'd put over 200 miles on her car, as he'd just worked on it the day before & had then taken note of the odometer reading.]

   We knew now that she'd bear more watching. The boys kept her car keys. We told her Duane was fixing her car.)

Sun.4-22: The Johnson gang was here for Easter. 21 for dinner & 29 for supper. Garys left their camera here, & Kelly lost his retainer. (Kelly called to say he might have lost his retainer while out looking at our calves & asked if we'd go check there. Bill called him back & told him we went out to look for it & found a black calf wearing it. Actually, that wasn't true, but we did find it, unbroken, in the feed bunk & returned it to Kelly).

Sat.4-28: Bill put on anhydrous. We loaded hay. Bill & I went to prom.

Sun.5-06: Alan was confirmed. Company here. Very hectic day.

Thu.5-10: Went out 7:30 a.m. to chore & Bill to incorporate. I did several loads of laundry, paid some bills, cut some sour dock. Moved sows & pigs to white house & cleaned red house crates. Chored again. Put hot wire around cows. Came in about 10 p.m. Worked on planter.

Fri.5-11: I learned how to incorporate herbicide. Bill started planting.

Sun.5-13: 1/2" rain. Mother's Day. Moved crib pigs out N. Cleaned crib. I mowed lawn. Did laundry. Bill planted. We went to Jerry's graduation (Gary & Betty's boy).

Fri.5-18: Bill planted beans. I disked alfalfa.

Mon.5-21: Kids & I weaned pigs in white house. Took sows out W. Mowed the yard. Bill was incorporating on the S. place. He came home about 2 a.m. Rained 1.1"

Sun.5-27: Went to church. Went to David Andersen's 25th anniversary, & then to Bill's 25th class reunion at Steak House in Avoca.

Mon.5-28: Memorial Day. We drove to Shelby, Avoca, & over home for supper. Jerod stayed at the folks'.

Tue.5-29: I painted brown on porch & window trim. I think Bill must have sprayed fence rows.

Thu.5-31: Bill went to ASC & after parts. Kids & I ground sow feed; Al hoed on Grandma's field; Bill & I incorporated & planted beans on S. place. Got done with chores 11:30 p.m.

Mon. 6-04: Vet came & we worked calves. Lost one nice big one due to broken blood vessel or smashed trachea.

Thu.6-07: Bill hauling corn to Oakland feedlot. Bill & Al hoeing. Helen locked herself out of her house & lost her keys. (The Alzheimer's was playing tricks on her again.) I picked her up for dinner. A terrible wind blew a big (70') pine tree down on our porch.

Sat.6-09: Bill repaired the haybine. We cut up & hauled away the big pine tree.

Sun.6-10: Went to 4-H picnic. Bill mowed some hay. We went to Lori's confirmation gathering (Duane's daughter).

Tue.6-12: Went to horse races with Duanes, Waynes, Garys, & Dennises (for Wayne's B.D.) There were Tornado warnings as we were leaving races. Nothing bad for weather at home.

Thu.6-14: Folks came for Al's B.D. Turned some hay over, but it rained. Ground for sows & crib.

Sun.6-17: Alan left for 4-H camp at Madrid.

Tue.6-26: Duanes & us made hay. Rain & hail about 6:30 p.m. After chores, we put last of Duane's bales in barn. Al went to moped class in Harlan. Kris to ball game in Macedonia.

Fri.6-29: Got up at 5:30 a.m. to sort sows. Sold 66 @ 559 lbs. @ $47. Rod & Jerry Brewer fixed the porch roof.

Sat.6-30: Al got his moped permit & driver's permit.

Wed.7-04: Went to parade in Avoca.

Wed.7-05: Al mowed hay. Kris & I walked beans. Baled hay.

Thu.7-08 & 09: Cultivating & making hay.

Sun.7-15: Fifty people here for dinner to see Calvin & Sis. Some went to see arm wrestling at Harlan fair after dinner.

Sun.7-21: Bill combined wheat at Herb's.

Thu.8-02: Al, Willy, & I picked 72 doz. ears of sweet corn & took them to Harlan grocery stores. (The sweet corn venture was a 4-H project of Alan's.)

Fri.8-03: Bill & Al ran both balers at Duane's & then helped unload bales. Jerod & Kris shot B.B. gun through kitchen window. They misbehaved all day. (I was peacefully working on a sewing project, when I heard an unusual "pop" at my west kitchen window. As I went to investigate, I saw fine glass on the window sill first, & then I saw a tiny round hole in the window —"Ah ha!" I said. "A B.B. gun."

Two little backsides caught my eye just as they were scrambling into the garage to hide. When I confronted them, I heard, "B.B. gun? No I didn't have one."

I said, "Jerod, I know better."

"Kris did it!" he replied in a whine.

"Jerod, you were shooting at the cat pan," Kris added.

"I didn't aim at the window!" he quickly replied.

"It wasn't me," the other suspect added. In frustration, I spanked them both, which of course, they thought was quite unfair.)

Sat.8-24: We picked 127 doz. ears of sweet corn.

Sun.8-05: Very hot & humid. Kids & I worked on sweet corn for the freezer. Bill helped Duane with bales. We took the kids swimming at Prairie Rose.

Sun.8-19: We went to State Fair. Boz (Jerod) got lost twice. Once for about 2 1/2 hrs. (He didn't think he was lost — he had a camel ride, & did all sorts of things, & saw all sorts of sights while we looked all over the fairgrounds for him — he knew where the car was, & he wasn't a bit concerned, even though he was only seven years old.)

Mon.8-20: Bill & I both baled here. Duane hauled in. Terry, Al, Jason Schnack, & Dallas Klindt helped mow bales away. We ate supper at 1 a.m. After the guys left, Bill & I went out to put bales away & pick up bales.

Tue.8-21: Bill & I got in the house 5 min. until 5 a.m. & it soon started to rain. We went to see *Gremlins* (the movie).

Wed.8-22: Kids got on bus at 7:40 a.m. for 1st day of school. Bill & I picked sweet corn. Bill mowed & I turned over hay until my tractor died. Bill finished. Bill baled on cemetery field. Broke needles in the baler.

Thu.8-23: Making hay here. Alan got 1st half of his braces off. We got Alan a moped.

Sat.8-25: (Finished tearing down old corn crib at Christian Home place & burnt it.)

Thu.8-30: Alan got his braces off & got his retainer.

Fri.9-21: (Still making hay) Bill combining beans.

Sun.10-07: We went down to Duane's for turkey supper & watched the Reagan-Mondale debates.

Tue.10-09: Bill did first corn of the season.

Sat.10-20: Did corn on Louie's. Grain bin stirator ripped its wires overnight.

Sun.10-21: Yield ck'd corn N. of place. (Later won 1st place in Shelby

County Yield Contest for 195.08 bu. corn/acre.

Mon.10-22: Yield ck'd beans. (Later we learned that we'd won 1st place in the county yield contest with 54.65 bu/A.)

Wed.10-31: Unloaded beans in the rain. I went to Jerod's Halloween Party at school. Bill took him trick or treating.

Sun.11-04: I painted latex top coat on house. Finished beans at S. place.

Tue.11-06: Bill & Duane finished True's beans. I sewed on Jerod's suit. Went to vote. Kids leveled off bean bin. I cut out Kris' dress.

Thu.11-08: (I loaded corn trucks for Mike & Jack to haul to Oakland.) I marked hogs. Boys are combining.

Fri.11-09: We sorted hogs. It was pouring while we loaded. I worked on Kris' dress. Took Boz to wedding rehearsal.

Sat.11-10: Bill & Duane each took load corn to feedlot. I finished Kris' dress. We went to Duane Bornholdt (my cousin) & Janelle Clayton's wedding. Jerod was ring bearer.

Tue.11-13: Bill & Duane combining. Jack & I hauled in last of corn from Christian home. I went to Oakland for corn check, to ASC for bean loan money, & to PCA. I painted some on the N. side of the house.

Thu.11-15: Custom work is DONE ! We worked all forenoon on combine, & combined here til 10:30 p.m.

Fri.11-16: Worked on corn in N. field.

Sat.11-17: We finished corn out N. about chore time. Got 47 cows from Colorado.

Fri.11-23: Sherry & Ken came for turkey dinner. (Ken closed a bathroom window over our tub & drywalled the room.)

Fri.12-07: I cleaned frantically. Went to Harlan for groceries, etc. Dad came to get Jerod after school. Garys, Duanes, & Waynes here for Christmas supper.

Fri.12-14: No School, snow. We sorted & took 3 loads hogs to Harlan. Al & I cleaned off the pit lid. Bill got 200+ pigs at salebarn. He went to a Rocky Mountain oyster fry in Walnut. I cut out a corduroy skirt.

Mon.12-24: Jerod left a note for Santa to bring something for Cole (our dog).

Tue.12-25: Jerod was up at 5 a.m. He got kids up at 7 a.m. & we had our Christmas. Went to Duane's for dinner & supper.

Wed.12-26: Went to Mom & Dad's for late dinner & Christmas with Sherry & Ken's. Sis had flu.

Thu.12-27: Bill & Alan are very sick. They started vomiting about 4 a.m. I went to lunch at Kathy Voge's (with my old office bunch). When I got home, Alan was throwing up in a bucket on the washer, & Bill was on the pot.

Mon.12-31: To New Year's Eve dance in Minden with Duanes.

1985

Tue.1-01: I did farm books so we ate dinner late. I went to Avoca Vet to pick up some medicine, & stopped at the Stitch Shoppe sale. Got super buys on some really nice fabric.

Thu.1-03: Bill went out to work with hogs & then worked on cash flow figures. I started figuring income taxes.

Sat.1-05: Bill helped Duane load a tandem hay truck with pup (750 bales). I sewed. Club at Judy Babbitt's. Enjoyable afternoon. Bill loaded our truck with bales.

Fri.1-11: We took our truck to Harlan to Wilson Seeds to pick up 225 bu. of seed corn.

Mon.1-14: (Met with PCA to review our financial situation & set up new loan.) We have improved enough to qualify for middle interest rate. Stopped at Shelby County Mutual to add insurance coverage to garage contents to cover seed corn.

Wed.1-16: Got up 5 a.m. & got ready to head to Mexico with the Wilson Seeds group. Mom was here to get the kids off to school. Everything went fine at the airport & we took off about 8:30 a.m. (After a plane change to a big DC10 in Dallas, we arrived at 2 p.m. in Acapulco, where it was a very hot steamy 93°. We caught a bus to our motel & checked in to room 2802 on the 28th floor where we were greeted by a beautiful blue bay scene from our room's window. [Although our one suitcase was lost, after several trips down from our room, we finally found it at the front desk about 11 p.m.] Next we walked around & had our first supper in Mexico, at a Denny's restaurant, with our friends Pam & Dean Bauer, & Duane & Louise Hillyard.)

Thu.1-17: We were up early to see the sights (took a city bus tour, shopped, saw the cliff divers, had a delicious evening meal at our hotel, listened to a band, & had a good time. [Two crazy women at the hotel were dancing like wild animals & put on quite a show.])

Fri.1-18: (Our young guide, Simon, & six of us, crammed into a cab with the driver, & had a riot in the crazy traffic on our way to gov't stores & open air flea markets, where we bargained with shop owners for souvenirs, & had lots of laughs. We went out on the beach where Bill, Dean, & Louise went para-sailing; & we swam in the hotel pool ["swam" is used quite loosely because I don't swim, I drown!]. That evening we took a cab to a fancy Mexican restaurant. Even though our driver could speak very little English, when he got upset at other drivers in the crazy Mexican traffic, he swore at the "California drivers" in perfect English!)

Sat.1-19: (Back in Iowa) Duane & Terry loaded a truck (with 750 of our hay bales). (In Acapulco), we took a taxi, with Bauers' & Hillyards', to the pier for a glass bottom boat ride to La Roquetta Island. (You see, while sunning on the beach Friday, we were approached by a nice looking man in a business suit, showing attractive brochures for a glass bottom boat tour of the bay. For $12.50 per person we would have a tour of the bay, with open bar on the boat, dinner on the island, & use of an exclusive beach for the afternoon. We thought it sounded good, so the six of us bought tickets for the next day.

When we got down to the crowded pier Saturday, we stood in line where we were told we'd board for our tour. We saw big double decker boats & were excited about the trip!

As the line shortened, the big boats left & we were finally pointed toward our boat: a little, dumpy, creaky looking wooden boat with a tattered striped canvas sun shade. It had crude white painted wooden benches around its perimeter, to seat about 15 people, & a regular two-paned house storm window [with a crack across one corner, I might add] set into the center of the boat floor, to make it a "glass bottom boat"!

Harry, the Indian, was our guide on the dumpy disappointing boat. As we stepped past him and his cooler by the motor at the back of the boat, he announced that today was his birthday & there was only enough beer for him [so much for the "open bar" on the boat!].

He popped open a beer & took a few chugs, as he started the motor. Clouds of white smoke quickly engulfed us all, as the Johnson outboard motor puffed, coughed, & came alive.

As he eased us away from the pier & then on out to open water, he haughtily announced, with beer in hand, "I hope you can all swim cause I don't carry no life jackets." [We looked quickly about & he wasn't joking: there were none!] We were on for the ride now & hoped the island wasn't far.

Harry did have a teenage diver with him who jumped overboard, with a sea urchin in his teeth, & lured some pretty fish, under the storm window bottom of the boat, so that we could see them.

At the island we disembarked & that quickly, Harry sped away in his boat & left us there. We were to have lunch at the island restaurant — it was just up the hill — & the area around it was much less than attractive & stank of livestock manure.

Inside the filthy open air restaurant, a big goat [with a bad case of scours] was roaming among the tables. His apparent owner picked up a brown bottle of beer from a table to show the crowd how the goat could drink beer. The goat had it way in his mouth, glugging anxiously. The man sat the bottle back on the table; & the lady seated there, who had been visiting, & had not seen the goat trick, picked up her bottle & took a drink. Ick!

We had been warned not to drink the water away from our hotel, & at this buffet, we were afraid to eat the food, as well, because the place was just not clean! The food didn't look too appetizing either: there was some kind of gray and green stuff on half shells that looked like something a clam may have regurgitated. We only ate fresh fruit & little else. So much for our "included dinner meal"!

We left the filthy restaurant for the beach. It, we discovered, was an "exclusive beach" all right: exclusively Mexican; & we got dirty stares like we should not be there. It wasn't nice anyway, with broken glass & litter all over.

To pass time until our return boat was to arrive, we sat on some huge rocks, took pictures of all of us pretending to be cliff divers, & joked & visited about our "glass bottom boat tour."

Determined not to go back on the same boat, we were first in line at the dock, & got on a big double decker boat for our escape from the island. [This was a boat of richer, fancier dressed people.] Soon after we sailed, a man in a spiffy navy blazer, white slacks, & captains hat came around with a stack of 5"x7" photos [they had been taken of passengers on the trip out as a token]. He looked & looked through his stack & couldn't find any of us. He kept saying in his Spanish accent, "I don't know why we no have your pictures, Señors. Took everyone's pictures!"
— We tried to quiet him so as not to draw any more attention to ourselves.

If that wasn't enough for our adventurous tale, the young diver who was to jump overboard to lure fish under the glass bottom, did his thing; & when he got back aboard, I watched him go behind a wooden partition at the back of the boat, where he proceeded to grab a pail & bail water out of the boat! — Oh, fine! We had traded our dumpy, little, glass bottom boat & Harry the Indian, for a bigger, classier boat that was sinking!

Well, finally we did make it back to our hotel. We cleaned up for cocktails & a Mexican buffet & show at Acapulco Plaza Hotel; & we talked of our glass bottomed boat tour in Mexico that we'd never forget!)

Sun.1-20: Montezuma's revenge got me about 4:30 a.m., & I was sick all day during our long journey toward home [of course, I blamed the island!]. Bill & I got up at 8 a.m., ate breakfast with Pam & Dean, & walked around. I bought a hand painted floral pottery duck from a vendor by our hotel.

We also walked out to the beach, where we saw a darling little dark-eyed, pig-tailed Mexican girl of about 5 yrs. of age, who was selling necklaces & a puppet. I asked to take her picture & she said, "Sure, 300 pesos!"

Bill said, "No, too much, 100 pesos."

She quickly replied, "No, 300 pesos!" She finally agreed for us to take her picture & buy her puppet for 300 pesos. By then, we had to hurry to get our bags & catch the bus to the airport.

Our plane was having mechanical troubles & we had to change from noon to a 4 p.m. flight. I had a very upset stomach the whole time, & we had to sit on the floor at the airport: there were no chairs or benches ...

When we landed in Chicago, in a near blizzard, we couldn't taxi up to the terminal because of ice & snow on the runway; & because the door of the plane was iced shut, we got out an emergency exit & ran about 1/4 mile to the terminal in 0° F. weather with our 97° weather clothes on.

As we went through customs, an officer told me to cover up my duck, which was sticking out the top of my carry-on bag. He said the drastic temperature change could break it. Also at customs, they asked if anyone had any fruit, or leather goods, specifically sea turtle. A man said he had sea turtle cowboy boots [$350-$400 ones], & they confiscated them — no reimbursement — [sea turtle is an endangered species in the U.S., but not in Mexico].)

We got to Omaha, & then on home about 2:30 a.m. Mom & the kids woke up to visit & see all our goodies. Mom & Al worked with hogs all day, cleaning pens etc. — very cold.

Mon.1-21: Kids went off to school. Bill & I were both feeling punk today — Montezuma was getting both of us.

Tue.1-22: We worked on figures for taxes, loaded 2 wagons of hay, chored, & came in. Neither of us felt too good.

Wed.1-23: (Bill & Duane finished loading a hay truck, & we loaded another truck for Forrest Rutherford & Elvin Barnett [regular hay customers of ours from Missouri].

Fri.1-25: Our PCA man came down & we signed papers for 1985.

Sat.1-26: Kris & I went to an all day 4-H sewing workshop. (Kathy Barrett, Betty Graybill, & I helped the kids learn to sew.)

Mon.1-28: (Bill & Duane loaded hay trucks. Al's school jazz band contest. I was on hall duty during the contest.)

Thu.1-31: (We traded 2 small tractors for a 7000 Ford. We went to my folk's 40th anniversary supper.)

Sun.2-03: Kids misbehaved all day (naturally, I was trying to clean for company)! Louise & Duane, & Pam, Dean & boys came for supper, & to look at each others Acapulco pictures.

Mon.2-04: Went to Pork Producers Banquet: Bill was voted in as a director for the Southwest District for a 3 yr. term.

Thu.2-07: Bill put on fert. I spent 3 or 4 hrs. preparing a pork presentation & went to Harlan for all the groceries.

Fri.2-08: (I left at 7:30 a.m. for Harlan High School, where Judy & Rhonda Babbitt, Dorena Christensen, & Jackie Blum helped me present pork info, food samples, & slides to 130 home ec. students during the day, for Porkettes.) I came home to relax; & watched *Dallas* & *Falcon Crest*.

Mon.2-18: I marked hogs & we took 42 to Harlan @ 230 lbs @ $49 cwt. We tagged new calves. Bill went to school brd. mtg. Jerod, Kris & I started cutting 5" blocks for a quilt for Jerod, after he picked out the colors from my fabric scraps.

Thu.2-21: Daffodils south of house are coming up. Rained a lot in early a.m. hrs. I took Kris to choir practice at 7:30 a.m. & then sewed on Jerod's quilt. Bill & Duane to Omaha.

Fri.2-22: Jerod took his quilt for show & tell.

Fri.3-01: Lovely day, this 1st day of March. (The mud did cause some trouble in getting the truck up to the loading chute: Bill loaded 2 cows for the sale barn that had lost their calves. Kris had a bike wreck on our cemetery hill road after school & had to be taken for x-rays of her shoulder. She got some pain medicine & we brought her home.)

Sat.3-02: Kris came to life & started asking questions about how she got hurt. She didn't seem to remember anything about her wreck or going to the hospital.

Sat.3-04: Took Kris to Dr. for another x-ray (her collarbone was separated from her shoulder blade, & swollen).

Sat.3-09: (Al's Southwest 4-H club toured Wislon's seed corn plant in

Harlan & I served them dinner.)

Mon.3-31: Bill & Alan went to Pork Producers Barrow Show In Kimballton. Bill won 1st in judging contest, Alan 5th. They came home very tickled.

Wed.3-20: 1st day of spring & my 1st purple crocus bloomed. I raked yard, Bill went to a sale.

Sat.3-30: Al & Bill took hogs to Harlan. I helped put pizzas together at school for a band fund raiser. We went to the school play, *Harvey*. We got several inches of snow.

Sun.3-31: Went over home. Dad didn't feel good & we ended up taking him to the hospital. We headed home to ck. cows, & one had feet hanging out, so we got her in & Bill pulled the calf. Calf was OK.

Mon.4-01: We ck'd cows & one had feet out, so after much running in the deep snow, we got her in the cattleshed & pulled her baby. He came back feet first, but was OK. His mother didn't claim him though. (We came in to get dry clothes on, & went back out & ran all the cows in the yard, got gates to partition off the cattleshed, locked up the new cow & put her calf on the teat, sorted off some other close cows, & got in the house about noon to clean up & go to the hospital. Dad had kidney stones & high blood pressure, we learned. We visited & headed home to ck. the cows.)

Tue.4-02: Judy Babbitt & I did a pork presentation for Jerod's class at Shelby School (Judy brought a live 3 day old pig). After school, we all loaded a hay truck.

Thu.4-11: (Dad had a kidney stone removed at Jenny Ed.)

Sat.4-27: Bill & I went to prom (school brd. members were guests). (He got me a neat daisy corsage & this was only the 3rd time he's gotten me flowers in the 20 yrs. I've known him, so it was very special to me).

Sun.5-19: Al was harrowing; I was incorporating (herbicide); & Bill was planting. We quit to go to Shelby's graduation & then Bill planted again until dark.

Mon.5-20: Bill & I went to funeral visitation for Zeta Hamdorf (a neighbor & member of my Happy Dozen Club).

Wed.5-22: We went to Paul Nielsen's funeral (a relative of Bill's). Lots & lots of people.

May 5-29: Went to Kris' 1st softball game of the season.

Sun.6-2: We started building a tree house in the grove, & went to 4-H club picnic, & to Kris' ball game.

Tue.6-11: Helen saw a specialist for a CAT scan & tests. He said she has Alzheimer's disease. (Named for the German Dr. Alois Alzheimer, who first described the disease in the very early 1900's, it's a degenerative disease that attacks the brain & causes worsening of memory, thinking, and behavior, & currently has no cure.)

Fri.6-14: Jerod took Alan up breakfast in bed for his 15th birthday.

Sun.6-16: Al went out to ck. cows & found one with her head caught under the plank lot fence (I have no idea how she managed it). We knocked off a plank to free her & pulled her to upright her, but she later died.

Sat.6-29: (Alan left on the Shelby County 4-H interstate exchange to Warsaw, Indiana.)

Wed.8-07: We started to mow away bales before 8 a.m., & put in over 7 loads (about 100 bales to a rack or wagon load) before the guys came in for dinner. Later we loaded our truck with bales & Bill took it to Omaha. Kids & I baled up broken bales, & Al went to 4-H, Kris had band practice, & Bill had a school board meeting.

Mon 8-12: I didn't sleep much during the night, as I kept flying up to make sure Boz wasn't getting up to get a drink: he wasn't to have any water after midnight. We got up at 5 a.m. & left for the hospital. Jerod had his tonsils & adenoids taken out.

Mon.8-26: We were making hay.

Tue.8-27: We baled up 12 racks of hay.

Wed.8-28: (About 8 a.m. we started to unload bales into Elsie Hintz's barn. Mike put them in the elevator, & Jo, Duane, Willy, & I mowed them away. We ate in town & went back to unload 4 more racks. Duane & I turned over hay. We had a malt from town & baled 3 more racks. We were going to pull them in a crib & quit, but they wouldn't fit, so we unloaded them & mowed them in the barn until we nearly died — no air up in the barn, & hot, & bales were so <u>super</u> heavy. I got home 9:30 p.m., showered, & was ready for bed.

Thu.8-29: Rained.

Mon.9-02: (Kids marched in Labor Day Parade in Neola. My folks & Sherry's came for dinner.)

Sun.9-29: It's SNOWING! Yuk! The first of the season.

Thu.10-03: Bill's 44th birthday. He & I worked on combine. Al went to soils judging contest with Ag class. Bill helped Pork Producers grill burgers on the Harlan Square.

Mon.10-07: Combining beans. Worked until after midnight. Did 60 A. It was 1 a.m. when we got done showering.

Tue.10-08: Betty & Gary took Helen to the Salem Lutheran Retirement Home in Elk Horn. (Because of her Alzheimer's she just couldn't stay in her home any longer — we couldn't be with her all the times she needed us.)

Thu.10-10: Rainy. We took Helen some of her things & visited. "Al ordered his ring" (this was in Alan's handwriting) (To him, ordering his class ring was worth a journal entry).

Fri.10-11: Did yield ck. N. of creek. 182 bu/A.

Sun. 10-13: Started on corn on the S. place.

Wed.10-16: (Guys combining.) I went after groceries. Cleaned some pens & feeders in the finisher. Moved a load of pigs out N., & kids helped move 3 loads when they got home. Al leveled corn in drying bin. We all showered up & I cut everyone's hair. Folded some clothes. Al rode his moped to jazz band, & we had a pizza when he came home. It was 2:30 a.m. when Bill came. He had cut 80 A. of beans at Herb's.

Fri.10-18: Bill & Bob Konz grilled pork burgers at Shelby's homecoming. Kids went to dance. Jerod & I watched *Dallas*.

Fri.10-25: Bill combined until about 2 a.m. & finished Herb's beans.

Sat.10-26: (Combined beans here) Bill worked til 2 a.m.

Sun.10-27: (We loaded a hay truck & then combined beans.)

Thu.10-31: I helped Jerod carve his big pumpkin & put a candle in it on the porch, before he went trick or treating. Bill & Duane finished beans about midnight.

Mon.11-04: Bill & I went out right away to start repairing the combine: we'd broken a back wheel spindle last night. Bill had to go to Macedonia for a spindle.

Fri.11-08: We were making hay & combining. I raked hay. It was freezing cold in the wind. So-o-o-o COLD!!! I came home for some hot chocolate & hot soup & went back to help move big bales off the field.

Tue.11-12: I cleaned for club. Bill went to Dunlap salebarn. Bought cows. I went to Harlan to PCA, ASC, FB, & got groceries. Irwin Andersens, Bill Babbitts, & Bob Browns came for club supper.

Sun.11-24: Combined & hauled bales home. Worked til 3 a.m.

Tue.11-26: We continued to whittle away at corn out N. We broke another spindle on the back wheel & couldn't find parts anywhere. Bill called Rich Goshorn, who had a combine like ours, & borrowed the wheel & spindle off of Rich's & we did our last load. Done with corn! (I remember Bill was so ecstatic about being done, that he came zooming in from the field with the combine, singing away, & quickly started to back it in the shed; however, he hadn't remembered to put the grain tank extension down, & it hit the top plate of the machine shed & bent all to pieces.)

Sat.11-30: Our 17th anniversary. Did nothing special. I worked on books. Bill went after pickup parts. It was snowy & blowy so we stayed home.

Tue.12-03: I went to club Christmas luncheon. It was decided our Happy Dozen Club would no longer meet: many have jobs in town & it was hard to find a day or time to meet anymore.

Thu.12-05: I washed dishes at church's annual abelskiver supper. Kris had confirmation. Al had 4-H, Bill had a school board mtg.

Sat.12-07: I got myself a Singer serger & got our Christmas tree. (My serger is one of my favorite items. I'd definitely recommend one to anyone who sews, as I love to do.)

Fri.12-13: Bill got 28 cows at salebarn.

Fri.12-20: I sewed on Mom & Sis' sweatshirts. Bill got 14 cows at salebarn.

Wed.12-25: Kids were up about 7:30 a.m. & we opened presents. Went to Betty's for dinner & supper.

Sat.12-28: My folks & Sherry's came for Christmas.

Tue.12-31: Bill & I went to new year's eve dance in Minden with Duanes, Garys, & Waynes.

1986

Wed.1-01: Slept late. I went to Barb's fabric shop sale.

Thu.1-02: Kids went back to school. Hurray!

Sat.1-18: Got up at 7 a.m. so Al could go to a jazz band contest. We loaded a Wisc. hay truck. We invited Duanes & Waynes up for supper & cards. We had a swell visit & some good laughs while playing cards.

Tue.1-28: I had heard on the radio that the Columbia Space Craft had blown up only a little over a minute after launch. I then watched coverage on TV, & Bill came in to watch too.

Wed.1-29: I brought a gray calf home in the cab of the pickup (we were surprised to find an early arrival when we went to round up cows at the S. place, to bring them home).

Sat.2-01: Kris got a "I" rating on her bells at Jr. Hi solo contest. We loaded hogs, & raked yard.

Tue.2-04: Kids made snowmen when they came home from school.

Fri.2-14: (As I was bringing the kids home from a ball game, I was giving them driving tips about coming down an icy hill to an intersection where we wanted to turn. Just as I had told them not to go too fast, & to abort the turn if they started to slide through the intersection, the ice caught our car; it wouldn't turn at the intersection; & we started to slide into the ditch! We teetered on the edge of the ditch, stuck in the snow, & Al walked to get Tom Rihner, who pulled us out with his pickup. (Wow! What do think of this lesson plan?)

Sat.2-15: (Al's team got 2nd in livestock judging contest at Beef Expo in Des Moines.) We sold hogs. Bill helped Duane work cows & calves. Al & Kris went to Valentine's dance.

Mon. 2-24: I did a pork presentation for Harlan High School home ec classes, with help of Debbie Burton, & Beth Reinig. Bill had school brd. mtg. Also went to PCA & FHA.

Wed.3-05: (Bill picked up & delivered seed beans; I sewed.)

Tue.4-01: (loaded 2 hay trucks.)

Wed.4-02: (loaded 3 hay trucks)

Mon.4-07: Bill helped Duane load a hay truck. Boys & I went to 4-H. I showed slides on how to give a presentation.

Tue.4-08: Bill & Duane spent 7 1/2 hrs. loading 3 Dakota hay trucks. I chored.

Thu.4-10: (Duanes & us helped each other load many semi loads of hay this year [for Dakotas, Wisc., & Mo.]. Sometimes we'd load 2 or even 3 trucks in a day, but today was particularly memorable because 6 trucks were coming!)

(We got up at 6:15 a.m., ck'd cows & had vet come to pull a calf. Two trucks came, & we had one half loaded when the driver decided if we didn't have enough of one kind of hay to load his truck, we should unload him. We did, & nothing would suit the other driver, so he left. They then loaded 4 trucks at Duane's. Finished about 9:30 p.m.)

Wed.4-16: We loaded hay all day. Later Bill had a school brd. mtg., Al went to jazz band, Kris had a track meet, I went to FFA banquet.

Fri.4-18: Bill & Derald Graybill went to Colo, Iowa, to ck. out a school superintendent candidate.(The superintendent search involved many school brd. mtgs. for Bill this year.)

Sat.4-19: I put meat outside on the grill for dinner.

Wed.4-23: We loaded hay trucks for John Salesman & Duanne Heins (from Monroe, Wisconsin area. They have been regular hay customers, as well as friends of ours, since 1983 when we met them through a 4-H Interstate Exchange program.)

Thu.4-24: Bill put on anhydrous, I pumped 10 loads from pit.

Fri.5-02: Bill was putting on dry fertilizer. I planted a mum, geraniums, sultanas, & petunias (I love flowers both, inside & out). Boz had his 1st pee wee baseball practice.

Sun.5-04: Kristin was confirmed this morning at church, & we had a whole house full of company for dinner.

Mon.5-05: (Bill's Mom moved back home from the retirement home, & a lady was hired to live in, & cook & care for her. [Helen had days at the retirement home when she was like her old self, & kept asking to go home: the family decided she might have to spend years in a nursing home later due to her Alzheimer's, & hence wanted to let her try to enjoy the comfort of her own home while she still could.])

Wed.5-07: (I disked. Bill started planting.)

Sun.5-11: Jerod fixed me breakfast in bed for Mother's Day.

Tue.5-13: I mowed yard, spaded flower patches, & planted columbines, cosmos, & pansies. Bill seeded, went to a sale, & a school brd. mtg. Al had Driver's Ed.

Sat.5-24: Bill planted beans, & I springtoothed. We went to Shelby Alumni Banquet, visited with a lot of people, & had a super good time. We visited at Helen's afterwards.

Sat.5-03: I hauled manure, Al disked it in, Bill planted a little patch to corn.

Sun.6-01: Bill Babbitt's big 90' tall silo fell over. We went up later & helped clean up some of the mess of spilled corn, & splintered feed shed it had fallen on.

Mon.6-02: Gave hay to cows. Al went to Driver's Ed. Bill & I went up to bale mid morning. Al brought more wagons when he came home. We blew 2 tires. Kris had dinner ready for us, & we went back to bale. Had 8 racks when Duane came to help. It got too dry so we quit about 7:30 p.m. Al & I went after groceries, & then picked up Boz & Kris from ballgames.

Wed.6-04: We helped Duane on hay on Ann's. It rained us out about 5 p.m. Rained hard — got 1 1/2".

Sat.6-07: Al went to FFA Judging Contest in Ida Grove. Kris to 4-H. Boz to ball practice. Bill chored. I went to Harlan on errands. Ck'd on Helen when I picked up the kids.

Sun.6-08: Al windrowed on Jack's. I went to Atlantic after twine. We went to 4-H picnic. We made hay with Duanes.

Tue.6-17: We all turned hay, windrowed, & mowed hay away. We went to FHA to sign papers for a guaranteed loan (to supplement our PCA loan).

Fri.6-20: Bill & I had a PCA appt. Finally got all papers in order for new '86 loan. Bill cultivated. Al & I went in to Kris' ball game, & worked in food stand. Bill came later.

Tue.6-24: Bill & boys went to Grand Island, Nebr., to get a windrower conditioner. They got twine & dropped hay samples at A & L Labs in Omaha (for protein tests). I ran errands.

Sat.6-28: Sherry's & folks came for supper for Kris' B.D. Al picked up Kevin, his interstate exchange 4-H'er from Indiana.

Wed.7-02: Al & Kevin went with 4-H group to Des Moines to Adventureland & to tour the capitol. Bill & Duane went to Hay Expo in Alleman, Iowa. I mowed Helen's yard while kids were at ball practice.

Fri.7-04: Cows were out at 6 a.m. so we chased the bats in. Baled hay. Went to watch mud volleyball, play softball, & see fire works in Avoca.

Sun.7-O6: Slept late. Went to church to be greeters. Folks were here for dinner when we got home. Mom brought sweetcorn & it was delicious.

Went for a drive & then had ice cream.

Tue.7-08: Jerod's 9th B.D. He got a Tonka roadgrader & Nerf boomerang. We unloaded racks of hay. Bill tried wheat. It rained really hard about 7 p.m.

Wed.7-09: We unloaded more racks of hay. Al went to FFA judging contest at Atlantic. I went to Harlan to Pamida's Grand Opening. Kris had a game. Bill had school brd. mtg.

Sat.7-12: Bill & kids went to Shelby Fun Days.

Wed.7-16: We combined our oats.

Thu.7-17: Bill combined. Al & I hauled oats to bins — so darned hot! I scooped after dinner to fill the bin & thought I was going to die — so hot!

Fri.7-18: Al & I baled straw. Bill was combining wheat.

Mon.7-21: Unloaded straw in Richard's barn. Al went to fair to water his pigs. I worked in fair food stand after dinner.

Tue.7-22: Al showed in several classes at fair hog show.

Wed.7-23: (We started making hay on Jack's [Bornholdt].)

Sat.7-26: (I got up 5 a.m. for Atlantic Craze Daze.) Got some neat buys. Home at noon. We raked, baled, unloaded hay.

Tue.7-29: (We were unloading hay at Jack's. On last rack I was mowing a bale, & another one came off the conveyor & hit me in the leg & dislocated my right knee. It hurt like crazy! Kris brought me home to put ice on it. Guys finished baling on Jack's finally. [I went to Dr. next day & he said it had already popped back, to put ice on it & stay off it.])

Sun.8-03: My brother, Mom, & sister called me for my B.D.

Wed.8-20: Bill called the sheriff as the big motor off an auger, & 2 hydraulic cylinders on the planter were gone at the Dr.'s farm. [They were never found.]

Thu.8-21: Bill helped serve at Pork Producers Food Stand at the State Fair.

Fri.8-22: Went to my Grandpa Bornholdt's 85th B.D. supper.

Sat.8-23: Al won the individual division of FFA Livestock Judging Contest at the Iowa State Fair. His team got 8th.

Mon.9-08: (I was taking some hay wagons to the field with our big tractor, when a drawbar pin jumped out, & a couple wagons went in the ditch S. of Al Schue's. Cotton Krieger & his road grader happened along & helped me pull them out of the ditch.) (Cotton is gone now, but he always greeted me with a smile, & was really a nice man.)

9-29: We went to funeral visitation for Bill's great aunt Jenny (His Grandma Kate Damgaard Johnson's sister).

Fri.10-03: Bill's 45th B.D. Alan got a red 1977 Pontiac Grand Prix from Jack Ploen. Bill & I went to PCA for a review. Bill & kids went to a ball game.

Wed.10-08: We went to Ivan Nelson's funeral. (a friend, a fellow school board member of Bill's, his wife Sharon was in Bill's high school class, & his son Waylan was in Alan's class. He'd had a sudden heart attack & died.)

Fri.10-09: Bill & Duane were combining beans. (Al, Charlie Pattee, & I baled 3 racks of hay.)

Sat.10-11: Overnight & through the day we got 4" rain.

Sun.10-12: Everyone slept late. Al, Bill, & Duane vacuvated beans. I started our oil burner for 1st time of the season.

Mon.10-13: Only 28° this a.m. First freeze.

Fri.10-17: Mom & Dad brought Grandma Bornholdt to school for Grandparent's Day with Jerod. I helped fix soup at Jr. class soup supper. Parents night for cross country & football.

>Bill wrote this poem for today's Grandparent's Day:

>>It's been some time since you were in schools,
>>So today we've decided to suspend the rules.
>>We've got our globes, and our rocks that we touch;
>>Of course our teacher, and our computer and such.
>>We add and we multiply and long division comes soon.
>>We can act out a play or sing you a tune.
>>We want you to know we do more than just play;
>>So we welcome you all to "Grandparent's Day."

Sun.10-26: (While unloading corn into a grain bin late this afternoon, I needed to take a potty break, & as I headed into an old building, I slipped & tore my hand on a board that had an old screen door hook sticking out of it. Since the Dr.'s office wasn't open today, I cleaned & wrapped up my hand, & kept unloading corn ... We were to go to the Kids' 4-H awards banquet tonight, & I didn't want to go to the emergency room at the hospital this evening.)

Mon.10-27: I went to Dr. & got a tetanus shot & 8 stitches in middle two fingers on my left hand. We were still combining.

Mon.11-03: (We put the torch in the bucket of the crawler to raise it up toward the top of a grin bin & cut a pulley off the cross auger to get a bad bearing repaired. We then did corn on Louie's. The belt burnt off the cross auger. I got a truck stuck in the field, & we couldn't get it out even with both tractors. We came in about 10:30 p.m. Had soup & hot chocolate. Bill was getting the flu. I took out the bright blue nylon stitches in my hand just before I went to bed.)

Tue.11-04: We set up an elevator to unload the stuck truck in the field, & then were able to get it out.

Sat.11-08: My folks came for supper & we went to *Dumb Luck* (Al's Jr. class play). It was funny & Al did a good job as "Mr. Fletcher."

Sun.11-09: Two speed broke on the truck. I felt absolutely horrible all day. I finally went to bed 6:30 p.m. Al helped until 11 p.m. Duane got done with all his corn, fixed the 2-speed, & helped haul for Bill til nearly 3 a.m.

Mon.11-10: Snowed.

Sat.11-22: At 3:08 p.m. I brought the Big Case & the last wagon out of Louie's field & we were <u>Done With Harvest</u>!

Tue.11-25: We moved 4 loads of cows to Dr.'s farm.

Wed.11-26: Took James a get well card & gift. He was miserable with chicken pox. (Duane & Jo's boy.)

Thu.11-27: We took my folks to Sis' for Thanksgiving dinner.

Fri.11-28: We left Sis's in Iowa City, stopped at the Botanical Center in Des Moines to tour it, & came on home.

Wed.12-03: (Bill took 50 new cows to S. place, & then went to Arlin's (my Dad's brother) to help neighbors & friends harvest Arlin's crops, as he was quite ill.)

Sun.12-15: Bill went to Donna Oehlertz's funeral (her daughter Janetta married Bill's brother Charlie). I had the flu.

Thu.12-25: We went to Betty's for Christmas dinner & supper.

Sun.12-27: Went over home for turkey supper & presents with my folks and Sherry & Ken, Jessica, & Laura.

Wed.12-31: Bill helped Leonard finish his corn. John Salesman came for a semi load of hay. $65/T.

1987

Thu.1-01: Everyone slept late. I went to Barb Brown's birthday fabric sale. Bill & the boys chored & worked outside. Kris & I took down the tree & all the decorations, & put them away. We had sandwiches & chocolate sodas for supper.

Thu.1-08: Bill got a trophy for 1st place in the Shelby County Soybean Yield Contest for 60.48 bu/A.

Sun.1-11: After dinner of ham & broccoli casserole, we went to see *Crocodile Dundee* in Atlantic. It was good — funny — & a pleasant happy ending. We visited my folks & then Helen.

Tue.1-13: I got my hair cut & styled in Avoca.

Fri.1-16: (We loaded 160 straw bales to take to salebarn. Bill went to Bob Schuster's to play cards. I sewed.)

Mon.1-19: (Worked on income tax figures. Brought last of cows home from S. place. I sewed on trip clothes.)

Wed.1-21: (Bill & I left for Omaha airport with a group of fellow Wilson Seeds dealers. After boarding our plane at gate 13, we took off & climbed to 35,000 feet, & landed in Denver just before 9 a.m. In about an hour, we were flying again, partaking of airline cuisine, & watching the movie *Karate Kid*. It was 5:47 p.m. [Iowa time] when we landed & were given a pretty lei at the airport.

[I could hardly believe that just hours before we were shivering in Iowa with our cattle, hogs, & kids, & now we were tourists among the palm trees, gorgeous flowers, bright blue sunny skies, and warmth of Honolulu, Hawaii!]

[Alan was going to handle the chores back home, & friend Gertie Thies was going to stay with the kids, to see that they got up for school, to cook for them, & keep them from killing each other.]

To top off our 1st day in Hawaii, we went to a reception with all the Wilson people we were with, had supper outside on the hotel terrace, & saw our first live hula show.)

Thu.1-22: I woke up at 3 a.m. (7 a.m. Iowa time) & read until it was time to go to breakfast. Today we went on a city bus tour: our driver, "Cousin Mike," said the waters are about 6000' deep, 1 million people live on 11 inhabited islands, gasoline is 23.9¢/liter, & the big Bengal Banyan trees we're seeing are from India. We saw Punchbowl National Cemetery, the governor's house, & Queen's palace. (Later we went with Pam & Dean Bauer, on the free Navy tour of Pearl Harbor: we saw a film of the Japanese attack in WWII, & took a boat out to the Arizona Memorial, & walked above the ship that now rests on the bottom of Pearl harbor, with hundreds of its men still entombed there. We went on a catamaran dinner cruise this evening, where we watched a spectacular sunset, & later, the beautiful city lights from out on the ocean.)

Fri.1-23: (Today 12 of us rented 2 mini-vans & toured Oahu. Donnie & Jean Christensen [from Harlan] had been to Hawaii before, so led us with one van, while Pam & Dean Bauer, & Duane & Louise Hillyard, followed with us in the 2nd van.

We stopped at a pretty lookout spot: a man was taking souvenir pictures of people with his parrot. Louise had the bird sit on her shoulder, where it chose to relieve itself, which gave us some laughs. She later called the parrot man a "mindless twit." This sort of thing made for a really fun day, as we picked up shells & lava rocks on Sunset Beach, toured Waimea Falls Park, saw pineapple fields [where someone just happened to find a pineapple]; & got souvenirs at Dole Cannery & roadside shops.)

Sat.1-24: (Today we flew on to Maui. On a trolley ride, our driver was joking about the native habits, & he said, "I'm going to have octopus for supper — shake & bake." At lunch in a whaler's village, Bill sat in a mess of spilled cola, with his white shorts. We had a country western buffet this evening & danced. Went to bed fairly early.)

Sun.1-25: (First we had the Wilson Olympics where 4 teams of 20 each had fun with contests, like an obstacle course relay where we had to run with swim flippers on, jump in a sack and hop to a mark, ride a tiny tricycle, & swim to retrieve a marker. Our team, The Thunder Lizards, took 2nd over all.

Then we drove to the summit of Haleakala Volcano — about a 38 mi. road trip. There were breathtaking, beautiful rainbows all the way up. We tasted a stalk of sugar cane in a field on our way back to our hotel. We had supper in a nice restaurant [I had a delicious sirloin for $9.95, while some paid $17.50 for fish].)

Mon.1-26: (Sight-seeing with our gang in a rented van. We passed the lepers island & Bill said, "They have a prison there for all the really bad people. The inmates are called *lepercons*." ... We went to Iao Needle, & around the N. part of the island on super steep, super windey roads— absolutely beautiful sights! We watched pineapple pickers working in fields on our way back. We stopped briefly so I could buy some fabric, & went on to a ceremonial pig roast & luau. [I didn't like anything but the salad — poi is not my thing.]

Tue.1-27: (Spent the day packing, shopping, & seeing sights. It was after 9:30 p.m. when we left, seeing all the lights of Honolulu, as we flew away from these beautiful islands.)

Wed.1-28: (Landed in Denver about 6:30 a.m., & learned our flight to Omaha had been cancelled. We had to go home by way of Chicago, & finally arrived in Omaha at 2:30 p.m., & got home at 5 p.m., where we unpacked our souvenirs & visited.)

Thu.1-29: Bill ck'd critters, & I ran errands.

Fri.1-30: Larry & Donny Buboltz were here to put on my new S. door. (Our narrow entry door needed replaced, & they widened the hole to normal size while they were doing it.)

Sat.1-31: I called my brother to see how he was doing: he'd had his appendix removed in emergency surgery on Wed.

Tue.2-03: (Loaded out some seed oats. I sewed a shirt for Bill from fabric I got in Hawaii. I baked 2 apple pies [this is worth noting because, as a rule, I don't do pies].

Feb.2-04: (Loaded a hay truck & such.) Bill & I went to computer class in Shelby. #61 cow had a calf, heifer #61.

Mon.2-09: Bob Hundt came to start installing our new furnace (until now our home's heat source was a clunky, box-shaped, disgusting, oil burner stove in our dining room).

Tue.2-10: Bill went with school brd. to state legislative mtg. in Des Moines. I went to Porkettes. Locked my keys in the pickup at Fareway — wasted about 1 1/2 hrs. there trying to get it open: policeman couldn't get it open, so we broke a hinge on the little door window to open the lock.

Wed.2-11: FHA was here to go over '87 cash flow figures. I sent a bunch of Valentines. Polyurethaned S. door & trim.

Sun.2-15: My folks, Sherrys, & Calvin were here for dinner. (Our uncle Arlin is quite ill & Calvin & Sherry had come home to see him.)

Thu.2-19: I did a pork presentation in Irwin School.

Fri.2-20: I did a pork presentation in Harlan High School home ec classes, with help of Donna Peters, Lori Ohms, Beth Reinig, & Lorrane Thraen.

Wed.2-25: I hung out chore clothes. It's 43° F but the strong winds & the wet clothes sure made my fingers cold!

Sat.2-28: We went to Wilson Seeds pot luck supper & looked at everyone's pictures from Hawaii.

Mon.3-02: Saw our first robin of the season in the E. yard.

Tue.3-03: Black birds were singing in the grove this noon, & my 1st crocus was blooming. Thermometer says 65° at 2 p.m.

Fri.3-06: Bill loaded seed oats for Tom Rihner. We took 2 pickup loads of straw to salebarn. I went to school to watch Jerod in spelling bee. He won 4th grade division & was very excited! Bill got 19 cows at the salebarn. (We had just sat down to supper when Scott Hess called. He lives about 8 mi. S. of us, but could see an orange glow up our way, and asked if we were on fire at our place.)

(We hurried to look out & could see a fire all right, but it wasn't ours. Bill could tell it was Tommy Rihner's barn from its outline of fire in the darkness.

We jumped in the pickup & headed over. From the road N. of Tom's, the sight of the huge skeleton of the burning barn was so eerie & threatening! The barn's every crack was spitting fire, as if to try to rid itself of this evil demon. But in retaliation, the fierce flames ROARED! & flared even higher as if attacking the night sky as well.

Along the road N. of Tom's, we jumped out to help other neighbors stomp out spot fires that had started in the field from burning bits of the barn. Flaming pieces had started his windbreak trees on fire first, & then were whipped on farther N. by strong winds, where they started fires in the dry cornstalks. Some embers even landed in the field, over the road, 1/4 mi. N. of Tom's.

People of all sorts, including the fire dept., soon came to Rihner's farm, but the barn was all ready beyond saving. However, the volunteers did work to protect the other buildings, & finally extinguish the windbreak fires, & spot fires. For this night the ordeal was over, & the cruel demon had been exorcised, but not before it had devoured the barn.)

Fri.3-13: Bill loaded out seed oats, ck'd cows, went to a Wilson Seeds mtg., to the salebarn, & then to plow. I did 3 pork education tapes for KNOD. Paid bills & ran errands.

Sun.3-22: (We got word that Pam & Dean Bauer's boy Danny had died. He had cerebral palsy. He was 4 years old. My heart aches for his parents & family. We went to his funeral visitation this evening.)

Mon.3-23: (Alan went to the hospital at 6 a.m. to have his tonsils &

adenoids removed. [They were quite infected & he'd had several bouts of strep throat.])

Fri.3-27: Al went back to school. Didn't stay for track.

Sat.3-28: It was snowing & Bill & I worked with cows all afternoon, trying to get the ones penned in who were going to have calves. We were having a genuine blizzard!

Sun.3-29: Bill went to ck. cows on Leonard's about 2 a.m. & ran the pickup off his driveway. He walked home & got me, & we took the big Case down to pull it out. (Bill thought it might be snowed under if we waited until morning.) It was snowing & blowing like crazy & almost impossible to see the road or tell where we were at! It was really scary, even coming just the 1/2 mi. home! ... No Sun. paper — roads drifted. Kids painted frog designs on a set of tea towels.

Mon.3-30: No school. Roads still closed.

Tue.3-31: Parent-teacher conferences. I went to last Soils Course mtg. in Harlan, & got a completion certificate.

Sun.4-05: Bill bought me an antique roll top desk at Bob Boysen's sale in Avoca. (I've wished for one for ages.)

Thu.4-16: (This afternoon while doing books) I found a cancelled check to The Exchange with a note on the left side that read, "Attn. Karen" & an arrow to the "for" line — it was filled in "poker." It cracked me up.

Fri.4-17: Jerod had 3 teeth pulled at the dentist, & he was going to pull 2 of Kris' baby teeth (because he said they should have come out by now), but I asked him to do an X-ray first. As it turned out, she hadn't lost the baby teeth, because she had no permanent teeth above those two. (He'll fill those baby teeth to save them as long as possible.)

Sun.4-19: Johnsons here for Easter dinner & supper.

Sat.4-25: Alan's Junior Prom. Bill & I chaperoned. Jerod mowed the yard for the first time of the season.

Wed.4-29: Bill started planting corn.

Fri.5-15: (Making Hay.) Mom called to say Arlin had passed away.

Mon.5-18: (Bill finished plowing & I raked hay. He stayed to work on hay & planting & I went to Arlin's funeral.) I hurried home to take Kris to an awards banquet — no one had picked her up from practice. I found her walking home, & she was mad. She cleaned up & we went to Shelby just in time for her name to be called for her 1st award. Shortly after we got home, Bill came home mad as a hornet — he'd run out of seed corn. He went back & finished the field. (Trying Day!)

Sat.5-23: Dad called to say Calvins had a little girl yesterday: Olivia Jean. I cut out a yellow & white fake fur care bear for her & worked on it when we weren't ck'ing hay.

Sun.5-24: We went to Lori's high school graduation at Avoca (Duane & Jo's daughter).

Tue.5-26: Raining. Shelby had some tornado-type damage.

Thu.6-04: I ate my first garden ripe tomato of the season.
  (See my poem "Surprise" in Section VII.)

Sat.6-06: Went to Kelly Johnson's graduation party .

Mon.6-08: Got up before 6 a.m. & headed to hay field. Jerod rode his bike down after a while. He caught 2 baby bull snakes & a field mouse, & looked them over. He put pheasant feathers in his cap that he found on the ground ... finished baling by 11 a.m. Bill went after parts, & we unloaded racks until 5:30 p.m. Had lunch, & Bill went to spray. Al went to wash his car. Kris went to ball game. We ck'd cows.

Sun.6-14: Alan's 17th B.D. Mom & Dad came at 6:45 a.m. to have breakfast with Al. We went to Al's 4-H club picnic & tour. Kris made Al a cake & we had it with our supper.

Tue.6-16: (Duanes & us went to check out nursing homes for Helen. [The lady who'd been staying with her was leaving & we couldn't find anyone else.] We'd had Helen to specialists again, hoping we could find something to help her, as her memory loss was getting much worse [she often didn't know where she was or even know her family]. It's so hard to watch Alzheimer's take away someone you love so dearly, and not be able to do anything to help them.)

Fri.6-26: I weeded Helen's flowers (the flowers she used to love so much), and cleaned in her house. We went to Elk Horn to take Helen some things for her room (Her family had moved her to Salem Lutheran Nursing Home there).

Sun.6-28: Kris' 15th B.D. We got ready to make hay after dinner. My folks came. We baled 8 racks & hurried to get them all in as it started to rain about dark.

Mon.6-29: Al went to State 4-H Conference in Ames.

Wed.7-01: Bill, Duane, James, & Jerod went to the hay expo.

Wed.7-02: Bill combined wheat at Herb's.

Sun.7-05: Bill & I met Duanes, Charlies, Bettys, & Delores in to Helen's, to clean out cupboards & drawers, & decide on a household sale.

Mon.7-06: Al left for Iowa Ag Youth Institute, in Ames. Bill & Duane went to Helen's to help auctioneers make sale bill.

Wed.7-08: Jerod's 10th B.D. Folks came for dinner & brought him a cake.

Fri.7-10: I went to Harlan Sewing Center & got my new Ultra Unlimited 6268 Singer Sewing Machine. I practiced on my new machine.

Tue.7-14: Shortly after 8 p.m. it started to pour huge drops & then hailed for probably 20 mins. or more. It flattened the oats out N. & really stripped up the corn on Louie's. Bill was combining at Bill True's.

Tue.7-21: (We went to watch Al & Jerod show their hogs at the fair. Worked on straw until 8 p.m.)

Fri.7-24: (I took Al to Harlan at 6 a.m. to leave on the 4-H Interstate Exchange, to Flasher, N. Dak. Boys came to unload straw at 7 a.m. [we'd been making straw or hay for a week] I was shot. They unloaded racks & I did chores. We baled straw after dinner & hurried home when it started to storm, spent until 9:30 p.m. getting all the loads in the sheds.)

Sat.7-25: (Kris & I went to Atlantic Crazy Daze & my folks'. Bill & Jerod went to Avoca Fair.)

Sun.7-26: (All the family met early at Helen's to put items out in the yard for her household sale.) The house seemed so different after everything was taken out — there'll be no more going to visit at "Grandma's house" after today — The end of a special part of our lives.

    Lord, why did Helen have to have her last years be this way? ... We got home about 8:30 p.m. & looked over "our treasures" purchased at the sale — items that we can save for years to come, to savor the memories they awake of years never to be again, & of people in our lives never to be forgotten — treasures to save, with stories to pass on to our children, of their grandparents & ancestors.

Mon.7-27: I called Alan In North Dakota.

Mon.8-03: I tried to clean house. Kids were fighting, yelling, throwing things, & wouldn't help with anything. Happy Birthday to me. Al & Jerod had 4-H. Bill, Kris, & I went to Mickel's for supper.

Tue.8-04: Calvin, & his boys came home. We took them to the Cass

County Fair. Bill had to stay home to wait for the vet to post a cow, who had died in the windbreak (just like with a person, an animal is posted, or has an autopsy, to determine the cause of death).

Wed.8-05: (It was early evening, on this very still, warm, muggy day; I was at my sewing machine, & the bobbin had just wound wrong & jammed — Jerod came running in & said all the hogs were dying! We hurried out N. to the hog house.

[Bill had just pumped 4 loads of liquid manure out of the pit.] [However he hadn't been aware that his pumping was agitating the manure, & allowing poison gases to be released, that were killing the hogs — until Jerod happened to look in at the hogs, & noticed lots of dead ones.] He yelled at his Dad! & then came to get me.

We worked from 7 p.m. to 10:30 p.m. getting live hogs chased, pushed, & pulled out of the building into fresh air; & then moving out the dead ones. There were so many, we had to get the Bobcat loader to haul them out. We had headaches when we came in & Bill & I didn't sleep all night.)

Thu.8-06: (The dead truck came about 7:30 a.m. & we started loading all of the dead hogs. There were well over 100 head, about 75 of them were market weight, & the rest were various sizes down to 140 lbs.

We saved a hog to have it posted: our insurance man said our insurance wouldn't cover the hog losses, but would pay for a postmortem on one ... Bill said later, to him, "Did I tell you that our veterinary charges $10,000 to post a hog?" [It brought some chuckles to lighten the mood.]

Veterinarian, Dr. Roy Schultz, came to look things over shortly before noon & post the hog. He was sure hydrogen sulfide gas was what most likely killed our hogs. [This deadly gas can be present in manure pits, under certain conditions, & was brought to the surface & released when the pit pumping stirred the manure.] [Our pit had been pumped *many* times before, but this time, a different bacteria may have been working, and just a different combination of conditions.]

[Hydrogen sulfide, you may remember from chemistry class, has an odor like rotten eggs. We had not noticed this smell in our hog incident; & Dr. Schultz said that this gas can kill, at even a .05% or 500 ppm concentration; but that at a higher concentration the olfactory nerves (the nerves of smell) are immediately paralyzed and often no odor is noted. The offensive odor of rotten eggs occurs at very low concentrations: .0001 to .0005% or 1-5 ppm. He also said that it's a dense gas that is heavier than air, & usually hydrogen sulfide gas dissipates quickly when released into the air.]

However in our incident, even though all the doors on all 4 sides of the building were wide open, the still day, with practically no air movement, & the hogs leisurely resting & not stirring around, allowed the dense gas to engulf them in there pens & kill them before they knew it.

Dr. Schultz said we could have been killed by the gas, as well, while we worked to get the hogs out. I'm detailing this information to impress upon others how <u>it's absolutely essential to be cautious around manure pits</u>. **Take no chances!** Until you seek an expert's help! And remember, too, <u>it doesn't have to smell to be able</u> **to kill you!**

Fri.8-07: I didn't sleep too well again tonight.

Sat.8-08: (Went to Donna & Greg's wedding in Elk Horn & their reception & dance in Corley. [Betty's daughter.]

Sun.8-09: Went to a big picnic at Mom & Dad's for Calvin's. There were 54 of us. Even Ross & Donna Miller, & Jack & Bertha Manz (old country school days neighbors).

Tue.8-11: (Bill caught his fingers in the back side of the tractor door & had to have 3 stitches. We took Calvin, Jason, & Clinton to the airport to return to San Diego.)

Sun.8-16: We went to Wilbert & Bernice Jacobsen's Golden Anniversary in Avoca.

Sat.8-22: Coyotes had killed a yellow calf on Louie's.

Sun.8-23: (We made hay. Al had 4-H County Council here.)

Mon.8-24: (Jerod stayed at my folks', Kris went to volleyball, rest of us went to St. Fair. Had car trouble & had to stay the night in Des Moines.)

Mon.9-14: (Bill started combining corn at Herb's.)

Tue.9-22: Finally finished the last of 4th cutting hay.

Sun.9-27: Al took hay to cows at Cave's. Bill was combining beans. I took Jerod to S.S. Al, Kris, & I unloaded a rack of bales. Jerod came running out yelling, "Dinner's Ready!" We came in to macaroni & cheese, salad, & apple sauce. (Kids can do neat things once in a while!)

Mon.10-19: 8 a.m. — midnight. Finished corn on Dr.'s farm.

Wed.10-21: Unloaded 3 racks hay. Vet came & we worked 3 groups of cows & calves. Then combined until 10 p.m.

Thu.10-22: 8:30 a.m. - 7 p.m. Fixed fence.

Fri.10-23: Fixed fence. Bill & kids went to soup supper & last home football game.

Sat.10-31: Rainy. Kris got her school driving permit.

Sun.11-01: Sorted calves. 37 little. 62 big.

Mon.11-09: Athletic Banquet. Kris got letters for softball & volleyball, & Alan got a letter for cross country.

Sat.11-14: Vet came to work on a cow's eye. (She'd been shot by an unknown person, probably a hunter). Vet found pellets all around her eye & had to take her eye out.

Wed.11-25: My folks went with us to Sis's in Iowa City.

Sun.11-29: Went over to Betty's for Helen's birthday.

Tue.12-08: (Put up Christmas tree when kids got home.)

Wed.12-09: Duanne Heins came for hay. It was muddy so Bill pulled him in & out (of Louie's) with the big Case.

Sun.12-13: (I won $100 playing Christmas Bingo in Avoca.) One other person had a bingo & we had to cut cards. The other person cut first & got a king. I cut and got and ace! Wow! What a neat Surprise!)

Sun.12-20: Bill took Jeord to S.S. We went to Atlantic to Christmas shop & went to my folks' for supper.

Mon.12-28: Today the cow who'd been shot in the eye (Nov.14) had to be put to sleep (she ended up paralyzed from pellets in her brain.)

Thu.12-31: James stayed the night with Jerod, & Corene with Kris. Bill & I went to supper with Duanes & watched movies.

1988

Fri.1-01: Kris had practice at 10 a.m. & Corene went home. I went to Barb's sale.

Sat.1-02: Cleaned frantically. Sherry's & folks came for Christmas presents & a lovely turkey supper.

Sun.1-03: We visited Bill's mom. She was pretty perky & got out more words than usual.

Sat.1-09: I went to Atlantic. Found some _super_ buys on Anthony's 1/2 of marked down price sale. Got $202 worth of clothes for $62. We sold 22 cows in Denison.

Mon.1-11: I stopped at Avoca Building & got paint for my dining room, living room, sewing room, & bedroom. Also got a house paint brush, a trim brush, some patching plaster, a paint roller w/guard, & a smooth roller — this used up my Christmas bingo winnings of Avoca Bucks. We went to the S. place to capture cows & load them. Had them pregged at the vet's in Avoca, then brought open ones home & took others to Leonard's 80.

Sun.1-24: Took Jerod to S.S. Painted my kitchen cloud blue. 6 p.m. we had a strong rain, then snow, even lightning.

Tue.1-26: 8° below zero.

Sat.1-30: James came up to keep Jerod company, & we went with Duane's to see *Three Men And A Baby* & ate out.

Feb.2-02: I scrubbed the porch & painted walls & ceiling.

Thu.2-04: Had Wilson Seeds customer open house, & 4-H here.

Sun.2-07: Went to the mall & saw *Good Morning Viet Nam*. (Robin Williams was so good in it, & it was a superb movie that was especially meaningful to me, because my brother served a year in Viet Nam, & through his letters home, I know some of how hard that war was on the troops. [For example, our soldiers fought, and some died, to take a hill from the enemy, & the next day, they were ordered to fall back & let the hill go.] These sorts of political games were messing with their minds, & morale was awful. They weren't allowed to fight to win while they were there.

The Viet Nam War was our government's big game to win political gains, but it was at the unnecessary risk of our people's lives. The Viet Nam War was the biggest mistake of this century. We never should have been there! But those who died there did not die in vain: because this war angered so many Americans, & taught this country's gov't an invaluable lesson — don't ever again get our people involved in a war, half way around the world, that we can't hope to win! This lesson has helped to spare perhaps thousands of lives, since our country has stayed out of unwinable wars for nearly 20 years since Viet Nam. [Desert Storm was another political maneuver in our government's chess game, but we can be thankful it didn't backfire & turn into another Viet Nam.]

Wed.2-17: I painted dining room. We loaded a hay truck.

Thu.2-25: I gave a pork presentation for Earling School 2nd graders. Went well.

Fri.2-26: (Gave pork presentation all day for Harlan High School Home Ec. classes. Karen Harper & Kathy Keane helped.)

Fri.2-27: Duanes & us went to Dinner Theater at Harlan. Delicious steak supper — funny plays — nice evening.

Thu.3-03: (Bill went to Denison to watch our 17 heifers sell. I did a pork presentation for grade school kids in Panama, with a baby pig brought by Bob Schmitz. I painted the bedroom. Bill went to play basketball. Boys to 4-H.)

Sat.3-12: Kris had a softball clinic at Storm Lake.

Mon.3-14: (Loaded hay trucks. Dallas Klindt helped. 888 heavy bales.)

Tue.3-15: Man came to clean seed oats. Men came to get oats.

Fri.3-18: Bill bought $10,000 worth of pigs. We went to school pancake supper & to see Bill & Jerod play in basketball fund-raiser.

Sat.3-19: Went to Shelby Fireman's Dance. Had some good laughs. Good 50's & big band music.

Sat.3-26: We went out early to chore. Bill went to plow. (We loaded a hay truck about 10 a.m. As Bill was following him to Shelby to weigh, the trucker hit rough spots, going too fast on a curve, & lost the big part of his load of hay in the ditch beyond Gene Wahlings'. We spent until 3:30 p.m. carrying bales up out of the ditch, & loading them back on the truck again.) Alan & I went to the County Democratic Convention at Harlan. Al was made a delegate, & it was very interesting.

Mon.3-28: (We got word that Pam & Dean Bauer's son David died yesterday. David was 12 & had cerebral palsy). Bill disked. Bill & I stopped to see Helen, & went to Exira for David's funeral visitation.

Tue.3-29: We went to David's funeral. (So sad for Pam & Dean & their family. [Their son Danny died just over a year ago.] [Pam & Dean have two other sons Michael & Brian.])

Thu.3-31: Jerod found a balloon by our river bridge that had a card attached saying it had been launched by a 3rd grader in Cumberland (about 40 mi. S.E. of here).

Fri.4-01: Bill finished drilling oats & alfalfa on well field. Jerod & I were watching Lambey all day: she was ready to lamb. I cut out Kris' Easter dress. About 5 p.m. Jerod called the vet. I pulled a dead lamb & the vet pulled a second dead one when he came. Jerod was so disappointed! (Lambey was his pet, & he was so looking forward to having his first experience with newborn lambs.) This turned out to be a horrible day for me. It rained about 1/2".

Sun.4-03: Easter Sunday. Kris ushered. There were 32 here for dinner & supper. I was glad when the day was done.

Mon.4-04: I was very tired. Hay truck came about 11 a.m. & we had him loaded by 1 p.m. Bill rolled oats. Jerod & Bill took out some electric fence through Richard's. I slept an hour & then did dishes, etc. & made tie backs for Al's Curtains.

Tue.4-12: I planted 12 tomatoes, 2 peppers, 2 parsley. (Bill put on anhydrous. I chored & went after anhydrous tanks.)

Wed.4-13: Went to school to see Kris inducted into National Honor Society.

Mon.4-18: The crew set poles for the hay shed. Larry Buboltz worked the day on it. Alan & I disked.

Fri.4-29: Bill & I went to Aunt Edna's 95th birthday supper.

Sat.4-30: Bill started planting corn on Louie's. I got Alan's graduation announcements done & mailed. Alan field cultivated. I chored. Kris & I raked & picked up sticks in the grove. Got a new calf. A sick cow died.

Mon.5-02: (We loaded a hay truck) Bales were heavy & we were short on help. Extremely windy. Bill finished planting corn about 10 p.m. <u>Done with all corn</u>. (Jerod & I went to Mom's for her B.D. & took steak, salad, & garlic bread, & fixed supper there.)

Sun.5-08: Jerod brought me breakfast in bed for Mother's Day. Bill took Jerod to S.S. & we all went to church to see Alan & the seniors recognized.

Mon.5-09: (Bill & Al delivered seed beans. I painted on S. side of house.)

Wed.5-11: I painted on house. Bill planted beans. We went to Shelby to Alan's baccalaureate.

Fri.5-13: (Larry finished our hay shed) (Since we've made a lot of hay, we've had to rent barns for inside storage: we decided to put up more storage of our own for hay.)

Sat.5-14: (My folks came & brought Alan a pretty red potted rose bush for part of his graduation gift. I planted it by the house.)

Sun.5-15: (My folks came for dinner & went with us to Alan's High School graduation. Alan gave a good salutatorian's speech. Dad sat next to us & clapped when others clapped, etc. We greeted grad's outside afterwards, & took some family pictures. There was a lot of excitement & activity among people, as is usual at a graduation.

However, Dad was saying some unusual things: He said he didn't hear Alan's speech at all ... [I thought he was just emotional about his first grandson's graduation, & I passed it off.]

My folks went on to our place with us, & Dad didn't recognize their pickup in our yard; & he asked where we got the pretty red rose bush. [I thought he was joking — teasing — to cover his emotions.]

Dad said he & Mom would head home as he was tired. [That wasn't unusual as Dad likes an afternoon nap.]

After they left, we dashed on to several graduation parties. I called Dad when we got home, & he sounded OK.

I called my sister that evening & told her of some of the unusual happenings of the day. I was concerned about Dad, & I decided I'd call him the next morning.)

Mon.5-16: (I talked to Dad first thing, & he wasn't OK: he said he didn't remember anything about Al's graduation yesterday beyond the first speaker on stage; he said he didn't remember going home from our place; or anything about last evening. I told him I'd be over right away & we'd get him to a doctor to find out what was happening.) ... Well, the doctor thought Dad had had a T.I.A.: a type of temporary stroke where a piece of fatty deposit from an artery wall had broken loose, & went up & lodged in his brain, shutting off oxygen for a time, before dissolving. This mini-stroke caused the temporary memory loss ... The Doctor set up an appointment for Dad with a vascular specialist in Omaha, & prescribed medicine to prevent a stroke in the interim.)

I got home about 4 p.m. Painted on the wash house awhile; & then the kids & I went to the Fine Arts Awards at school. From down the road a ways, as we were coming home, it looked like our house was on fire! I nearly had heart failure.

William The Great had the whole grove, just N. of our house, burning like wildfire! (He had set stick piles on fire in the grove to get it prettied up prior to Al's graduation party, & they were burning so brightly. The fires were leaping clear up into the trees & came very close to getting out of control ... we had to watch the fires for about an hour until they died down some ... What a day!)

Wed.5-18: I cleaned like crazy! Alan, Bill, & I put up ceiling fan in living room & dining room, & kitchen light fixtures. I painted the dining room ceiling 3 coats & plastered the kitchen ceiling.

Thu.5-19: I hurried with cleaning all a.m. We took Dad to Omaha to see Dr. Waltke, a vascular specialist, at his office near Methodist Hospital.

Fri.5-20: (I hurried like crazy with cleaning, etc. We had about 130 people for a buffet/picnic supper for Alan's graduation party. Everything went pretty well. I was so tired, but my knees hurt & I couldn't sleep. Got up & took aspirin.)

Mon.5-30: (We baled hay, picked them up, & stacked them in the new hay shed [we used our new bale accumulator & loader attachment].) Worked from 8 a.m. to 10 p.m.

Wed.6-01: (I think today was the day Dad had surgery to remove a severe blockage in his left carotid artery. [The T.I.A. had been a warning sign of a worse impending health problem, & had pushed Dad to get a full checkup.])

Fri.6-10: (We baled & hauled in hay all week, loaded a hay semi yesterday). I did chores while Bill spent nearly all day at ASC getting approval to make hay on government ground. Feeding little square bales to 88 cows isn't any fun. Bill helped me load evening bales & went to cultivate. I fed cows corn & hay. Petted calves & talked to the new ones.

Sat.6-11: Cows out 6 a.m. (Hay truck came at 8 a.m.) Jerod & I went after hydraulic oil. (Guys mowed gov't ground.) I planted two purple leaf plum bushes by the wash house.

Tue.6-14: Bill went to big bale at 6 a.m. Cows were bawling, so I got up & put bales in for them & watered them. Today is Alan's 18th B.D. Al went away (for the day). (Kris had Driver Ed & later a ballgame. I weeded flower beds, & chored. Bill had a school board mtg.)

Sun.6-19: (Went to Corley airport to watch planes at annual flight breakfast. Al, Bill, & Jerod took a plane ride. We went to Walnut's annual antique walk; & on to my folks for supper. Stopped to see Helen, & Bettys.

Wed.6-22: (Alan & I went to his orientation at Iowa State University in Ames.)

Sat.6-25: Bill got up at sunrise to round bale. I went to water cows, & a calf had his head stuck between the front wheels of the 830 Case tractor. (Who could even guess what he was thinking when he did that! Al & I had to take one front wheel off to free him.)

Sun.6-26: Went to Johnson picnic (at Avoca Park). Had a nice visit. Jerod, & Al, & Kris swam.

Tue.6-28: Kris' 16th B.D. She had Driver's Ed & then a softball game this evening. (Bill & I got the combine ready to go & he went to Herb's. Al was windrowing oats.)

Wed.6-29: Got 1/2" rain — first rain in about a month. No water, no electricity . (A downed electric wire by the crib had to be repaired.) Bill discovered a wagon load of our big round bales in Bobby Schuster's field. (Jerod had parked it yesterday, but it wasn't sitting level & had rolled way down a hill, & through a fence into the neighbor's field.) Also found a hog of Jerod's dead. Nice day so far.

Fri.7-01: Kris stepped on a toothpick in the living room carpet & rammed 1/2 the pick into the ball of her foot. (It was hurting her terribly; I took her to the Doctor. He was unable to get it out, gave her some antibiotics for infection, told us to watch it, & we came home.

Tue.7-05: John Salesman came for two loads of hay.

Sat.7-09: Kris got her driver's license.

Mon.7-11: Dr. renewed Kris' antibiotic & said to continue to watch her foot.

Wed.7-13: We baled wheat straw. It was so hot!

Thu.7-14: I raked straw all day. It was so hot & rough. Bill & Jerod took a load of hay to Omaha.

Fri.7-15: (Baled straw. Baler broke. Had blowout on front tire of little Ford. Rain storm came up, & I had to bring a cableless tractor home. Kris lost a load of bales in the ditch by Mohr's. This evening, after Kris took a shower, she worked with her foot wound, & was able to get hold of the toothpick & finally pull it out. It was 1 3/8 inches long.)

Sat.7-16: Bill & the boys took their hogs to the fair.

Sun.7-17: I wasn't feeling good — too much heat & too many hours. We put rained on straw in the barn & crib. Rained.

Mon.7-18: Alan got 2nd in class for truckload of 6, & 1st in two other classes. Jerod got blues & a red. (Fair hog show.)

Thu.7-21: Alan left for San Diego to visit at my brother's.

Sat.7-23: Made hay from 7:30 a.m. to 12:45 a.m. Sun.

Sun.7-24: Didn't rain so we made hay 8:30 a.m. to 8 p.m.

Tue.7-26: Sorted hogs before 7 a.m. Loaded 127 for I.B.P. Made hay and such. Had supper 10:20 p.m.

Sat.7-30: Kris & I went to Atlantic Craze Daze. Stopped to see Grandma Bornholdt, Aunt Lois, & my folks. Went to Larry Allen & Traci's wedding reception. (Relative of Bill's)

Mon.8-01: (We hauled big round bales home. Alan came home.)

Wed.8-03: I got some perfume & a couple necklaces with B.D. money from Mom & Dad. Sherry & the girls came.

Wed.8-10: (Alan stayed home to do chores; the rest of us left for Montana on a vacation. 93,620 miles on the car's odometer.)

Thu.8-11: (Today we headed from the corn palace in Mitchell, South Dakota, across to the Badlands, & Wall Drug. Here we had ice water out of the original natural well that was discovered in the 1800's; & a man built a drugstore around it. We saw Mount Rushmore Memorial & stayed in Rapid City in about the last available motel room in town, for $58.)

Fri.8-12: (We went to Reptile Gardens [Jerod picked this out & loved it]. We got stopped for speeding in Belle Fouche [the officer talked to Bill & then told him, "Take the $30 that the ticket would've cost, & take your family out for supper tonight, just don't come back to Belle Fouche again. Have a safe trip."] We crossed into Wyoming & on to Montana where we stopped at Custer's Battlefield, & drove on to Lewistown where we stayed the night.)

Sat.8-13: (We visited with Bill's cousin Don Nelson & his mom Alta & family. [Bill's mom was from this Moore area of Montana. Helen was half sister to Alta's husband Archie; & Archie's dad, Charlie Nelson, was a brother to Bill's great grandmother Henrietta Nelson Johnson. Helen's mom, Mary, was Charles Nelson's 2nd wife]).

Sun.8-14: (We visited with cousins Jim & Joyce Turner & toured their ranch. Went to Crystal Lake with Don's.)

Mon.8-15: (We visited with cousin Gary Nelson & his kids, before leaving relatives to head on southwest where we ran into haze from the forest fires that were burning in Yellowstone National Park. After we got to the park, we saw lots of roadside signs that read, "Caution. Active fires in this area. Do not leave the road." We saw buffalo right on the road, & saw elk, deer, & moose. We got the last room for $53, with one bed; kids had to sleep on the floor in their sleeping bags.

Tue.8-16: (We went to see Old Faithful & the neat old main lodge. We visited with some people from Omaha, Al & Judy Barber; & they took our picture by the geyser ... the Grand Tetons were so pretty, as we headed back E. into Wyoming. We stopped at Hell's Half Acre: a really neat Badlands type hole down into a valley & really pretty. After a 45 cent chocolate ice cream cone here, we headed on to Douglas where we stayed the night.

Wed.8-17: Passed Wyoming/Nebraska state line 2:42 p.m. Stopped for dinner at Rete's, where Jerod pulled a loose molar. (We drove on east, got home about 11 p.m. [96,153 mi. on the odometer now].) Hot & stuffy. I cleaned up stuff. Did laundry, watered plants, went to bed about 2 a.m.

Thu.8-18: Cows out.

Sat.8-20: (Bill & Al pumped from the pit. My folks came for dinner. I did bookwork. We went to Leonard & Elva Peters' 50th anniversary reception.)

Sun.8-21: (Alan left for Iowa State University to get settled into the dorm for his first year of classes there.)

Wed.8-24: I got $45 worth of really neat fabric at The Sewing Box @ 75% off (Harlan store going out of business).

Tue.8-30: First Day Of School. (Moved corn & sold beans. Jerod, James, & I went to see *Who Framed Roger Rabbit*.)

Wed.8-31: (Bill started to combine corn at Herb's.)

Mon.9-05: Baled & loaded 8 racks of hay out N.

Thu.9-08: Bill & Duane did beans on Herb's. I windrowed.

Fri.9-09: Raked hay. Loaded a hay truck. Windrowed hay.

Sat.9-10: Vacuvated beans (to sell). Raked & baled hay.

Sun.9-11: Raked & baled hay. Boys combined. Vacced beans.

Mon.9-12: (Made hay. Loaded bales in the dark.)

Tue.9-13: Bill combined beans at Herb's until 2:30 a.m.

Wed.9-14: Bill was elected president of school board.

Sun.9-18: (Help came to unload 12 racks of hay into Louie's barn. We went to Eddie Skeets dance in Minden.)

Sat.10-01: We cleaned oats again. Went to Robert & Judy's 25th anniversary dance. (Dad's brother.)

Tue.10-04: We finished corn on Louie's. Bill & I went to the Creative Writing Class (through Iowa Western Community College) in Harlan taught by Edna Pike (Bill's high school English teacher).

Wed.10-05: Mom called to say Aunt Lois was to have surgery — she'd fallen & broken her hip. I went over to see her.

Sun.10-09: Stopped to see Arnold Rock for his 89th B.D. We went to

Genevieve & Edwin Doll's wedding reception.

Fri.10-14: <u>Finished corn & were done about 6 p.m.</u>

Sat.10-15: We had to hurry out to get cows ready to work. No one was in a good mood — everyone was tired.

Fri.10-21: (We chased in cows & calves & weaned calves.)

Sat.10-22: Calf was bawling right outside bedroom window, so we all dashed out of bed & spent next 3 hrs. or so chasing escaped calves back in.

Mon.10-24: (We took a corn sample to Wilson's for a protein test. Bought some items at Farner's going out of business sale [a department store that'd been in Harlan for years]).

Tue.10-25: (We loaded a hay truck for Duanne Heins.) I wrote my McKinley bug poem (Section VII: Leptocoris Trivittatus).

Sat.10-29: Bill & I went to surprise 50th B.D. party for Dick Brown at the Avoca legion.

Thu.11-03: I painted wash house. Bill chiseled on Louie's.

Tue.11-08: (Bill went to a Wilson Dealer's mtg. I went to vote, & to parent-teacher conferences. At writing class, Pastor Stan Nielsen & Edna Pike told about the process of getting their book [The Picture And The Pen] printed.)

Wed.11-09: (Alan got a pin for 9 yrs of 4-H membership.)

Fri.11-11: James Walter's 10th B.D. We went to annual pork supper at Avoca Legion & to school play. Rained 1".

Thu.11-24: We went to Charlie & Jan's for Thanksgiving.

Sat.11-26: "Someone" put a pecan roll in the microwave to warm it, & wasn't paying attention to it at all. It burnt to a crisp & filled the house with smoke, on my just washed curtains & walls. What a pleasant way to start my day.

Mon.11-28: (Bill went to see seed corn customers. I did some mending, & started a quilt for Alan out of half blocks from Bill's denim jeans, & purple corduroy.) I believe I like a zigzag pattern best.

Tue.11-29: Got up before 6 a.m. Duanne H. was here for a load of big round bales.

Sun.12-04: (I visited Edna while Jerod was at S.S. She played a 45 rpm record for me of her son Bernard talking to his folks (it was made while he was in the service in Texas, shortly before he was shot down & killed in WW II. He was a tail gunner in a war plane). I worked on Al's quilt. We cut a Christmas tree. It was fun.

Tue.12-06: Bill won a prize for the 3rd best bale of alfalfa hay at the Hay Fair in Atlantic. He was on the panel of experts for a question & answer session.

Wed.12-14: I stitched decorative squares around the binding of Alan's quilt & finally finished it.

Sat.12-17: (We went to Ames to pick up Alan for semester break.)

Mon.12-19: (We poured cement for a cattle waterer platform on Louie's.)

Sun.12-25: No one seemed to be exactly elated with what they got. So much for all the shopping, etc. I think everyone should just buy their own gifts & wrap them & then maybe everyone would really get what they wanted. We went to Betty's for dinner & supper.

Tue.12-27: I did books all day.

Wed.12-27: Kids went to the dentist. I still have a cold & was really tired & yucky today.

1989

Sun.1-01: We went to Mom & Dad's for dinner (& visited with Sherry & Ken). We went to funeral visitation for Norman Oehlertz (Jan's dad).

Mon.1-02: We went to Norman Oehlertz's funeral. (This evening, the 5 of us went to Atlantic to see the movie *Dirty Rotten Scoundrels* & then had pizza.)

Wed.1-04: (Took the Christmas decorations down & the tree out. I rearranged plants, etc. & cleaned until noon. Alan & Bill chored. I went in & painted Edna's kitchen for her.)

Thu.1-05: Dark & rainy. (Duanne Heins was here for a load of hay & then had breakfast with us. Bill & I went to PCA for our annual review. Bill had a school brd. mtg.

Thu.1-12: I'm sending away Bill's Publishers Clearing House Sweepstakes. He said if he won, he'd buy hay & send it to Lawrence Erhardts (dairy farmers we know in North Dakota who are having a tough year); and we talked about building on to our house: a utility room, second bathroom, a big sewing room, & a closet along the bedroom, all with a basement underneath for Bill's tractors, trophies, & collectibles. I'd refinish a round oak table for the kitchen, & use the current one in my sewing room. I'd also pay off ALL our debts & we'd never borrow money again, for anything!

Fri.1-13: 10°.(We loaded calves for the Avoca salebarn.) Bill often gets hyper immediately, so loading cattle seldom goes well. (He went to the sale & Al & I went to visit Grandma Bornholdt, Aunt Lois, & my folks.)

Mon.1-16: (We took Alan back to Ames. Stopped to see the Kate Shellie Bridge [a really high railroad tressel just east of Boone].) I love to listen to trains on the track & see all the different colors, conditions, & kinds of cars.

Tue.1-17: I sprayed some McKinley bugs (box elder bugs) outside, & sucked them up inside. They're everywhere! I hate them! They're making horrid spots on curtains, walls ,etc. Weather was mild today, a lovely day for January. Spring can't come yet — I have too much to do yet.

Mon.1-23: Mild, clear. I worked on income taxes from 8 a.m. to 4 p.m. Only stopped about 5 min. for a snack at noon. Bill hauled big hay bales home from Dallas Klindt's.

Wed.1-25: School's running late because of thick fog. Big wet flakes of snow started to fall & ground was white before the bus came. Bill dashed to Wilson's with a truck of (seed) beans. (Then had a tax appt. at the lawyer, & then our PCA man was here to set up a new loan. We didn't have our dinner until about 5:30 p.m.) I had a horrid dream last night about driving the brown pickup through a mud hole in the cattle lot.

Fri.1-27: (We went to Myrtle Johnson's funeral [relative of Bill's] [Harry Johnson's wife].)

Tue.1-31: Above 60° F. Sunny & Beautiful! (Jerod was home with a cold. Bill looked at the new calf.) It was so nice out today — just like springtime — even grass was greening from Sat. night's rain.

Thu.2-02: 8° Below Zero. Before the radio came on (at 6:45 a.m.) Kris came in (to our bedroom) to announce that there was no water. I ck'd the temperature & we decided the well pipes are frozen. (As we looked out it was blowing & snowing so Bill was imagining how much fun it would be to hang down in the top of the well to try to thaw the pipe, considering today's weather conditions.)

Fri.2-03: 16° Below Zero. No school anywhere in this area because of extreme cold temps. We slept a little later & then had Malt O Meal. (Hog) waterers were frozen (in the finisher) & Bill had to borrow an LP heater to thaw them.

Sat.2-04: 10° Below Zero. Bill worked on cattle & hog waterers that were frozen. 830 (tractor) wouldn't start.

Mon.2-06: Cold. (We sorted & loaded hogs.) I guessed them at 242 lbs.: they weighed 246 lbs. We went to Charlie Mayhugh's funeral (a neighbor). Richard & Pola Peters went with us to the Pork Producers Banquet. I was surprised to be named as Bell Ringer Award winner (for my pork education efforts).

Tue.2-07: (About 7 a.m. we loaded a hay truck for Duanne H. He came in for breakfast. I had a paper-towel-covered plate by the skillet on the stove where I was forking out cooked bacon: the paper towel caught on fire. As I dashed past the men at the kitchen table, to put out the fire in the sink, Duanne said, "She's really a short order cook; she cooks it on the way to the table!" I told him that I bet he didn't get this kind of entertainment with breakfast in town.)

Tue.2-14: Got a Valentine & letter from Alan. Went to funeral visitation for Bill Barrett, Sr. (an area trucker).

Sun.2-19: Bill & Boz took 9600 to Klindt's (repair shop) — something wrong with Dual Power. (Boz & I went sleigh riding on Louie's, & then Bill tied our sleds behind the pickup & we went for rides in the hay field. Rod Andersens were snowmobiling & took Jerod for a ride.) It was snowing lightly, about 20°F, and no wind, so it was fun.

Mon.2-20: Bill & I got a cow in & pulled her calf. #5 bull.

Thu.2-23: Helped pull a calf. Tractor wouldn't start so Bill was mad. Kris put her car in the ditch on the way home from school: hit & icy patch, spun around & slid backwards into a deep ditch. Bill drove her car down the ditch to where we could get a tow rope on it & we pulled it out, unharmed.

Fri.2-24: I was very depressed. Has been an unpleasant week. I often think about how different my life might be if I had finished college, & pursued a career in art, design, & sewing & textiles. I like living on a farm, but I'm liking life on a farm less & less every year. So much hard work, & we never seem to get anywhere: so much debt. I hate owing money — so much money.

Sat.2-25: Hay truck came for big bales. Bill got tractor stuck putting bales in for cows. Bill & I went to Pork Producers Banquet in Minden & dance. The Competition played. They are so good. Bill & I had a great time dancing.

Fri.3-03: No school — icy. I typed up a bunch of Bill's poems. Bill & Jerod went to the salebarn after dinner.

Sun.3-05: Kids & I went sleigh riding in the driveway & across on Minnie's. Went great on the ice!

Tue.3-07: (Bill left for three days, with a group of local people, to tour John Deere factories in Waterloo, Iowa, & Moline, Illinois.)

Wed.3-08: I went out before 7 a.m. to check cows & do chores. Everything was fine here, & I checked cows at 10 p.m. for the last time today.

Thu.3-09: (I ck'd cows at 7 a.m. then took a wagon to Herb's for seed oats. Fed bales to cows.) Beautiful out today. Sunny & mild. I cleaned all afternoon. Bill came home.

Mon.3-13: I hurried to get the house in order & left for Sis' In Iowa City. (Al & Bill went to Harlan. Al had a Drs. appt. & they ran some errands. There was a new calf dead in the cattleshed when they got back: still in the gut.)

Tue.3-14: Sis & I visited & shopped. Bill went after a replacement calf. Kris had her French (class) supper at school, & she was mad because Boz was there. Bill forgot to go & get him.

Wed.3-15: (Sis & I went shopping & to the art museum. Had a swell day. Bill loaded a hay truck with big bales, & then he & Al went to the machinery show in Omaha.)

Thu.3-16: I left Sherry's about 8:30 a.m. & came on home. The house was kind of a mess, so I swept up McKinley bugs, cleared the table, sorted & washed several loads of laundry, did dishes, folded clothes, & shook rugs. Bill & Al went to Lindeman Ford's open house. Well, I had a nice time at Sis's & a good visit. (Got nice bargains on our shopping trips.)

Sun.3-26: (Took Edna to church & then we went on to Jo's for Easter dinner & supper.)

Mon.3-27: (Picked up my folks at Omaha airport. They'd been out to San Diego to my brothers'.)

Fri.3-31: (We went to Wilbur Johnson's funeral, Bill's uncle. Went to Bill & Jerod's ballgame against Creighton.)

Sat.4-01: Bill seeded red clover. Jerod watched gates while I put bales in to all cows. (Kids, & I raked in the yard & burnt leaves. Jerod roasted hot dogs: he wrapped them in foil & put them in a gallon can in the fire. He brought buns, catsup, relish, & mustard out; & I had two of his delicious hot dogs. Bill came from disking & had some too.)

Mon.4-03: (Worked outside all day.) Had supper at 9 p.m. I hate Daylight Savings Time all ready! Why can't they leave it one way or the other, & never change it? We get up at the same time, by the clock as always, but we work an hour or two longer every day since it's light out longer, so I'm tired all spring & summer. I hate it!

Wed.4-05: Bill drilled oats. I harrowed.

Tue.4-11: Bill got 2 loads of cows in Dunlap.

Wed.4-12: I cut out Kris' purple satin prom dress.

Sun.4-16: (We picked up my folks & headed to Ames & ISU for a Freshman Honors Society induction for Alan. About 25 mi. west of Ames, our car's oil light came on, & we pulled off at a quick shop near Beaver, Iowa [population 85], to make some calls. This being a Sun., we found no car repair shops open, & finally called Bill's brother Duane [he's a good mechanic] — he'd come, but he still had chores to do, & then it's a 2 hour drive up here, for him, from home.

Just as we thought we were stranded & would miss Al's ceremony, a lady we'd never met offered us the use of her van: Laurie Doran had been in the shop picking up some items, when she overheard our calls & conversations. She lived a half mile away, & said she'd call her husband Doug to come & get her. He came right away; we visited with him a bit; they handed us the keys to their van; we climbed into it, & went on to Ames in time for Al's ceremony.

When we got back to the quick shop, we refueled the van & took it back to the Doran's, where they invited us into their home to visit & wait for Duane to come. These two kind, caring, trusting people had helped to save our day; & to top it off, Duane came, with the part he knew we needed, had our car fixed in half an hour, & we drove on home!)

(I wrote the poem "The Doctor," Sec. V1, this evening.)

Tue.4-19: (We loaded a hay truck of sq. bales. Loaded out some corn. Bill hauled manure. The drawbar broke on the 9700, & Boz & I went to Audubon to get another one.)

Sat.4-22: Kris looked nice in her purple prom dress, with her hair in a French braid, & new black patent shoes. (Bill & I helped with dishes & casino night at prom.)

Sun.4-30: Jerod acolyted his 1st time at church. (We went to Aunt Edna's 96th B.D. party.) I took nice pictures, but later discovered I'd had no film in the camera. Our oats & alfalfa are dying from herbicide carryover.

Tue.5-02: Bill started planting corn on the 13 A. field.

Thu.5-04: (Bill planted on S. place. I disked on Louie's. Mike Johnson, our nephew, wrecked his car tonight & went to hospital with neck injuries, bruises, and such.)

Thu.5-18: (I went to Ames to get Alan & all of his stuff for the summer. We hurried to Jerod's school musical. He was a raccoon.) Jerod did a super job in the musical!

Sun.5-21: (Kris handed out programs & Bill handed out diplomas at Shelby's high school graduation.)

Thu.5-25: Windrowed hay.

Sat.5-27: I cleaned house frantically all day. (Bill windrowed. Al turned hay. Went to Shelby Alumni Banquet, & then about 15 people came out for Bill's 30 year class reunion.)

Mon.5-29: (We made hay all day. I didn't feel good & finally came home about 5 p.m., threw up, took aspirin for a super bad headache, & layed down.) Kris woke me up (when she came home from ball practice) & I told her I'd been sick, & felt awful. She said, "Oh, Mauble. Poor little Mauble. Boo! Hoo! Hoo!" in her light, sarcastic manner, as she stood near my bed. Then she stalked out through the dining room, turned quickly, & humorously ordered, "Just don't make a mess!"

Thu.6-01: I went to Grandma Bornholdt's, cut her hair & gave her a permanent, so it'd be nice for the Bornholdt picnic.

Sun.6-04: (Making hay so we didn't get to go to the picnic.)

Tue.6-06: (Made hay all day.) Johnny Carson, in his *Tonight Show* monologue, said a few solemn words for a graduation, "From the Halls of Montezuma, to the shores of Tripoli, I've seen a lot of ugly people around the world, but nothing like row three." (Johnny's monologues are tops to ease the tension at the end of a long hard day!)

Thu.6-08: 55/100 rain. As much as 4" at S. place. (Al took Jerod to 4-H camp at Madrid.) (We went to S. place to ck. rain damage. Corn looks terrible there from Septor damage.)

Fri.6-09: 45°F at KMA. Record low. (Bill baled hay. I mowed weeds. Al turned over hay. Guys brought big bales home.)

Sat.6-10: (Got up 5:45 a.m. to sort & load 90 hogs for IBP.) We went to the creek field to load bales. I had a pickup & rack. I ran over Mac (our new yellow Lab pup). It's the most heartbreaking thing I've ever done in my life. I cried & prayed, & was devastated from what I'd done. He was such a sweetheart & we all loved him so. Why do such terrible things have to happen?

Sun.6-11: Bill & I went to Madrid after Jerod. He introduced us to all his counselors, & he'd had such a good time. (After we got home) I told him that Mac had died. He was tired anyway, & this was terrible news for him.

Wed.6-14: It's Alan's 19th B.D. (We're making hay. A calf died that we had the Vet out for. A cow broke her leg, falling in a creek, & we took her to slaughter.)

Mon.6-19: Turned bulls out. I painted on house. Kris fixed dinner & did dishes for me. Bill worked outside.

Wed.6-28: Kris' 17th B.D. We went to her ball game.

Mon.7-03: Hot & Humid! (We raked hay — Duane & Jo, & Larry Krummel's came up for burgers & polish sausages on the grill, & homemade ice cream.) (Larry is Jo's brother.)

Sat.7-08: Jerod's 12th B.D.: he got 2 sets of Construx, so he built new deals with them all day.

Mon.7-10: (Al left at 6 a.m. to take windrower hydrostats to Roland, Iowa, for repair. Bill repaired tires. We made hay. He square baled until 2:30 a.m.)

Wed.7-12: Jerod entered his cows photograph, & Construx framed picture at fair. He got 2 blues, & a lavender special recognition on his cows.

Mon.7-17: We unloaded racks of bales into hay shed. Picked up all big round bales off the field.

Wed.7-19: Al turned hay & baled some. Kris went to Adventureland. (Bill & I made new electric fence for cows.)
    (See story in "Observations & Thoughts" section.)

Sun.7-23: (We took Kris to Ames to ISU for a week long engineering workshop.)

Mon.7-24: I marked & sorted hogs while Al & Bill unloaded a truck load of pallets (we store our hay on pallets). I did some book work & raked straw. Bill did Gene Sorensen's oats. Al & Bill picked up big round bales on creek field.

Tue.7-25: (We turned hay over & made straw.)

Fri.7-28: Baled straw on McCarthy's & brought 10 racks home.

Sat.7-29: (I went to Craze Daze, but was home by 8 a.m. as it looked like rain. The guys had 2 layers loaded on a hay truck when it poured. We quick put racks of straw in sheds, & when the rain stopped, we unloaded the wet hay bales, & loaded the hay truck with dry bales.)

Tue.8-01: Walked beans. Unloaded rack of straw.

Fri.8-04: Over 100°. We unloaded 3 racks of straw before dinner. It was so HOT!.

Sat.8-05: (We were loading big round bales for Duanne H. It started to blow like crazy & dust got in our eyes & teeth: never did rain — went N. of us. We unloaded straw racks.)

Tue.8-08: Al mowed hay on the well field.

Thu.8-10: Started baling — came in about 11 p.m.

Fri.8-11: Made hay. Brought home 10 racks.

Sat.8-12: Made hay. Came home with 12 racks.

Sun.8-13: Jerod was crucifer. I helped usher. Al & Bill loaded some hay. We went to Bill's "over 35" slow pitch softball game in Walnut, & ate supper out.

Mon.8-14: Bill picked up big round sorghum bales on Leonard's. Al mowed hay out N.

Tue.8-15: Kris had her senior pictures taken. Al mowed. We brought big bales home from Klindt's.

Wed.8-16: Hauled big round bales.

Thu.8-17: (Made hay.) I'm tired — extremely tired. This afternoon my head was super stuffed up from dust & weeds.

Wed.8-23: Rain. (Today was the day our world turned upside down.) (We slept some later than usual, since we wouldn't have to hurry out to make hay. Then Bill went out to chore, & Jerod went out behind him. I sat down at my desk to pay bills & do book work. Alan left for Harlan for a doctor's appointment, & Kris was getting ready to go to practice.

Sometime later Jerod came in the house, & I asked him if he'd helped Dad feed cows. He said, "No, I wasn't with Dad, I've been in the shed." With that I sent him to watch gates for his dad & check on him; & I continued my book work.

Shortly Jerod came bursting back into the house saying, "Call

Duane, call the ambulance, & call Babbitt! Dad's upset the tractor!"

I told the kids to make the calls, & I raced out west, over the hill, with the pickup. In the middle of the steep, muddy cow yard, I saw the tractor wheels in the air, & Bill pinned facedown underneath, his legs sticking out one side! Dear God, He was alive!

He asked me if I'd called Duane & the ambulance, & I said yes, the kids did. I said, "What do you want me to do?"

"Get the big Case & a chain," was his reply.

I raced back to the yard for the tractor, where I met Jerod, & asked him if they'd made the calls. They had, & he helped me find a chain. I told him to stay at the yard & tell the ambulance where to come; & I headed out west with the big tractor. I was backing it into position when Duane & Mike came. Duane hooked the chain over the back tire of Bill's tractor & wedged a railroad tie under the tire for it to catch on, to make the tractor flip up off of Bill; & then he asked me, "Do you know how to drive that thing?"

I said, "Yes," & crawled into the cab of the big Case & drove it ahead at Duane's signal. The bent tractor came up off of Bill, quickly flipped upright onto its wheels, & Bill was left in the clear.

Duane was quiet & white as a sheet. Bill was a terrible grayish yellow color, but he was talking to us. He said he'd been beating with a drawbar pin, trying to make noise so someone would hear him, & come.

The Shelby ambulance soon came & then Harlan Medivac; & the Life Flight helicopter was ordered. I guess lots of people were here by this time; but I didn't see most of them, as I was kneeling on the ground by Bill, where I'd helped to cut off his clothes, & was holding his arm straight for an IV. Over the ambulance radio, I heard the helicopter pilot say, "We're about 3 minutes out"; & then, "We can't find you." My heart sank, & I froze ... but then the next transmission was, "We've got you spotted." Tears came as I heard and saw the chopper overhead.

People at the scene had helped to chase the cows & calves away from Bill & up into another yard so that the helicopter had plenty of room to land ... I remember seeing the helicopter crew, in their flight suits, running down the muddy hill in the cow yard toward the chopper, with Bill on a stretcher.

The Life Flight got him to Saint Joseph Hospital in Omaha in about 14 minutes (an hours drive from home).

The ambulance took Jerod & I; the other kids followed in the car. All the way to Omaha I cried & prayed, "Please don't let him die, Lord! Please don't let him die!" I prayed the Lord's prayer & talked to God non-stop as we sped toward St. Joe. The kids & I arrived about 1:05 p.m. & were shown to a waiting room. A chaplain came in to talk to us, & I do remember that his kind caring words reassured me, & made me feel better. I knew Bill was going to be fine, & I knew he'd come home again: I never once had any thoughts otherwise.

The priest told us what he knew about Bill's condition & kept us informed about what the emergency crew was doing with Bill, who his doctors were, & later how his surgery was going. He also told us about the hospital, & showed us where restrooms, waiting rooms, phones, food, etc. could be found.

It was nearing 8 p.m. when we finally got to see Bill. We had learned that he had internal bleeding, a triple fracture in his upper left leg, his pelvis was fractured in 4 places, he had a large pressure wound on his left thigh, his urinary tract was torn in two, his hand was bunged up, & his eyes had oil in them. The kids & other family & friends went home towards late evening. I stayed the night.)

Thu.8-24: I went down to peek at Bill at 6 a.m. He was to have x-rays & lab tests; & orders were to remove his stomach tube & oxygen, clean up his hand, shampoo oil out of his hair, & get him an eye specialist. (His eyes were solid blood red, partly from the pressure he had been under, under the tractor, & partly from the oil he'd gotten in them.) I was with him all day & went home about 9 p.m. with Duanes.

Fri.8-25: (I woke up real early & started making lists of things to do. Ross [my uncle] came; & he helped me cover a haystack since it'd started to rain. Duane & Mike came up to chore. Alan gathered his stuff & left for Ames & ISU. I got to Omaha before noon & Bill went to surgery to have his leg wounds flushed. I went to eat my first food of the day at 5 p.m. Lots of people called or stopped to see him, he chattered & joked for his guests. [I told him that this morning Duane said, "I came up to take care of Bill's work, but I didn't know whether to play the right or left jack." Bill chuckled & said, "Oh he did, well that bird."] I met Emma Jeanne Shipley from Nodaway, Iowa: her husband's in for heart surgery. We enjoyed each others company in days ahead.) I left for home about 8 p.m., made calls, & checked lists.

Sun.8-27: (There were a lot of calls & guests today, both at home & at the hospital. I stayed the night again, by Bill.)

Mon.8-28: (I ck'd on Bill & freshened up. I called IBP & sold a load of hogs for $47.50. Bill had written a poem in the night. Tom Tavarone, a young med student from New Jersey who's assigned to Bill, writes poetry too. Tom told me more after the surgery today than the doctors did: he keeps us well informed. Today the leg wound was debreeded again. Bill got an air bed today, & different traction.)

Tue.8-29: Duane & Mike helped me sort & load hogs. Mom got the kids off to school. I got to ICU to Bill at 2:30 p.m. Bill had two whole stacks of get well cards.

Wed.8-30: Jo came to the hospital to have breakfast with me, & then went to pre-op with Bill & I. Today he went to surgery again to have the thigh wound debreeded, & his Dr. said it looked better than it's looked yet. They'll plan to take him Fri. for another good cleaning, & to put the rod in his left leg, & start the grafting on his thigh. After surgery he was very lost & confused, maybe the morphine.

Thu.8-31: I called Alan & Sis. I ordered protein for calves & hogs, & mineral blocks for cows. Ck'd the hogs. Duane & Mike came up to help. I got to Omaha before noon. Cutting down on pain medication today, he was hallucinating this a.m. He had 3 kinds of laxatives today. I talked with Margaret Mitchell from Tennessee: her father is in ICU with cancer. (Bill goes to surgery again tomorrow so I stayed the night.)

Fri.9-01: Bill finally had some B.M. relief (an unpleasant subject & an act many of us take for granted; but when you're bedfast, it becomes a topic of concern). (Today Bill was in surgery for over 6 hrs. to get a 15 m.m. diameter stainless steel rod put in his left femur, from his hip to his knee, & his first skin graft on his thigh.) I sat with him until midnight, & then slept in the waiting room.

Sat.9-02: I cleaned up & went to see Bill before 6 a.m. His doctors were all in to talk to him, & said yesterday's surgery had gone well. Al & Jerod came to visit. Jerod & I went home at 3:30 p.m. & mowed the yard. Duane had hay down for us. I called Calvin's & then Leonard Klindt's to ck. on him. His chemo makes him sick & he's having a rough go.

Wed.9-06: I stayed around to see if I needed to rake hay. I payed bills, made calls, sent cards, went to bank, mailed insurance claims, ck'd with Mike on hay. They ended up baling without me raking. I fell asleep about 2:45 p.m. & woke up when Dad called about 4 p.m. I ck'd on the baling with Duane. Boz & I went up to visit Bill at 6 p.m.

Thu.9-07: Bill was down to whirlpool (very painful for him to be moved).

Fri.9-08: It was raining. We got over 4". I left home before 7 a.m. & hit hard rain in the city. (Bill went to surgery for second skin grafting.) ... Some area schools were running late due to flooding. The river was out at Avoca & Hancock. Red Oak & Shennendoah had water 2' deep in the streets. A tornado touched down N.W. of Harlan. Kimbalton got 8" rain. Most areas got at least 5". Lots of thunder & lightning ... (Lots of cards & visitors continue to come. Bill got a letter today from Beautiful

Sunshine with money for an in-town shave, because he said it always makes him feel like a million dollars!)

Sun.9-10: (Al & I chored. He put in a new yard light for me, while I ground calf creep feed. Kris fixed dinner. I went to St. Joe, & when I got home Kris was doing homework, Boz was asleep, & Al had gone back to Ames.)

Mon.9-11: Made grilled cheese sandwiches for breakfast since we're out of milk (need quite a few groceries). I filled feeders in the hog house. Ck'd cows. Put 2 big bales in middle yard. Fed rest of critters. Called the Clerk of Court to get Bill excused from jury duty on the 12th. Cleaned up & went to Omaha. Bill was back from physical therapy (physical torture, he renamed it): his leg wasn't ready for whirlpool yet. I talked to Shirley Lisle: her husband Merle is here for cancer treatment (ranchers from Ft. Laramie, Wyoming).

Wed.9-13: Duane & Mike helped me move bales off the creek field. Kids & I went to visit Bill after Boz' confirmation.

Fri.9-15: I chored, got a new muffler put on the car before I went to Bill's. (An ICU nurse was up to see him today and Bill told me she said, "They actually wondered if I'd make it or not when I was down there.")

Sat.9-16: (A funny thing happened today: a couple students took Bill to physical therapy, & when they redressed his grafts, & wounds, they wrapped him up like a mummy. Later he called for a bedpan to do his thing, the nurse put it in place & left the room. It seems there was no hole left in the dressings for such actions ... Bill said it felt like pooping in your panty hose! ... When the nurse did come back she couldn't believe her eyes, or control her laughter! The nurses laughed about this one for days.)

I chored & windrowed hay on the well field, & David Andersen helped me. Went to Omaha with Gary's this evening.

Sun.9-17: I chored & raked hay on Louie's. Boz & I went to see Bill.

Mon.9-18: I raked on well field, helped Duane rake on Jack's, Duane & Mike baled & I raked. Got home about 10:30 p.m. Didn't call Bill because the phone didn't work.

Tue.9-19: Richard Peters helped me rake hay on the well field. Duane & Mike were baling. Went up to Bill at 7 p.m. He had a tiring day: passed out on a slant board.

Wed.9-21: I chored & hauled big bales home. Broke a wheel on one hay wagon. I watched Kris serve to win her volleyball game at school before I went up to Bill ... Hurricane Hugo with 135 m.p.h. winds, was coming ashore in the Carolinas. Did tremendous damage in Puerto Rico, St. Croix, & little islands ... Duane started combining beans ... Bill wrote more combining notes for Mike (he operated our combine for Bill).

Sun.9-24: Boz & I went to see *Honey, I Shrunk The Kids* at the mall, & then we went to see Bill.

Mon.9-25: (Bill had therapy, x-rays, tests to assess nerve damage, time on the slant board: quite a day. I hurried all day at home with chores, books & bills, errands, & chores.)

Wed.9-27: (I windrowed all day. This was Bill's first day in a wheel chair.)

Thu.9-28: (We worked cows & calves here: several fellas came with the vet to help out) ... Bill tried a walker for the first time: he said he walked too far out in the hall & crashed, & had to call a wrecker.

Fri.9-29: Mom & Dad went up with me this evening. We had Mc Ribs, fries, & a Pepsi with Bill.

Sun.10-01: Boz & I went up about 3 p.m. We took Bill out on the deck in his wheel chair. I cut his hair.

Tue.10-03: I was planning to go up to see Bill for his B.D., but the starter on the car stuck & burnt, so I stayed home. I was zapped anyway, as I'd been scooping corn to load out the bin of corn on Louie's.

Wed.10-04: (I had corn trucks here to empty grain bins. Alan Eggers came to help me scoop, & Paul hauled away from Duane & the combine.)

Thu.10-05: (Bill had surgery again. Three doctors did their thing.)

Sat.10-07: 7 a.m. We got up to sort & load hogs. Al took them to Harlan. He helped me move big bales in from out N. & back on Louie's. Jerod helped too. We didn't have dinner til 3 p.m. We went to get more bales, & it started to rain.

Sun.10-08: Slept until 9 a.m. Then we sorted off open cows. I was sure glad to get that task over. Al cleaned up & went to see Bill. Jerod helped me feed bales & then I ground calf creep feed. I made a homemade pizza for dinner, as I'd promised Bill I'd bring him a couple slices. (Hospital food leaves a lot to be desired & Bill was hungry for pizza). (We did a little shopping on the way to Bill, & then the kids got their food in the cafeteria, & came up to Bill's room to eat with him.) Alan had a ride back to Ames at 7 p.m.

Mon.10-09: I was extremely tired today. I chored & worked outside, ran errands, & got ready to load cows in the a.m.

Tue.10-10: We loaded 15 open cows & a bull for Northern States Beef in Omaha. I chored, cleaned a grain bin, & then went over to Bill. (ICU nurses came today to see him. They said they'd almost lost him, that his blood pressure dropped to nothing.)

Wed.10-11: (I was painting rusty spots in the W. grain bin, & didn't know until afternoon that Bill had gotten moved to Immanuel Medical Center (It's known for its rehab. program). Betty & Gary took me over to see Bill this evening.

Thu.10-12: I helped with the Senior Class Soup Supper & then dashed the cow ck. to PCA, & went over to see Bill.

Sun.10-15: Duane & Mike did our beans on the cemetery field.

Mon.10-16: I was so super tired but I chored & worked outside all day. Bill called me about 10 p.m.

Wed.10-18: Bill got stitches taken out of his inner thigh wound & knee.

Sat.10-21: Warm & mild. I went to Immanuel after Bill (This was Bill's first trip home, but just for the weekend.) (Part of Immanuel's rehab program was to allow patients to come home on weekends to learn how to get along with their disabilities.) He's been in the hospital 60 days. We looked at calves, etc. & then got him & his wheelchair & walker in the house. He ate lots of potatoes & gravy, pork chops, & pork & beans for dinner. We went to look at the crops & see Duane & Mike combining. Bill slept real good until 4:30 a.m. & then he had to have pills & a pillow under his leg. It was so good to have him home!

(We were new at handling him & he wasn't sure what he was capable of yet. Alan & I would each get under his arms to help him about. Well, we were trying to get him outside, but we had to let go of him at the door to fit through, & Bill went down on us like a rag doll. We had to roll him down the two steps and then upright him when we got him to the bottom ... he wasn't hurt & it was good for some laughs.)

Sun.10-22: Another beautiful day. Jerod fixed us pancakes. Bill watched us sort calves. Dad helped me move creep feeders & get them filled. Tom Tavorone stopped by & we took him to see the combine working. He had supper with us & then He took Bill back to Immanuel on his way home.

Sat.10-28: I went to get Bill again. He was more steady in his walker this week than last. We went to The Heritage for supper & he enjoyed that.

Sun.10-29: We weaned calves. Lori (our niece) took Bill back to

Immanuel on her way home to Blair.

Tue.10-31: Bill had a Halloween party this afternoon at Immanuel: he had big glasses, a tie, cigar, & an elephant nose. (Here at home the bill came today from Saint Joseph Hospital. It was in a big 8x10 envelope & was 72 pages long. $104,297.69. I'm so glad we have good insurance!

Wed.11-01: Run, run, as fast as you can: that's what I did all day today, never even stopped for dinner ... Friends & neighbors had a picking bee for us today and did 92 A. of white corn on our S. Place. (So many people called, stopped, helped with lunch, or harvest. there are lots of good people in this world!)

(Bill went to surgery again today, to have a left upper thigh wound opened that wouldn't heal: The Doctor took out some tissue & sewed it up. Thought maybe a deep stitch had failed to dissolve.)

Thu.11-02: (I went with Bill to St. Joe to see his urologist. Bill was hoping to get his super pubic catheter out, & he did, but Dr. put in a new one. Bill was disappointed & so was I.)

Sat.11-04: Bill went to therapy: went for a round in his walker & then tried a 4 legged cane. He did really well! We came on home. Mike combined corn here & I hauled in. We got done combining about 4 p.m.!

Sun.11-05: After dinner Duane helped haul 45 cows to the Dr.'s. farm. Then we put wagons & machinery away. I took Bill back to Immanuel.

Tue.11-07: Bill rode home with Jo, & he & I went to Edna Pike's writing class at Ia. Western in Harlan. Had a nice evening & Bill got to read 2 or 3 of his poems. I took him back to Immanuel & was home about midnight.

Wed.11-08: Bill had a pass from his Dr. to go to a school board mtg., so I picked him up, got him to the mtg., & got him back to Immanuel after midnight, & headed on the long lonely way home. It was after 1:30 a.m. when I got home.

Sat.11-11: I left just after 7 a.m. to get Bill. After dinner we moved cows to Ronnie Eggers'.

Sun.11-12: Duanes came for dinner & then Waynes came & we played pitch, & had a good visit. I took him back to Omaha.

Tue.11-14: (Bill walked with a regular cane, even outside on the rocks & grass.) I visited with Charlotte Mander (Bill's roommate's mom): Jeff had his car wreck Aug 26,1989 & they found him in the ditch about 2 a.m. on their way home. Must have been horrifying for them.

Wed.11-15: I scooped up spilled corn (by the augers). Moved the creep feeder to the E. yard. Put 3 big bales to calves. Moved all pigs from W. side to E. side in the finisher, & covered all unused waterers, closed all doors etc. I drove two steel posts in the hay field gateway, covered the well, put bales by the W. cattle waterer to protect it. Ate dinner about 3 p.m. After I showered the hog stink off, I was chilled & couldn't get warmed up. I took Jerod to confirmation & visited Edna until time to pick him up. I actually watched the 5 o'clock news — the first time in weeks.

Fri.11-17: Bill got dismissed from Immanuel & got to come home!!! (109 days in the hospital.)

Sun.11-19: We went to ck. cows. Bill even got out to look at a beaver dam in the creek. He didn't get along too bad in the cornstalks with his cane on one side & me on the other.

Tue.11-28: (Took Bill to therapy in Harlan, as we've been doing.) Went to Elk Horn to see his mom for her 78th B.D.

Thu.11-30: (Our 21st wedding anniversary) (Bill went to St. Joseph Hospital in Omaha for out patient surgery: he had his torn urethra lined up with scopes & a Foley catheter put in. [The catheter would keep the channel lined up, until the torn ends could heal together] ... after surgery there was some bleeding, and then complications set in: his kidneys partially shut down, & his out-patient surgery turned into a 3-week stay in the hospital. This time was a real booger, with stomach tubes, & IV's, & needle sticks a zillion times — he was a sick, sick boy!)

Wed.12-13: (The final bill came from Immanuel. $25,406.14)

Sat.12-16: COLD. (I had had nothing but trouble with hogs in the finisher: waterers were frozen everyday, & I spent hours carrying buckets of hot water to try to thaw them only to have them freeze solid again overnight; hogs were dying from piling up. I'd had it! Today the whole kit & kaboodle were on their way to the salebarn in Denison ... [As it turned out, this would be the last of our hog raising: we decided to give up hogs permanently because of Bill's injuries.])

Mon.12-18: I had great plans for this day & all the things I was going to get done. All my plans soon went by the wayside after I got a call that the cows were out. I got them in, fixed fence, chopped a hole in the ice in the creek for them to drink, got back to my car & it had a flat tire. Rats! Why can't something just go right! Everyday is full of such surprises. I couldn't get the fender skirt off the wheel well to get at the tire. George & Franny Wise happened along to help & I really appreciated it. I later took my tire to town, & was told it couldn't be fixed ... fine, now I have no spare ... The kids helped me put up a Christmas tree. The top almost touches the ceiling. It's so pretty ... we should have had it up a long time ago. Now if Bill can just make it home, we'll have a nice Christmas. I miss him so much when I don't make it to Omaha ... Nasty weather today.

Thu.12-21: Super cold: -24°. No school because of cold. I had just come in from chores about 10 a.m. when Bill called, & said he could be dismissed today! I had to finish chores, so it was noon when I left for Omaha. I got Bill home, & decided I'd go after Alan while the car was running. I got to Ames about 5:30 p.m., we loaded Alan's stuff & headed home. Got home around 8 p.m. It was great to have Bill & Alan home & be in out of the cold!

Fri.12-22: 29° BELOW ZERO. No school again because of cold.

Mon.12-25: We had a nice time opening packages, & later went to Betty's, where we had a nice dinner & supper, & fun playing cards & Tripoley.

1990

Mon.1-01: (My folks & Sherry's came over. Later we went to Jo's & played cards with them & Charlie's. I was tired.)

Sun.1-07: (We were called to the nursing home early this morning: Bill's mom was having breathing problems. We spent the day with her, here & at the hospital; she passed away this afternoon.) (To me she was a very special person, I'd spent as much time living close to her as I had my own mom.) (Helen loved to play cards, but Alzheimer's had tricked her into a game she couldn't win. My heart aches for her & the joys we could have had with her if this dread disease hadn't stolen her away from us.)

Wed.1-10: (Today was Helen's funeral. A very hard day.)

Thu.1-11: (Duane came up to load a hay truck for us, & then Bill & I headed to Omaha for a visit to his urologist. Bill got his Foley catheter taken out.)

Mon.1-15: (To the urologist again — he thinks scar tissue is closing down the channel & he scheduled surgery next week.)

Thu.1-18: (Bill went to therapy, at Harlan hospital as usual. I went upstairs to visit Bob Schuster: he had just found out that he had a large mass on a lung — a very sad time for he & Darlene.)

Fri.1-19: I took Alan back to ISU. Chored when I got home.

Sun.1-21: (After chores, I worked on taxes.)

Wed.1-24: I went to chore by 7 a.m. We had a PCA appt. at 9 a.m. Had to be to Immanuel at 12:30 p.m. for a therapy evaluation. Saw Dr. Manahan at 1:30 p.m. He thought Bill was improving nicely — still weak muscles, but thought he didn't need to go to Harlan for therapy anymore. He said we needed to buy Bill a good pair of hi-top tennis shoes, & we did before coming home.

Thu.1-25: I had to chore by 6 a.m. & we left for St. Joe. Bill went to surgery, but Dr. just injected dye to have a look — didn't want to open the blockage with scopes.

Wed.1-31: I dropped off a flower arrangement at Klindt's for a memorial for Leonard (another good neighbor gone) ... We went to a supper for my folks' 45th anniversary.

Sat.2-03: (We went with Duane's & Charlie's to the Funnybone in Omaha for Jan's B.D.)

Mon.2-05: Sunny. 50's. We had our Wilson Seeds open house.

Fri.2-09: Sold calves at Avoca salebarn.

Sat.1-10: Bill & Jerod went to Herb Rock's sale. I got my hair cut & styled in Harlan.

Mon.2-12: The Dec. bill came from St. Joe for $29,731.09.

Wed.2-14: (We headed to St. Joe for Bill to have surgery [we now refer to it as "The Valentine's Day Massacre"]. He was cut from his navel to his hemorrhoids to have scar tissue taken out of the urethra, & fresh ends sutured together [in hopes that scar tissue won't form to block the channel again] ... Nurse MaLinda Stolinski helped settle Bill in his room [her dad is Art Stolinski, an Omaha Stockyards commission man we've known for years. His son Jim was in Viet Nam in my brother's infantry unit [Jim lost his life there].)

Thu.2-15: I headed to Omaha to see Bill. They wanted him to try walking, but he was so taped up it hurt him to move ... It was slick when I left the city & our roads were solid ice & snow — slicker than snot.

Fri.2-16: COLD (I chored & went up to Bill.) A German Dr. came in to take Bill's bandages off & yanked out one of the abdominal drain tubes. Bill said it hurt sooo BAD! It must have been hooked to one of his testicles!

Sat.2-17: The kids & I chored, cleaned up & headed to Omaha. When we got there Bill was sitting up, in a chair, all smiles, & said he could go home.

Mon.2-19: Worked on filling out the disgusting financial aid forms! (for Al & Kris' college student loans).

Wed.2-21: (Worked all day getting cows home from Eggers' & the Dr.'s. farm. Ronnie, Paul, & Allen Eggers' helped round them up, & Duane & Mike helped chase & haul. Ed Patee was just passing by when he could see we were having trouble chasing, & he came to help.)

Fri.2-23: (To Omaha. Bill got staples out of his incision.)

Mon.2-26: (Duane & Mike came up to help load a hay truck for Forrest Rutherford from Missouri.)

Wed.2-28: We went to my Aunt Lois' funeral (my grandmas's mother's sister). She was quite a special person. I'll always remember going to visit her as I grew up. She once told me about washing an enamel pan in home ec class at ISU: she ran chips of enamel under her finger nails & it hurt terribly. Her hand was bleeding & she wrapped it in a towel, & ran to the infirmary. Her instructor didn't realize she was hurt, & was furious because Lois had left class without permission & without leaving her smock. She later ordered Lois to the Dean's office for the incident. "The dean was very understanding, & was such a nice lady," Aunt Lois said. The dean was Mrs. McKay — the home ec building at ISU is now McKay Hall — and Aunt Lois knew the lady it was named for. Aunt Lois graduated from ISU in 1917.)

Tue.3-06: Bill, Duane, & I drove to Phelps City & St. Joseph, Missouri, with white & yellow corn samples, looking for buyers. We saw several fields dotted with ducks & geese.

Wed.3-07: I paid bills & waded through Blue Cross insurance stuff. (I finished making a black canvas book bag for Boz.)

Sat.3-10: Bill & I went to Julie Behrens' & Dean Knindt's wedding reception, & on to a dance in Minden. I had a great evening. Hadn't been anywhere to visit for ages. Bill & I even danced a couple slow dances.

Mon.3-12: Went to St. Joe hospital. Dr. de Souza took out Bill's lower catheter. We talked to Tom Tavarone, & Doctors & nurses Bill had had. We went to Clarkson Hospital to visit Clarence Johnson, but he was in surgery, so we talked to Ida, Linda, & Lon (his family).

Tue.3-13: Crocuses are blooming south of the house.

Thu.3-15: No school. Several ins. of thick, super wet snow.

Sun.3-18: We went to Bob Schuster's funeral. Lots of people — church was full upstairs & down. A nice service full of love & remembrance for

Bob. He was only 57 years old. Cancer is such an inconsiderate killer. Why not pick a bad person. Why does this happen to good people who are so loved & have good to offer their families & the world? Why does life have to break our hearts & cause us so much pain? ...

We went to Jerry Buman's to see our share-a-calf. Smokey is doing just fine. We met Alan leaving for ISU, just as we were coming home. He'd left us a nice note. I hated it that we'd missed saying good-bye to him.

Tue.3-20: Loaded 2 hay trucks. Deep well wasn't working.

Wed.3-21: (Bill had surgery to have scar tissue removed, rotor-rooter style, & a Foley put in again.)

Thu.3-22: (Bill had stayed the night in St. Joe, & was dismissed today. [We stopped at Johnson Pharmacy in Council Bluffs to get a good leg bag [the kind with a twist valve on the bottom are the nicest to use] ... Mike loaded a hay truck for us. Plumber put in a new deep well pump.)

Fri.3-23: It was cold. I cut daffodils for a bouquet: they're so pretty!

Sun.3-25: My wax plant (hoya) from Grandma Marxen is blooming! I've had it for years & it's never bloomed. I remember Grandma's was always blooming in her S. kitchen window ... The blooms are beautiful! So unique!

Tue.3-27: (The car transmission went out as I was to take Boz to the orthodontist to have his brackets put on. I was just at Rihner's so left the car & went on with Al's car.)

Thu.3-29: (We loaded a hay truck.) I went to Harlan on a whole myriad of errands (didn't get home until 4 p.m.). Bill had left a note, "Went to ck. on car. I left just before you got here."

Mon.4-02: (Hauled cows home from S. place.)

Tue.4-03: (We went to get the last of the cows in at the S. place.) The 9 head we left yesterday had magically turned into 10 head. We captured the calf. Bill couldn't get him into the pickup, & I hurt my knee trying to heave the calf in & hurry to get out of his mother's way ... We came home to get the truck & brought the cows home ... I took Jerod to get his top wires on his teeth. Bill was loading a hay truck when we got home. A couple guys came after seed oats. We chored & tagged a couple new calves. I fixed supper & typed a transportation recommendation committee report for the school boards. I helped unload 50 bags of seed corn.

Mon.4-09: We had to tie up a cow who wouldn't claim her calf. It was the 1st try for Bill to rope & tie a cow since his accident. Fortunately she wasn't too uncooperative.

Thu.4-12: (Bill had out patient surgery again, to have his urinary tract looked at with scopes; & while he was under, Dr. Crosby took the screw out of Bill's leg rod, above his knee. It only required a small incision & a couple stitches.

    Later, just as we got home, a cow was having trouble; & Bill had to pull her calf. His knee was sure sore after this ordeal.) ... (Today's surgery deserves special notice because it was Bill's 13th, & FINAL SURGERY!!! Hurray! Hurray!)

Sat.4-14: Jerod set out Easter baskets this evening for he & Kris. For himself he put a "Boz's Basket" sign on my big willow clothes basket, & he made an inch square white paper basket for the bunny to leave Kris' goodies in.

Sun.4-15: (We went to Easter at Duane's. We came home to ck. on a cow & she had feet out ... we weren't able to pull the calf & called a vet: finally a live Easter baby was born.)

Sat.4-21: Super foggy this morning. We loaded one hay truck of big round bales & one of sqs. Bill plowed. I chored.

Tue.4-24: I disked on S. place. My tractor was running a little hot so I used a plastic K-Mart bag to get water out of the creek to fill the radiator.

Thu.4-26: Mike & I disked on Dr.'s. farm. Duane seeded gov't ground. I harrowed it in. Bill got planter ready.

Sat.4-28: I got Kris' dress done at 1 p.m. She went to prom.

Wed.5-02: Bill planted white corn on S. place. I disked.

Thu.5-03: Duanne came for big round bales. Bill planted on cemetery field & was almost done when it rained. He was soaked & muddy. I was disking on Louie's & my disk broke — it had been raining lightly for several rounds.

Tue.5-15: We cleaned in the garage all day. It poured & even hailed some.

Fri.5-18: Everything went fairly well for Kris' high school graduation party. There were 114 here.

Sun.5-20: (Kristin's graduation day ceremony. We went to lots of parties afterwards & visited with a lot of people.)

Tue.5-22: (Planting beans on Drs. farm.)

Sun.5-27: William & I went out to fill cow wagon with bales. Had breakfast on the picnic table & read the Sunday paper.

Thu.5-31: We went to Omaha for a Dr.'s. appt. Bill finally got his super pubic catheter out. He still is to use a Foley twice a day for maybe 6 mos. to keep the channel stretched.

 We saw a young man in the Dr.'s. office today who had practically no face. Every time we go to the hospital we see people so very much worse off than we have it — we have to be so thankful for what we have, & that we can walk & talk & get around.

 Lord, some people suffer with such horrible ordeals & conditions ... How do they get picked to endure such pain & heart-ache? ... Is their purpose to remind the rest of us how very lucky we are, & make us strive to do our best with what we have, to make our lives better? ... It makes me want to reach out & help anyone who needs help we can give.

 A smile & some caring & understanding can warm a heart & make someone's day, & it's so easy to give — so easy to be friendly.

Mon.6-11: Hauled bales from the well field all day. Hot, windy, & tiring. When we got home no dishes were done, clothes were all over the ground by the clothes line, the table wasn't cleared. It's so depressing to have kids big enough to help, & they won't do anything unless they're told to. Why can't they just see what needs to be done & do it.

Sun.6-17: Rain. Bill & I went to look at the flooding. Our whole hay field (the rural water well field) was under water & the road was closed because water was coming over it from Robert Andersen's field to the N. Flooded at Avoca Implement & got about 3 ft. deep by Wendelin's grain bin of our corn (W. of Zim's station).

Mon.6-18: Turned bulls in with cows.

Mon.6-25: We left to go scoop & vac the last of the hard, hot, stinking flood corn out of Wendelin's bin.

Wed.6-27: Bill baled until about 3:30 a.m. so we slept late. Alan & Bill went to hay expo. I went after groceries.

Sat.6-30: Went to Becky & Wayne Jacobsen's silver anniversary supper & dance in Minden.

Mon.7-09: Bill was cultivating beans. Al started windrowing hay on the well field. He had trouble with bottles, corn stalks, & trash that had washed into the field in the flood ... It started to rain about 8 p.m. The sky was full of frontal lines, dips, waves & whirls. It was really neat! Sometimes the patterns of the clouds are awesome!

Wed.7-18: (We've been making hay several days & are tired.) (This evening) the fence was shorting out (you can hear it snapping) across the road so I went to fix it & then darkness came, & lightning bugs popped up here & there. Nice breeze, not to hot, but BUGGY!!! ... A June bug is doing a tap routine on the picnic table. I have the porch light on to see but it is also attracting all varieties of flying pests. It could be so pleasant & peaceful without them. What good are they? But to annoy, annoy & disgust.

Tue.7-24: William & I went to Atlantic to see *Pretty Woman.* It was a good movie.

Thu.7-26: William & I, & Duane went to the lawyer. (Then Bill & I went to PCA to close the loan to buy Helen's farm.)

Sat.8-04: Bill, Jerod, & I went to Larry Madsen & Paulette Nielsen's wedding reception. (Larry was on Bill's tug-o'-war team.)

Tue.8-07: Calvin & his boys came (from San Diego).

Tue.8-14: (We all worked on some repairs on the old machine shed & then Kris & I painted on it.)

Wed.8-15: We went to the 4-H Share-a-calf mtg. Jerry Buman got Reserve Grand Champion overall with our calf.

Sun.8-19: Went to Sonny & Lee Weise's 50th anniversary open house. (Bill custom combined for them a number of years.)

Wed.8-22: Al loaded all of his stuff & headed to Ames (for his 3rd year of architecture studies at ISU.)

Thu.8-23: We fed cows etc., loaded up Kris' stuff & headed for Ames (for her first year at ISU in pre-pharmacy).

Mon.8-27: Jerod's first day of 8th grade, & his first day in Algebra I & freshman science went well. Bill went to Schuster's to help line up stuff for Darlene's farm sale. I windrowed. School got out early because of extreme heat: above 100°.

Sat.9-01: I turned hay together. Al windrowed creek field. Kris fixed meatloaf, green beans/mushrooms & onions, & baked potatoes for dinner. Bill, Jerod, & Kris brought first loads of bales home from well field.

Thu.9-06: We got our computer (a Tandy 1000 SL/2).

Fri.9-27: (We were loading out corn, but Bill had to go after a sweep auger belt, so he went to Avoca Auction's 40th anniversary sale for awhile.)

Wed.9-26: (I've been painting the crib & cattleshed, while Bill is gone custom combining.)

Wed.10-03: Rained over 1" during night. Bill's 49th B.D. & at least he didn't have to combine since it had rained. Went to Betty & Gary's for a fish fry supper.

Thu.11-01: Went out shortly after 7 a.m. — I got in 10 mins. after midnight, & Bill filled a wagon & then came.

Fri.11-02: Rain threatening, we dashed out the door just after 7 a.m. We emptied a wagon & Bill took off for the field. I thought the day would never end. I just kept hauling & unloading, & checking the bin, & leveling the fines wagon, & back to the field again for another load of corn. We finally finished about 4 p.m. Then put round bales in the hay shed, & put balers & wagons away. I went after Boz from practice, while Bill fed cows. I made chili soup, & took a nice hot shower. We watched a little TV & went to bed about 8 o'clock — we were exhausted! Never even stopped for dinner today. (Today ended all combining for this year.)

Sat.11-03: Raining. (Jerod had to go to the orthodontist [in Council Bluffs] to have a bracket replaced; so he, Bill, & I did some shopping, went to Johnny's for dinner, browsed in an antique shop, & had a pleasant day.)

Tue.11-06: It started to snow big fluffy wet wobs as we started chores. (We picked up stuff on the ground, cleaned up corn spills by the auger, filled both cow hay wagons, & leveled corn in two grain bins.)

Fri.11-09: (I went to Ames where my sister met me & we spent the day shopping and such. Visited Alan & Kris.)

Thu.11-15: Bill plowed at the well field. Gene Sorensen came with his tractor & plow about 3 p.m. & said he wanted to help Bill since he didn't get to last year (when Bill got hurt). (Gene helped him today & tomorrow.)

Sun.11-25: Sherry, Ken, & the girls, Mom & Dad, & Grandma Bornholdt were here for dinner.

Fri.11-30: Our 22nd anniversary. Bill & I made fence along the S. side of the cemetery field. Bill, Boz, & I went to Club 191 in Portsmouth for supper. There was a huge pretty full moon.

Sun.12-02: We learned at church this morning that Gary Damgaard (neighbor & relative) had been shot in a hunting accident.

Mon.12-03: Snow & blowing, no school, even no classes at ISU. Gary died this morning. He was only 53 years old, such a terrible tragedy. Will we ever know God's plan? So many unanswered questions ...

Wed.12-05: This evening we went to visitation for Gary Damgaard's family. People galore. They filed in non-stop for over an hour. Lots of beautiful plants. It's so hard to believe Gary is gone. How quickly our lives can end! We should treat each & every day as precious. Live each day to the fullest — not put off our dreams — care for people & reach out to touch other lives at every chance.

Sat.12-08: We cut a Christmas tree.

Fri.12-14: I worked on wallpapering my kitchen. Bill & Jerod went to soup supper & basketball game at school.

Wed.12-19: (Bill had ck-up with his Dr.'s. at Saint Joseph Hospital. Dr. de Souza thought he was doing fine. Dr. Crosby thought Bill & his leg were doing great! And the rod doesn't need to come out. [Dr. Crosby is to go to Saudia Arabia in a few days: his reserve unit has been activated for Desert Storm.] We also visited all the other nurses & people we know at the hospital.

Tue.12-25: We opened presents about 7:30 a.m. The Johnson family was here for dinner & supper.

Sun.12-30: 10° Below Zero. Boz fixed pancakes for breakfast. Bill & Al went to feed calves. I worked on tax figures. Kris went away with a friend.

Section V

A Laugh A Day Keeps The Doctor Away

First

"Gosh, it's hot in here! It's like I have a shell wrapped tightly around me. Maybe if I push real hard ... Oh! Oh! What was that crack I heard? I think I've broken something. Well, at least I can move and ... and even stand up. Wow!"

"Oh man, just look at all of these eggheads all lined up in rows in all directions. If I knew what a military graveyard looked like, I'd think I was in one."

"Look out! This whole place seems to be moving! These egg-shaped things are all cracking, and tiny heads are peeping out of them. Oh! What a mess this is!"

"So much for being lined up in both directions. If I'm not careful, I'm going to loose my identity here; everybody looks alike!"

"I do seem to be a little better looking and a little taller than the rest ..."

"Well lookey here, a little white feather sticking out of me. Now I can tell which one I am. Oh no! He's got one too, and him, and him ... wait, I've got two, three, four ... Oh man! Lost again!"

"What do I feel popping out of my head? I'd better get to the water fountain and have a look. Well, isn't this a nice distinguishing looking comb-like thing I've got here. The chicks will go crazy! Hey, guys, look what I've go—. So much for being advantaged."

"I wonder what that human is doing coming in here with that burlap bag and wire thing with a hook in the end. Hey! He's looking right at me. I must be a little taller."

My 4 Speed, Posi-traction, 4 x 4 Truck

One day I was just dreamin' down the road,
    When I met this Mack with an overload.
He was carryin' something that was wide, & way too high,
    So I got out in the weeds, just to let him by.
I stepped on the gas to get back on the road,
    But I fell in a hole that was overgrowed.
Before I knew it, I was slidin' down the bank,
    And into a pond, where my front wheels sank.
        Well, thanks a lot!
    I just about ain't never been stuck,
        With my 4 speed, posi-traction, 4 x 4 truck.

I locked in the hubs & shifted into low,
    But the gosh-darned thing still wouldn't go.
Well, that wouldn't stop this old fox,
    I had gov't. surplus chains back in the box.
That sure was a gratifying sight,
    When Uncle Sammy's chains started to bite.
But I was in for another good deal,
    When my tubeless tire slipped off of the wheel.
        Now what??
    I just about ain't never been stuck,
        With my 4 speed, posi-traction, 4 x 4 truck.

You'd think somebody would be comin' soon,
    Seein' as how it is just about noon.
I bet everybody went to the sale east of town,
    So I guess me & my truck are on our own.
Hmmm, I've got some cable here for my fenceline bunk.
    The contractor in town just gave me a hunk.
I pulled one end off of the roll,
    And tied it through the valve stem hole.
        Ah-ha!!
    I just about ain't never been stuck
        With my 4 speed, posi-traction 4 x 4 truck.

I wrapped it once around the wheel & crawled up the bank,
 Tryin' my best to hurry before the pickup sank.
My lucky day, I'm right in line.
 I tied the other end to the Budweiser sign.
I hopped in the cab and pulled it into gear.
 Then I let out the clutch and yelled, "I'm outta here!"
Well, — the pole crashed down and onto the cab,
 Blew out a tire & smashed the roof just a dab.
   Oh, Man!!
  I guess I just got stuck,
  With my 4 speed, posi-traction 4 x 4 truck.

  I just about ain't never been stuck,
  With my 4 speed, posi-traction, 4 x 4 truck.

***

Potpourri

 People, what a wide assortment of configurations,
Different colors from different nations.
 Some have bumps in all the right places,
And some have lumps all over their faces.

 Short, fat land barons on southern plantations,
Blotched skinned sun worshippers resembling Dalmations.
 Biceps, triceps, solar plexes,
From pumping, pulling, full thigh flexes.

 Some are able to run in marathon races,
And some can't reach their own shoe laces.
 But tall or short or thick or thin,
We'll all get along with a nod and a grin.

If you think you've got troubles, talk to me.

***

Did you write down what I owe you? Shoot!!

***

Your dog has the most beautiful hair I've ever seen.

***

We sat there in our shorts in the bright sunlight with our middle-age spreads and receding hairlines, reflecting.

***

    A derriere!

        Where?

            Ascending the stair.

                Please, provide me a chair,

                    My view not to impair,

                        By those who would stare.

***

As we were passing a tavern in a town billed as having settlers from Czechoslovakia, Bill said, "Did you know yesterday everybody in that bar got drunk? ... Its bartenders were bouncing Czech's all night."

***

Question: Did you hear about the 4 yr. old that couldn't walk?
Answer: His kid-knees weren't functioning.

***

Question: Did you know my wife is a crossword fanatic?
Answer: She's always yelling cross words!

***

Karen: Who said, "And miles to go before I sleep"?
Bill: Mrs. Standish.

***

Question: Did you hear about the rock group that came over from Nicaragua?
Answer: They were the Contraband.

***

Question: Did you hear about the big motel complex that blew up?
Answer: There were roomers flying everywhere!

***

Question: What did the scientist exclaim when he invented a battery charger?
Answer: What a revolting development this is!

***

>   Running for public office
> Is not unlike preparing to die.
>   You better have your "affairs" in order
> Long before you vie.

***

Bill: (After the movie *The Texas Chain Saw Massacre* was out) I get a lot more respect from my wife now ... all I have to do is get out my chain saw and start it on the porch!

***

Bill: Our 6 yr. old has retractable horns ... They disappear when he goes to sleep.

***

Bill was combining for Norman Trede and had dinner with them. They had just gotten up from the table when Norman asked Bill if he wanted a toothpick. Bill replied, "Oh, no thanks, I'm full."

***

Jerod: Why do they have King sizes bigger than Queen sizes? Some kings could be whimpy little short dudes, and some queens could be big ugly fat dudes.

***

Bill was eating supper one evening with some folks he was combining for. The hostess asked him, "Would you like a piece of yellow cake?"
He said, "Well, what color is it supposed to be?"

Potluck

I really love picnics with all of the food.
    Just grab a grape or two to get in the mood.
Not to try some of everything I'd consider rude,
        Unless it's the last helping, or to the pot seems glued.
            That is really Pot Luck.

We'd better get started, the youngins are starting to whine.
    All of the dishes are open and everything's fine.
"My Gosh," look at all of those kids in the line.
    There won't be anything left but mine.
        That would really be "Pot" luck.

"Just bring a covered dish," it said on the card.
    But after two months of eatin' out in the yard,
I look like I'm really laying on the lard.
    I can tell for sure when tying my shoes gets hard.
        I can't reach over my <u>Pot</u> luck.

Say, isn't that Aunt Martha just opening her door?
    I'm so full, but she always has good things in store.
I ran to the bathroom to make room for more,
    But the stool was plugged and running across the floor.
        Now this is really Pot-luck.

Maybe I can go all summer living off of my friends,
    Holidays and birthdays and what the neighbors bring in.
And then by fall when my welcome wears thin,
    I can coast till the meetings start & I'll start in again,
        With Potluck.

In

Who ran over the skunk?
It seems that no one knows.
If you are innocent,
We can judge you with our nose.

If we never from this country go,
And at home we seem content,
If a person didn't know,
We risk being thought in-continent.

My wife complains about the kids.
The things they do are unbelievable!
Asked if she would have any more,
She would like to think it inconceivable!

Our son is studying in Italy,
Our daughter takes classes in Ames;
But our youngest may be the ingredient
That will drive us both insane.

The kids worry about their inheritance,
"Are we over indulgent, inefficient, non-bequested?"
We don't seem to draw any interest,
Where we have our wealth infested.

Ne'er mind the nuts the squirrels have stored
Inside our family tree.
In all of this we are never bored,
We indulge in infamy.

A Fractured Fairy Tale

Once upon a time there was a bad little girl named Hepsabah Calamity Drizzlekirk. Although her mother had often told her, "Don't ever go into the forest alone, Hepsabah," she set off from home one day to do exactly that.

She told her mother that she was going out to play, and that she'd be back for dinner. With that, she grabbed a bag of corn chips to take with her, and quickly snuck off toward the deep dark forest before her mother could see where she was going.

Hepsabah wandered farther and farther into the dark forest and didn't really plan to be home for dinner, as she had told her mother she would be. She diddle daddled along and traipsed deeper and deeper into the woods, and danced about until she wasn't sure what direction home was.

She thought maybe she should be heading home, however she wasn't concerned that she was lost. She still thought she was smart. She had planned to find her way home by following a trail of corn chips that she had been dropping along her windey way into the deep dark forest. She looked about to find her trail of chips, only to discover that they were being eaten by a mean and heartless aardvark!

Now she was lost in the deep dark forest and had no way in the world to tell which way her home was.

"Ah hah!" she thought, as she took a magic bean from her pocket and planted it in the moist forest ground. She then laid down and fell into a deep sleep. When she awoke, there before her eyes was a giant bean stalk! It went up clear above the highest treetops, right into the clouds.

She grabbed one of the big leaves and pulled herself up and kept climbing up, up, up the giant bean stalk until she got to where she could see over the forest trees. As she gazed all around, finally she could see her bright red barn and knew which way her home was.

Hepsabah climbed down the giant bean stalk and headed for home. After a while she came upon her grandmother's house and decided to stop in.

Her grandmother said, "My, what big eyes you have, Hepsabah. You look as if you had been in the forest looking into the dark all day."

Hepsabah didn't tell her grandmother how bad she had been. She just sat down and had a bowl of cornflakes, but they were not too hot, so she tried some pizza, but it was too cold. Then she decided she must be the ugliest duckling in the world, as she caught a glimpse of herself in a mirror.

Backing away from the mirror with a start, she fell back and pricked her finger on a spindle. Again she grew very tired and went to find a place to lie down. One bed was too hard, and one was too lumpy, so she just laid down on the floor and shut her eyes.

When she woke up a huge green frog was standing next to her. Before she could move, he leaned over and kissed her, and she turned immediately into a pretty green frog. They fell in love with each other, got married, and lived happily ever after in the Kingdom of Always Always Land.

They lived in a glass house at the bottom of a giant lake, with their three darling baby frogs. From time to time she told her frog babies how she used to be a bad little girl named Hepsabah, who wandered into the forest one day ... after her mother had told her not to.

***

Kids Say And Do The Darnedest Things

We once had a big long-haired dog named Bud who ran down to Duane's, behind the kids on their bikes, one hot summer day, and ended up having a stroke; and he later died.

Later Jerod said about our current dog, "I bet Cole can run 50 hundred miles an hour a day and not even stroke!"

*

Kris' feelings are very easily hurt and she has always been the easiest to discipline. Once I ordered her, "Sit on a chair and stay there until you can behave!" ... she was still there the next day!

*

I had asked Kris to fold and put away a basket of laundry, and she took care of it promptly ... I didn't learn till several days later, when we seemed to be missing washcloths and underwear, that what she had done was take the basket of laundry upstairs and dump it into an unused dresser drawer.

*

The kids only called my office with extremely important matters ... like, "Mom, Alan is hitting me, and he won't leave me alone!" or "Kris won't play with me." or "What's there to eat?"

*

Alan, you can't coax a sow back into her crate by opening the door, hanging from the ceiling in the next crate, and hollering at her.

*

One day there was a square glass dish of fudge on my kitchen counter that Kris had made (you could stir it with a spoon); I draped a couple paper towels over it and consoled her with, "We'll cook it some more when we have time."

Meanwhile, the foot of a 6 yr. old went right smack in the dish of fudge, while the body attached to the foot was en route to snacks in the cupboard above the fudge. This spoon-style fudge then gushed out onto the fresh Sunday paper, which I hadn't even read yet, and onto a blouse pattern that was on the counter ... "And now, for the rest of the story," as Paul Harvey would say: the spoon-fudge never got cooked to a higher temperature, but I did enjoy destroying it! — somehow it helped.

*

There was another incident involving this same kitchen counter: I had a wool leisure suit cut out and all the pieces were laying on the counter, when a child (in training pants yet) got up on the counter to get at some snacks. Nature called and drenched one of the pattern pieces and its attached fabric ... (Fortunately I had enough extra fabric to cut out that pattern piece again.)

*

Jerod, what is a dodecahedron?
Answer: It's a left-handed homosexual.

*

While browsing in an antique shop, where the owner was ready to spray-paint an antique toy tractor and corn picker, a haughty lady customer rudely asked our 4 yr. old, "How would you like to have your shoes spay-painted green?"

"He shyly replied, "I hope your face Dies!"

*

Kris: Knock, knock.
Bill: What's the matter? You got a rod going out?

*

When a neighbor was leaving one day after a visit, our youngest said, very concerned and sweetly, "Good-bye, come back again sometime, come back again and stay and have dinner with us, come back sometime before your face rots off!"

***

Cutting Remarks

At our house I've given haircuts at all hours of the day and night, and sometimes in a pretty big hurry! I even cut Bill's once while he was on the throne. One of the boys went off to the bus one day before I was done with the last side! And I hurried to cut Al's one day when he asked me about ten minutes before his ride to Ames was to pick him up.

I did a nice job on Alan's, especially for such short notice and so little time. As I took the towel off his neck, I said, "That'll be $8.50 please." And of course he replied sarcastically, "Oh, sure!" ... (Just like Rodney Dangerfield, "I get no respect!")

Then there was the time Bill really needed a haircut when he was still in Intensive Care at St. Joseph Hospital in Omaha. I got permission from the nurse to do it, she helped me get a towel under his head to catch the hair and left the room, closing the door behind her. I got out my scissors and got myself a step stool so I could reach him. It was hard to get at the proper angle to do my work and still stay out of the way of his leg traction and all of his hoses and tubes. It went pretty well, but I had to get into some contorted positions at the head of his bed to get the job done.

Later one of the nurses said that Bill's haircut looked nice; but she laughed as she commented that I'd had quite a time with it. It was then that I learned I had provided entertainment to the whole ICU nursing staff, as they had all watched the haircut on closed circuit TV out at the main desk!

***

Bill: It scares me when I go into a doctor's office and see a sign that says, "Practicing Physician."

***

Bill: What good is a memory if you loose your mind?

***

Bill: I'd like to go up to someone and say, "Hi! I represent *Homely* magazine. Do you want to be our cover girl?"

***

Delicious?

Herb brought me an apple the other day.
    Of course I thanked him, what else could I say.

I laid it aside much to his dismay;
    I said, "I'm busy right now, I'll eat it someday."

The skin was all wrinkled. It looked 90 years old.
    One thing about it, it was easy to hold.

It was all yellow, I thought it should have been red.
    Lord knows how long the tree had been dead.

I just kind of wondered if I would get fat,
    Eating that little old yellow worm habitat.

I know you're not to look a gift horse in the mouth,
    But when that apple looked back, I thought I'd go south.

I guess it'll have to be my apple today,
    If I'm to stay healthy and keep the doctor away.

***

    Jerod said, "Maid! Maid! Get me some milk." And I said, "Listen young man, I'm not your maid, and anything you're capable of doing for yourself, you'll be expected to do." He jumped up, put his arms around my neck, hugged me tight, and boldly announced, "I can do this, but I can't do it to myself."

***

Daffy Definitions

Bonnie Sadir: What Irish electricians use.

Universal Joint: The tavern in the movie *Star Wars*.

Unprecedented: What a country is when it looses its president.

"Breathing Heifer": What 4 yr. old Jerod mistakenly called Alan's 4-H breeding heifer.

Things That Are Spotted

      Leopards
      Salamanders
      Glasses in your dishwasher
      Indians on the horizon
      Your underwear

***

Question: If you had an out house about 24' x 24' what would you call it?
Answer: Big John

***

Bill says he was 27 years old before he knew that all that jiggled wasn't jello.

***

Question: What were the Japs singing as they attacked Pearl Harbor?
Answer: The chorus to "Blue Moon."

***

Jerod once said during the Christmas season, "You just better watch it, or I'll punch you clear to Bethlehem."

***

Bill handed me the sugar bowl one day at breakfast and said, "Here, take your lumps."

***

Bill: Did you hear about an old Indian years ago who killed a buffalo and cut a tit off of it to keep, killed a beaver and cut a tit off of it to save, even killed a white woman once and cut off a tit to keep?
Karen: For peet's sake what for?
Bill: He was simply trying to keep abreast of things.

***

    One night the dog was barking like crazy, and I stuck my head out the door and asked the dog, "What's the matter?"
    From the other room I heard Bill say, "It's Tom."
    Puzzled by that I said, "What?"
    He replied, "You've heard about that Chinaman that's been running around the country? ... Peking Tom."

***

Karen: (At supper one evening) Jerod you better eat or you will shrivel up and die.
Bill: It'd be worse if he shriveled up and didn't die!

***

We were talking about how small Bill and I were as youngsters, and Bill said he was small in high school too. Jerod chimed in, "Well, welcome home puny dad!"

***

About the "powder" that's left in the bottom of a jar of dry roasted peanuts, Jerod said, "This powder tastes yucker than the darned peanuts!"

***

About two goose eggs on his forehead that he'd gotten from a fall, Jerod asked, "Mom, do you have anything that will fade these bumps?"

***

Karen: I just saw a yellow hearse!
Bill: That really was a hearse of a different color!

***

Bill: Sesame Street could donate a wing to a children's hospital and call it "Big Bird Wing."

***

When Jerod was about five, something on TV sparked him to jump up from where he was watching it, and remark to his dad, "I just hate it when you pet me. You just make me so mad! Sometimes you just pet me like a common dog."

***

A bull was carrying on with low-pitched groans and bellows one day as we turned him into a new field of cows, when Jerod said, "That bull must have a cold; he can't even moo right."

***

As we were leaving their house one evening after a visit, Jerod's grandpa asked him, "Do you hear my owl in the grove?" "What would you do if it were dark and he started hooting and scared you and made your hair stand up on end?"
Jerod calmly replied, "I'd comb it."

Mary's Kitchen

Have you ever eaten in Mary's kitchen?
If not, I'll bet you're just itchin'.
Andy says it's perfect, but Herbie's bitchin'.
You've got to decide if it's for eatin' or pitchin'.

To sit back and watch the others is key.
You may think a dish is a sight to see,
But is it a dessert or a main entree?
You don't dare ask what it's supposed to be.

Mary says, "Eat it, it's better than it looks.
It came right out of one of those centennial books.
I didn't have all the ingredients or as much as it took,
But it was sent in by one of those threshing cooks."

You can bet that by every young cook a tear is shed,
When after they toil all day to keep the workers fed,
The wild goose is burnt and the corn bread's red;
And Hubby says, "We'll eat in town instead."

Sometimes there's a new recipe to explore,
But if it comes out just as hard as the floor,
You just look behind that door.
That's what that five gallon bucket's for.

But at dinner time, no one has just sat,
We eat what's prepared and chit and chat.
What ever it was, it wasn't bad at that,
And everyone looks like they're getting fat

                ... even the cat!

It Must Come From Your Side

We have to hold in awe the miracle of birth,
    Our growth from a single cell.
We express our desires for what they are worth.
    The outcome we can't foretell.

Somehow we pass our color and height,
    Our looks and intelligence;
Whether we favor our left or our right,
    Our blood type, our common sense.

When we decide we want a daughter or son,
    We start the process and wait.
It gives us time to weigh our pros and cons,
    And pray for a recessive trait.

***

My Kingdom, ... Come

    When we first got married,
We couldn't get close enough.
    There were hugs and pets and kisses,
And all of that lovey-dovey stuff.

    But now that we have aches and pains,
That's not how we spend our nights.
    We retire to our kingdom,
And vie for territorial rights.

It's All Mine

What do I have?
    Well, let me see.
        I do my own thing,
            So I guess I'm free.

When I'm dreamin' down the road,
    And am a little too late to swerve,
        Folks tell me
            I've got a lot of nerve.

When the unknown confronts me
    And gives me the shakes,
        It's nice to know
            I've got what it takes.

I go where I like
    And that's not all,
        When I eat more than my share,
            It takes a lot of gall!

I've got my aches and pains and muscle strains,
    Worn out things and ketchup stains,
        But you'll have to listen hard to hear me complain
            Just as long as I've got warm blood in my veins.

I've got my family and friends
    And if that's not enough,
        Hidden away in my drawers,
            I've got my **"Stuff."**

Mystery Lunch

On a late summer day, Duane, Bill, and I were vacuvating soybeans out of grain bin rings in our machine shed. It was slow going because, as usual, the vac wasn't working very well; and we were having to do a lot of scooping! By afternoon when we were hot, dirty, and needing an energy recharge; I dashed to the house to make lunch.

Wanting to take them something cool and refreshing, I quickly cut watermelon into bites and put some into two small containers. I tucked the bowls back in the fridge to keep the melon cool while I made sandwiches, and fixed a water jug.

After I quickly plopped sandwiches into their brown bags, the last thing I did was open the fridge and grab the small containers. Putting one in each bag, I dashed for the door to head back out to the bin.

I sat their lunch bags on the hood of a tractor, because Bill said they'd finish filling the truck they were working on before they stopped to eat. With that, Bill sent me to do other chores and I didn't visit with him again until later that evening.

"Did you eat your lunch and your watermelon?" I asked.

"Watermelon?" he said. "What watermelon?" " I had a plastic container of some kind of brown powdery stuff. I didn't know what it was, so I didn't eat it."

Hearing that, I checked the lunch bags he'd brought back to the house and opened his container. There was the brown powdery stuff just as Bill had said — (it was breading for fish)!

The little container of watermelon bites he was to have had was still in the fridge.

***

The Joys Of Being A Farm Wife And Mother

My nephew was watching me clean my kitchen floor one day, on my hands and knees with a bucket of water and a scrubber. He said, "My mommy doesn't do her floors like this, she uses a mop." —OK, he was a bright observant 5 yr. old. —Then I got to the porch, which at our house is our entrance from chores —as I was about to back out the door and finish the floor, so I could pause for a few minutes rest, he added, "My mommy's water is never that dirty!"

*

As a neighbor who'd been helping us fill silo came in for dinner, he glanced beyond the kitchen and said, "If our house looked like that, my wife would have heart attack!"

*

Our outside door and our bathroom door used to open toward each other. A neighbor coming in for dinner happened to comment that the doors would form a nice pen. Since he was helping us fill silo, he was back the next day for dinner, and for a joke, I had a nice little pig penned behind those doors.

*

I was driving home about 11:30 p.m. after a particularly stressful day at the office. All the way home, I was thinking about kicking my shoes off and easing into my favorite chair to read the mail and watch a little TV to relax.

As I turned the knob of the front door and started to open it, it didn't open readily, but offered resistance. I discovered that there were some dirty clothes up against the inside of the door, and now they were caught underneath of it. After having to get down on my knees and reach my arm through the crack, I was finally able to partly dislodge the wob that was blocking my entry. I squeezed through the opening, only to trip over a chair that was on its side in the kitchen doorway.

As I looked up from where I had stumbled to, I saw something dripping off the kitchen table and onto the seat of a stool, and from there, onto a large blackish puddle on the floor — the same floor that had been mopped only the day before.

As I kicked a school bookbag aside and stepped closer, I could see that the substance was chocolate syrup. (I later learned there had been a fight over a malt-making affair ... Well at least it wasn't somebody's blood!)

I was ready to take this mess in stride and make my way to my chair, when I discovered half the contents of a box of Cheerios strewn in the doorway to the dining room and the empty box kicked up against the fridge. The TV was on, but no one was to be found; and I could only surmise that they'd all gotten tired of fighting and finally gone to bed.

All was not so bad though, 'cause if I'd been here I'd of probably had to do them some bodily harm. I sighed and said to myself, "It's been such a lovely rewarding day, I'll just kick my shoes off and sit down and relax."

*

My house often looks like a cyclone just struck! So I thought, I'll play their game, and I installed a dozen new coat hooks directly on the floor in miscellaneous places all over the house.

*

Once when we were first married I had vets and other men for dinner when we were working cows and calves. So far no one seemed to ever take a second cup of coffee at our house, so I decided to put an egg in it like the ladies used to do at the country school suppers. Well, let me tell you, in an electric percolator it doesn't work! And the coffee was some sad sight, with gross looking little floaters of cooked egg in it! The one veterinary, not wanting to hurt a new bride's feelings, was going to be gallant and drink his without saying anything, but as soon as I discovered the goof-up, I dumped his cup for him. ... (p.s. I'm a poor judge of coffee because neither Bill or I drink it.)

*

Some people don't do windows ... I don't do pies! The bottom crust I can handle — it's underneath and a patch or two won't show. It's the top crust that really gets me paranoid. I know I'm going to fail before I start, even though I take many precautions: I refrigerate the dough for easier handling, use a glass rolling pin with ice in it, use a no-stick pastry sheet with 9" and 10" circles printed on it.

Ah, yes, I have whipped out a perfect 10" circle with half a dozen beautifully executed strokes of my rolling pin; and then cut a pretty design of leaves in the center to make it attractive and vent the steam; and carefully put it on the pie, only to remember that I'd forgotten the dabs of butter on top.

When I pulled back the crust it tore in about sixteen places; or when I was ready to get the top crust off the pastry sheet in the first place, it wouldn't come loose; and I ended up pulling loose what would come and scraping off the rest. At that point I'd slap the crust on as is, slam the pie in the oven and vow not to do pies again!

*

I was almost eaten alive one day, while trying to screw iron blocks into sows crates for the little pigs ... the thanks I get for trying to see that their little darlings get the proper nutrition.

*

Hide! I Can't Let My Cornflakes Sog!

Bill had just poured the milk on his cornflakes one day when I saw a salesman drive into the yard. He said, "I don't need anything, and I don't want to talk to him now, or my cornflakes will sog!"

"Well, I can't go to the door, I'm not dressed yet!" I said, still in my pajamas. So I shut the kitchen light off and we hid.

Bill quickly dove under the kitchen table to get below window level, and lay face down, spread-eagle, and continued to eat his cornflakes. I dashed to the bedroom and quietly shut the doors. We heard the knock and we waited; soon we heard a car leaving.

We resumed our breakfast, thinking he was gone; but he'd only driven out north to our other driveway, and he was coming up the walk again! I still wasn't dressed so I hid in the bathroom and Bill crouched behind a chair in the living room.

He knocked again and when we didn't answer we heard our outside door open! We remained quiet as church mice, not believing our ears! The door closed right away again, and we soon heard a car start up and leave. We remained hidden a bit longer this time, and when we did come out, I found a note on the porch. It said, "Karen, if you're going to work today, your right rear car tire is low."

We got a good laugh out of this! This had been kind of a fun, exciting, unusual start to our day, and Bill did get to eat his cornflakes before they sogged.

***

Another time I remember a salesman was coming to the door that Bill didn't want to talk to. I had to answer the door, and when asked where Bill was, I couldn't lie, of course; so I said, "I'm not sure where he's at."

At that instant our five year old stepped up right behind me and announced, "I know where he is." "He's right there!" as he pointed to our dining room ...

And if we happened to be outside doing chores when we saw a salesman coming, we could of course hide in the barn or hog house; but instead of a five year old to give us away, there was a dog wagging his tail just outside of where we were hiding ... That's life, I guess.

***

I See You

I was sitting all alone at the kitchen table
Watching the markets as they came over the cable.
I knew that I had plenty to do,
But there was no one here to turn my screw.

Then the curtain from the window fell.
How to hang it back I could not tell.
It was definitely not my primal wish
To sit in here so conspicuous.

What if someone passed from who knows where,
And saw me here when I should be there.
So I picked my shoes from the back porch stores,
And headed outside to do my chores.

***

Karen: Look, there's a cardinal in the back yard!
Bill: Don't tell the Pope!

***

Bill: (He said this during the 80's) In the Midwest we don't have to worry about getting hurt in a tornado because I just heard the radio announcer say, "In case of a tornado, get in a depression."

***

Karen: I've always wanted to be in a position to laugh all the way to the bank.

***

Things Parents Used To Say

Put that down, you'll put your eye out!
I'll wash your mouth out with soap!
I'll kick your butt up-straddle your neck!

(It's that last one that always scared me the most. It sounded so painful that I always did whatever was necessary to keep it from happening to me!)

***

FOR SALE:

Industrial lots, will build to suit.
How about a house of ill repute?
Just like any other house but, instead
Of soft white, the lights are red.
One door up front and four behind,
For a man who is so inclined.
We wouldn't want to take a risk
So we'll subject you all to a friendly frisk.
The sign out front would clearly say
No exercise before you pay.
New jobs in town can't all be bad,
And what a lift for poor ol' Dad.
But wait, what if Mom should apply,
You know, try to make some bucks on the sly.
I think we'd better look at this thing.

Hmmmm, Let's put up another Burger King.

***

Q: Do you know what you get when you go to a prostitute and give her $20 when she only wants $15?
Ans: Sex change.

***

A man was leisurely reading his newspaper one day after lunch when suddenly something he'd read caught his eye. He jumped up from the table, and started for the front door, hurriedly calling back to his wife, "I've got to dash to town, there's something I've got to see."

Puzzled at what had excited him so, she looked at the page in the paper her husband had been reading, and there was a large add from a local clothing store that read, in big bold print, **"LADIES UNDER-WEAR 50% OFF."**

***

Bill: If I curl up with a good book, it'd better be soft cover.

***

Q: What's another name for a Halloween pigeon?
Ans: Boo Coo.

***

Over The Hill?

I take pills for this
    And drugs for that;
        I'm really getting in a groove.
I've got bladder leaks
    And libido peaks;
        And my bowels don't want to move.

On the same end
    My knees won't bend;
        They feel like they need some grease.
Without a doubt
    I've got the gout;
        And the pain doesn't seem to cease.

The muscle's gone
    That I used to dawn;
        And when I run I usually fall.
The warranty's up
    On my rotator cuff;
        So no one asks *me* to play ball.

My nose is new;
    I've got one elevated shoe;
        Oh, I'm sure you're all impressed.
I fill my pants
    With cheek implants;
        That's why it takes me so long to get dressed.

I've got cataracts
    And have mild attacks;
        And I'm starting to get crow's feet.
My teeth are few
    When I smile at you;
        But my heart still skips a beat.

I've got the trots
    And liver spots;
        It's hard for me to sit still.
But, as I look around
    At the rest of you clowns,
        I can't think that *I'm* over the hill.

Cents Of Christmas

No matter what your age or views
    Or degree of happiness,
It is this time of year that brews
    A warm feeling in all of us.

For twelve months we toil and sweat
    With new problems to address.
Then we give more than we get,
    All this adding to our stress.

It's more fun to give than to receive:
    To trade your wealth for bliss.
If that's what you believe,
    You've still time — to consider this.

Again it is that time of year
    With all of the hustle and the fuss.
It becomes so very clear,
    Why we call "Santa," "Saint Nickel-less."

***

Snowmobile

The Night After Christmas

'Twas the night after Christmas
    And much to my ire,
Someone had mistakingly thrown
    My new robe on the fire.

The glass balls were broken
    When the tree was tipped over;
And someone shortened our shag
    With their new plastic mower.

The house that once glistened
    And was as snug as a bug,
Has fingerprints on the windows
    And nut shells in the rug.

It was curtains for sure
    For that overstuffed mouse,
When someone *accidentally*
    Let the dog in the house.

We had cleaned for weeks
    With a three man crew;
And in less than a heartbeat,
    A tornado whipped through.

Oh! for a genie
    Who could grant me three wishes;
He could clean up this mess,
    And just help with the dishes.

Our home was a castle,
    But now, what a horrible sight;
As the "stuffed turkeys" departed,
    And we bid them, "Good Night."

Section VI

Observations And Thoughts

Savor It

Ahh! It's spring!

There's not a weed in the fields and
The way it looks, they won't be here to affect our yields.

Calves are being born on early spring grass;
It seems they are healthy from the first to the last.

The mother cat is dragging her newborn out to the sun,
And bathing them all carefully one by one.

And notice how perfectly clear is the air,
There probably won't be any insects this year.

It seems there is something missing here on the plain.
Will anything survive without any rain?

Moisture would sure help new plantings come through,
But then we'll have those ugly weeds too.

A new calf might come on a cold, rainy day;
And without careful watching, shorten his stay.

The poor kittens drowned where the barn roof leaks.
How could she know — it hadn't rained in weeks.

The bugs, I suppose, are a necessary evil,
The aphids, the flies, the dusty old weevil.

So when a perfect day comes along, stop and drink for awhile
For the difference sometimes is fleetingly fragile.

First Exposure

I followed his eyes as they darted from one new experience to the next, taking only enough time to explore, leaving analyzation to a more quiet time.

By the angle of his darting glances and the reactions of his mouth and facial expressions, it was more exhilarating for me to imagine which of the things he was looking at (things that I had seen for myself many times before) than it would be to share in his direct visual contacts.

What a wonderful thing to be able to look at something and actually see it.

***

See The Shape Things Are In

Outsized cylindrical structures stand,
Covered with silver-glinted skins,
Sporting circles that go round and round,
Like immense continuous grins.

Wearing clothing made of sheets with rows
Of rivets that go up and down,
Showing cones for the hats on their heads,
With augers angled to the ground.

Their lines and shapes and circles and cones,
Their ribs and rivets and sections,
Toy with the eye's imagination,
And make it dance in all directions!

Journey Just Before Dawn

Off to the southeast, toward town, at first the countryside appears to be strung with twinkling Christmas lights: white, yellow, blue — some red.

As my eyes focus, the scene overwhelms me, and I think, maybe I should holler, "Wake up world So you don't miss this spectacular show!" The sky at the horizon glows — just less than hot pink — and washes up to palest pink, that fades into softest baby blue.

My eyes travel on to take in what further delights are in store. They're drawn to streaks of horizontal clouds touched with lavenders and grays; and on down to white fluffy bands of fog that wrap the yet barely visible fields, and rope around out-croppings of trees that break the landscape's lines.

As the light is gradually turned up, I see that all the white is not just fog: the corn fields are white with our first major frost of the season on this October 17th morning.

As quickly as day takes the warm satisfaction from my journey across dawn's landscape, cold sadness grabs me.

Outside, just south of the window where I stand, I see my beautiful red daises; and realize they've stood directly in the path of this night's hit-and-run driver.

Their brave, but fragile petals still spread triumphantly, in their natural way — as if in suspended animation. But as soon as this erratic driver of the night speeds off with the warmth of the morning sun, my daises will be left by the wayside to breathe their last breath and go limp, like a shirt that's lost its starch.

Oh, if I had just picked one more bouquet!

The Old Folks At Home

They know more tales
Than the libraries hold.
    You should hear some of
The stories they've told.

    If you want to know the particulars
Of that shady land deal,
    Or someone might tell you
How they improved on the wheel.

    Go to the bench and sit and just rap.
There's a wealth of knowledge waiting for you to tap.
    You'll be surprised at the tales they can bestow.
More intimate facts than you could ever know.

    We take things for granted in this world today.
But take for instance — let us say,
    When it gets dark tonight, that's how it'll stay.
They can tell you what it was like before R.E.A.

    Take your kids down to meet that lonesome old man
Who carried the lantern, pumped water by hand.
    Followed the horses, that worked this land.
Let them hear his tales, then they'll understand.

    When the railroad came through they worked on the crews.
Another man I know used to make his own booze.
    You can live their life, walk in their shoes.
All it takes is some time, you've nothing to lose.

    Grandma can tell you all about that day,
When Grandpa first took her home in their sleigh.
    Find out what they did up in the barn in the hay,
And what it was like when your dad came their way.

    There's no way to experience the tales they relate.
How they enjoyed everyday, the jobs that we hate!
    Enjoy this treasure right now, don't wait!
Spend some time with these people, before it's too late.

The Hands Of Time

They were pale and soft and wrinkled as they rested on the arms of the wheel chair. They looked as if they had just finished washing dishes; and they undoubtedly had washed dishes several times in their long existence, but not recently.

At closer look, I could tell by their size and shape that they had gripped the handles of manure forks and scoop shovels, and an unbelievable number of corn ears as they were ripped from the stalk and hauled to safe storage.

There was a scar on top of his right forefinger where the whetstone had slipped and the tip of the scythe had taken its revenge.

The end joint of his right ring finger was missing. I could see him pulling the wet grass off of the mower bar and poking the muddy gopher mound from between the guards, just as the horses stepped ahead.

The large veins that had fed and replaced the very fiber of these vital extensions of his complex nervous system were dominately visible. Like earthworms forced to the surface by a spring rain, they had been pushed to the surface by the hard muscles that had for so long manipulated these long, crooked fingers.

Their every scar and enlarged joint had it's story to tell, but now they rested. Occasionally gesturing, wiping, or holding, but mostly ... they rested.

Pinnacles Of The Prairie

They were the pinnacles of the prairie.
The hubs of every 'stead.
Protectors of the bounty.
For the providers, they were a bed.

The focal point of each horizon,
Standing out amidst the trees.
Closed tightly against the north wind.
Open portals to admit the breeze.

A sanctuary for scores of pigeons
Perched above the mounds of hay.
Their bins were overflowing
With provisions for a colder day.

Now their skins are thin and broken,
Allowing dusty streams of light to pass.
Single-hinged doors are hanging helpless.
Quad-paned windows are void of glass.

Neglected because they're not needed.
Nostalgic reminders of bygone ways.
Like our world, they can fall down around us.
"We don't fix it unless it pays."

Consumed In The Night

The aging barn looked somewhat like a jack-o-lantern, glowing from within, showing a friendly, calm silhouette. Soon the flames within sought freedom. They lashed out from behind loose battens and from around closed doors, like the tongues of hissing snakes about to take their prey.

Dark smoke billowed from the cupola and partially open hay loft door. The smoke was barely visible in the blackness of the night, as it gushed skyward in the updraft.

Holes appeared among the wooden shingles. The oxygen of the night air aided the fire within to become more intent in its consumption.

The openings let the flames escape and run up the roof to the ridge and leap off into the darkness. More followed as if they were being sucked skyward.

By now the shingles and siding were consumed, exposing the skeleton of the massive old barn. Flames ran up the heavy timbers like spider monkeys playing in the jungle. The huge pile of old hay in the center glowed as if it contained no substance.

Weakened now, the cross members let go at one end and swung down into the inferno. There was a smell of red cedar as the long poles stood at attention, like a platoon of soldiers dressed from right to left and left to right by size. Then, they too fell victim to its voracious appetite, one by one.

The kill was complete. Now all the flames had to do was consume.

As the sun came up, all that was left was what would not burn, protruding from a glowing pile of ash. Tines of manure forks, hobbles, crumpled pails, and a twisted track, its carrier and hay fork. The door hinges lay in fours where they fell, and of course nails, thousands of nails, their task prematurely completed.

The only good things to remain were memories.

Gone !!??

I thought I saw him standing there—
    By the field corner,
        Watching the harvest before he went to town;
But it was just a once sturdy corner post
    Supported by braces, angling to the ground.

I thought I saw him standing there—
    Bent over his watermelons,
        Thinning them to give them space;
But it was just an old bushel basket
    Covering the tiller that would take his place.

I thought I saw him standing there—
    By the riverside,
        Checking his lines while trying to hide;
But it was just the stump of the once mighty oak
    He sat under with his feet in to soak.

I thought I saw him standing there—
    By the walnut tree,
        Taking them all because they were free;
No, it's the old corn sheller, now missing a screw,
    Standing there alone with nothing to do.

But, if he's not there we know—
    That although the things he's touched
        Are rusty and rotten,
One thing's for sure—
    He won't be forgotten.

The Best Laid Plans Of Man And Cows Often Go Awry

July 19, 1989: Because we had a group of cows who had eaten their current pasture down to nothing, we spent all forenoon getting an electric fence up around a new field of pasture for them. We dug several post holes and set wooden posts, hunted all over the farm to find enough white corner insulators to use; put in small, electric fence posts; strung wire, and electrified the new fence. Last of all we made a big 18' gate hole for the cows to get through from the spent pasture to the new one.

Three of us chased, coaxed, waited, and hollered; but we couldn't get any cows or calves to go through the new (once hot) gate hole.

Frustrated, Bill finally proclaimed that we'd "just walk away and let them go through on their own." We then headed in to our burnt-cheese-an-hour-late-for-dinner lasagne.

I wondered how long it would take the hungry critters to discover that they had access to new food ...

... I never even gave it another thought until the end of the day when I sat down at the picnic table to relax.

From the porch where I was sitting, I could see both cow pastures and still no cows had found the new gate hole.

Shortly at 7:58 p.m. the first cows started to appear along the crest of the hill in line with the new gate hole. They were bellering and hungry. First one and then another moved closer to the gate hole, nibbling right up to it, and then stepping back quickly. None of them wanted to be the first to try the once electrified hole.

8:00 p.m.: Bill went tearing out of the yard with the windrower whining and whirring loudly. The cows scattered east over the hill and clear away from the gate.

8:06 p.m.: Some started wandering back. Two pickups left the driveway, one going north and one going south. This time the noise didn't scare them as they continued chomping at the short tufts of grass in their old pasture.

8:09 p.m.: A brave black cow marched up and went halfway through the gate hole. "Ah ha!" they said as they started to follow and beller and then to stampede through into the fresh green food.

... My youngest son ran hollering toward me to tell me that the cows had found the hole ...

8:18 p.m.: His hollering scared three calves and they hightailed it east away from the hole, still on the spent grass side.

8:30 p.m.: The three calves came running up over the hill from the east bellering as if to say, "where are you, Mom?" "Where is everybody?"

8:32 p.m.: Seeing no one, they put their tails in the air, kicked up their heels, and headed east back over the hill, on the old side.

8:39 p.m.: Again I heard bawling as the three calves came into view, but again they dashed back over the hill, still on the wrong side.

8:54 p.m.: The cows were all coming toward my end of the new field. Once again the three calves appeared on the horizon, paused and ran headlong down toward the end of the old field close to the road across from me.

9:05 p.m.: One calf went through the gate hole!

9:07 p.m.: The other two started up the hill from where they were bellering, walked up to the gateway, but meandered away. After some dillydallying and ho-hum munching, they moved slowly toward the hole, and at 9:09 p.m. these last two calves finally found their way through the gate hole to the green grass side.

(It took them all afternoon and evening to discover that they had access to new eating. Of course if this had been during the night or while we were gone, they would have detected immediately that the fence wasn't working and all eighty head of them would have been out trampling and destroying our corn.)

***

We're Pulling For You

On a few occasions I have pulled pigs because my hands are small, and I was able to do more good for the sow than my husband with his bigger hands.

I once assisted a veterinarian with a cesarean on a sow who was having trouble giving birth. The sow had been in labor for quite a long time and seemed to be in such pain. I felt so sorry for her and just wanted to help her if I could.

I've helped to pull calves too. Sometimes the mothers need assistance just like we humans do.

Usually a cow won't let a human near at calving, her motherly instinct giving her more fight and an even less agreeable nature than usual; but I remember a cow we found laying down at chore time who looked to be in such pain: she let me walk right up to her to assess her situation, and I patted her on the head and said, "We'll get you some help, Mrs." and I hurried to call the vet and get Bill.

The vet had to turn the calf to pull him, he just wasn't coming right and that's why the labor had been so hard. We hung him upside down to let the mucus drain out of his lungs so he could breathe, and tried to rub him to get his circulation going, but his birth had just been too hard and he died. The vet also pulled a second calf that was dead.

This whole time the cow was just laying there letting us help her (she knew the birth wasn't going right and that she needed our help). She seemed relieved when the birthing was done, but I was sad for her, and "I patted her head and said, "I'm sorry about your babies Mrs. We tried to save them for you." ... Sometimes things just don't go the way we'd like them to.

***

Dress?

I hate to wear good clothes for everyday. They might get grease on them, or get torn on a fence or piece of machinery. I like comfortable, practical outfits, like jeans and sweatshirts. In hay making time I wear long sleeved shirts to keep from getting scratched from the hay and to keep from getting suntanned crooked ... In a dressy dress, with makeup on and my hair done, it looks goofy to have arms tanned up to short sleeve length or a tan "V" at my neckline.

In winter time I wear coveralls with a jacket and sweatshirt over them, a stocking hat, and tall green insulated boots (if I have to be out choring for hours when it's below zero I've got to be warm) ... I saw a cattle buyer (one who had talked to me several times at the farm) in town one day and spoke to him. He said, "I don't believe I know you."

I said, "I'm Mrs. Bill Johnson."

His reply was, "Oh, I didn't recognize you without your chore clothes on." ... that may have been a compliment? ... It's necessary on the farm to wear clothes to suit the work; and beauty and glamour get left by the wayside.

*

One night at a dance I was sitting at a table with a group of friends. A man I didn't know came over to our table and very kindly said to me, "Pardon me, but I just have to tell you that you're the handsomest woman I've ever seen."

I was flattered and my friends at the table had the nerve to laugh and say, after the gentleman left, "Boy, he's really plowed, isn't he?"

*

There is something less than glamourous about a farmwife in a sleeveless dressy dress if she has biceps like a weight lifter.

*

Chic designer jeans come in 27 sizes, but they don't fit me.

***

I would like to see "designer tractors" ... designed that is to fit me (5'2") instead of a 6'2" man! Come on, there must be other short farmers out there who have trouble stepping on the clutch as I do. I have to hold myself up on the edge of the seat by hanging onto the steering wheel to get enough pressure on the clutch to depress it completely. And the gear shift levers definitely need to be redesigned: I almost dislocate my shoulder getting our one tractor out of park, and some are so hard to reach if your arm isn't long.

Our big tractors are supposed to have adjustable seats, but they adjust for someone who is 5'10" to 6" 5" and that misses me by a long ways. When the seat is in its lowest position my toes still just barely touch the floor. In our one tractor the seat is high in the middle so it's like sitting on a giant rounded mushroom, and if you don't think that gives me a back ache after a day of disking, you're wrong.

And then there is our new $100,000+ combine: they should have consulted a woman on the cab design. The windows are terrible to get at to wash, and the cab floor very cleverly has ribs in the floor mat which would make it easy to sweep the dirt out the door, but there are big raised rubber "letters" all across the doorway that are impossible to sweep the dirt over! ... it's the little things in life that drive us crazy!

***

The Scheme of Things

Some folks believe that it would be neat
    If the human race wouldn't eat any meat.
They argue: the world would have excess stores
    If all the scores were herbivores.

They infer that cattle are inefficient converters
    of cornstalks, mesquite, and snow.
I'd like to see them feed that stuff
    To anything but a cow.

We were designed with our eyes in the front
    Which tells us we are expected to hunt.
This makes it seem so extremely dumb
    To assume we are to sneak up on a plumb.

It seems to me the old cow is better equipped
    To cope with the elements of class.
If grazing had been our Maker's intent
    We'd have dew claws, hooves,
            and a tail hanging from our ass.

***

People will look at and may enjoy
A painting even if they don't understand
What the artist is trying to say,
But subject them to the efforts
Of a book full of big words,
And they will leave it lay.

***

When your writings
    You, with ambivalence strew,
You draw some readers close,
      But push more away from you.
So if you desire
    Their continued interest in you,
Never use a big word
    When a small one will do.

My Least Favorite Job

I'm tired of fixing this old fence,
    So I'll put it in new and bear the expense.
I'll call the cat' to grub out the stumps.
    He can fill in the ditch and level the humps.

Barbed wire: $35.00 a roll is the cheapest he had.
    Maybe that I rolled up wasn't that bad.
The posts were 2.99 and he wouldn't jew,
    So I'll just go home and salvage a few.

When you're stretching barbed wire, it ain't no joke,
    Cause all of them barbs can scratch and poke.
"Now handle it careful," but as soon as I spoke:
    "Look out back there!!" The darn thing broke.

The posts I had were rusty, or orange, or green.
    This will be the darndest fence you've ever seen.
I looked and looked but this is all I found.
    I'll just drive the twisted part into the ground.

I tied a wire and need the pincher again,
    But now it's laying on the other end.
It's just a quarter mile, I thought with a grin,
    but by now I bet I've walked over ten.

It's not straight but who gives a hoot.
    The wire must have caught on that plum brush root.
Grandpa would have made it better; but still,
    If you look from the road, it's over the hill.

A Tear, "So What?"

    Your first born receives an honor
Or a compliment from an anonymous donor.
    On Memorial Day when the flag comes by,
The sun's shining brightly
    And there's not a cloud in the sky.
You know you're looking but you can't see. "Why?"
    It seems there's something in your eye.

    Sometimes when you're playing ball
And know darn well you gave your "all";
    The end draws near and the scores are high
But the other team goes right on by.

    If someone's sick, or someone dies
And the children come with all the "whys?"
    "Or," a little finger pokes you in the eye.
Now, there's a reason why!

    ***

If you can make it through the day and don't know how you did it, you're most fortunate.

    ***

Treasures

    Nipped by nostalgia
And an urge to recoup
    Forgive us the junk we drag home
To clutter our stoop.

    We scrounge through the shops
Our attics and sheds
    For toys and old records
And dolls with cracked heads.

    Can we find an old dry sink
Or Grandpa's roll top desk?
    Some fine china like Grandma's
Or maybe something grotesque?

    Let us keep what we find
Lest all be forgotten
    As we walk that fine line
Between rustic and rotten.

***

There is nothing so close that it doesn't have to be reached for.

***

If a bird in the hand is your primary wish, just be thankful you don't like to fish.

The "Doctor"

He's a very special brother.
There's no doubt about that!
He'll come and help us "Johnny-on-the spot,"
No matter where we're at!

He whips out his tools and starts to work —
So quiet you could hear the drop of a pin.
He sees what's wrong and soon, his face,
Is covered with his own unique little, "special grin."

Oh, yes, — the problem is what he thought,
And it's not the oil pump at all!
It's a special hex shaft that's rounded off ...
He'd made the "diagnosis" when we made the "call."

He had our car "cured" in minutes:
We started it up and, yes, it ran!
There was another rattle, so while he was there,
He put a washer on the air conditioner or tightened the fan.

He slammed the hood shut, washed the grease off his hands,
Said now we could drive our car home on our way,
We drove off, followed by our brother the "Doctor."
He had pronounced us "well" and saved our day!

Oohhh, It's DRY

As I looked out over the fields today,
The corn's burning up and there ain't no hay.
The cracks are so wide that you better stay away.

I put the cows back in but doubt if they'll stay.
The grasshoppers got the beans but, "say,"
There's some hemp in the ditch, maybe that'll pay.

I guess a little time off isn't a sin,
So I went to town and the banker asked, "Where you been?"
"Oh," I said, "I've been going backwards & couldn't get in."

He said, "Your notes are due!" and handed me a pen.
So I stuck it in my pocket with a sheepish grin,
And said, "It looks like I just got you again."

***

Déjà Vu

The 1980's were unbelievably harsh times on the farm economy. Contrary to popular notion, where in hard times the poor operators were the ones who got the axe, the '80's were non-discriminatory. As our neighbors passed from the picture in one way or another, we were more than willing to consume their responsibilities; and they were washed away, leaving but another empty farmhouse to mark where the school bus once stopped.

But, with fewer operators on the land, reliance on non-farm capital became greater and greater to those remaining. Hence, rising interest and deflating collaterals were beginning to slowly erode the soil from beneath the feet of even the most unexpecting.

This all reminds me of when Mom would dress chickens and of how the chickens must have felt. As she would take the roosters, a few at a time, the rest of the flock seemed not to notice their absence, but for the commotion at the time. It just meant more hens for those remaining. With their added responsibilities, Mom would leave the strongest and yank the legs from beneath the weakest, as she needed them.

Eventually, with even just three toes to count on, those remaining were able to see what was coming; but their assumed responsibilities were making them weaker and weaker.

What do we need roosters for anyway??

When It Rains ———?

At first, wary and unbelieving,
    They listen to the raindrops — individually.
        All is very quiet,
            As if not to chance disturbing the spell,
        The fragile cadence.

And then it stops abruptly.

    Like a no drip faucet,
        It is shut off.

All is quiet yet, and then slowly
    Conversation begins:
        "That wasn't enough."
        "That won't soak down to the dry seeds."

And then comments shift to
    Markets, weed control, and ball scores.

One of the players has left,
    But suddenly bursts back in.
        Shirt wet and grinning from ear to ear,
            "It's raining south of town
                And coming this way."

A loud clap of thunder
    Precedes the downpour into town,
        And the banter quickens.
Laughing, hollering, joking,
        And then — slowly somber.

"My New terraces aren't going to hold
        If this keeps up."
"I bet we don't get back into the fields
        For at least a week."
"I knew I should have forward contracted."
"I sure hope it isn't raining on La Salle Street."

Dirt Farmer

I came in late from planting corn.
I was cold, tired, aching and dirty.
Yes dirty! Dirtier than anyone should get.

There had been a 20 mph. wind blowing all day.
That wind, tiring in itself,
Carried the dirt the planter stirred up
Into my eyes and nose.

Going away from the wind,
I could occasionally smell the insecticide.
The worms weren't going to get it all,
At least not right away.

Although I'm doing what I enjoy doing,
At times I wonder if I'm working the soil
Or the soil is working me.

***

If you make hay when the sun shines, you'll have to sell it in the dark.

***

Jerod once said, "There was a worm slinching out in the field where we disked."

Peace Unquiet

As the sun slips between the horizon and eternity,
    The sounds of day change to the sounds of serenity.
The hustle and bustle of eking an existence
    Become the refueling time of little resistance.

The ever present warning of the tattletale jay
    Makes one wonder where he is at the end of the day.
The hawks eerie shadow sends the squirrel to his hole.
    The silent owl awaits emergence of the nocturnal mole.

Supper is ready when we come in the door;
    The cat is out hunting, the dog's on the floor.

"Mom!! Alan hit me and you know where,
    And now Jerod is sitting on my chair!"

At last, the kids go to town to join the crowd,
    As the lights flash on and the music gets loud.
At least now we can hear the cicada's song.
    Why don't the kids ever take us along?

***

    Listen to the earth after a warm spring rain.

***

    As a rule, you'll learn far more with your mouth shut
    than with it open.

The Key

There are but a few who can make us well
    When we go to them and ache and tell.
And for that relief, we will gladly pay
    Much more than we could earn that day.

What a small group we have indeed,
    Who choose the route to run and lead.
Someone is always willing to fill their sack
    By crossing their palms behind their back.

What about the jocks down at the park
    Who play their games from dawn to dark?
We willingly pay to sit and observe
    As they pass, shoot, swing, and round the curve.

So what if those guys out on the land
    Could close their doors and make a stand?
They feed the world: this minority.
    It would seem **that they hold the Golden Key.**

***

Our body is a very complicated and delicate mechanism. That's why something no more than a positive attitude can have such a profound effect on our well-being.

When The Dust Settles

I'm going to live forever!
    Oh, I know that's not true.
No one knows,
    I may go before you.

We'd all like to know
    If from then - we will be.
Should we live for now,
    Or for eternity?

Will we trod on our fellows,
    For a cold granite bust?
And walk away from our peers
    With so little trust.

When the dust settles,
    Where will you be?
And will you have
    Just company?

When the end comes it'll matter
    In whom *did* we trust,
That we may go on forever
    And not end up just dust.

***

If you've never heard a cornstalk grow, there are a lot of things that you don't know.

The Harvest

The combines roll into the naked soybeans,
    Separators engaged,
        Wide mouths open and gliding on the ground;
Like pelicans gleaning the water's surface,
    Taking in all,
        And spitting out what they don't want.
After the soybeans,
            The corn:
Still standing stately,
    Although dry and vulnerable,
        With its golden bounty partially hidden,
                partially exposed,
        To the drying breezes and early fall sun.
This bounty soon to be torn from its once nurturing parent,
    Like a babe from its dying mother—
        To be whisked off to a safer environment,
            Awaiting its place in the chain.
It will be traded,
    And bartered,
        And hedged,
           And hauled;
Its value and condition varying many times,
    Before its energies are taken from it,
        And they are consumed.

Dance With Destiny

I'm born on the white corn;
And I'll soon be freed,
As the combine captures the ears
For the farmer's need.

I'll be dumped in a wagon.
My life could soon end.
As the tractor starts up,
And I'm hauled toward the bin.

My life's in a whirl,
Like a winter's snow.
They want me gone,
But I'll decide where I go!

Shall I dance in her hair?
Or tickle her nose?
Shall I whirl in her eyes?
Or just play at her toes?

I can drift on the ground,
And make it white as the snows.
Or I can sail up and away,
To where nobody knows.

***

The sun bounced the colors of a hundred rainbows
through the dew's outline of a spider's artwork.

Harvest Time ... Down Time ...

The radio comes on and it's six forty-five.
The sun's barely up and I'm barely alive.
For we combined last night till we filled up a bin;
Got in about midnight and today we'll do it again.
I'd rather not get up but I drag out of bed.
I go to get kids up but they don't hear what I've said.
I put dishes in the washer, clear off the table,
Do laundry, and sweep, and whatever I'm able
Until it's time to head out the door on a run ...
I'm already tired and my day's just begun!
The boss is already mad, hollering, "Where have you been?"
In just half an hour, he's madder than sin!
This rubs me wrong, so I holler right back!
... For ruining my day, he has quite a knack.
We hurry to chore, water cows, and haul bales,
Check the hogs, set the grinder, for others fill pails.
We fuel up the tractors, the pickup, and truck;
Check their oil and their water to improve our luck.
Then it's ready — get set — on your mark!
We're off to the fields to combine beans or corn till dark.
He runs the combine as I haul the grain.
Trying to figure where he wants a wagon is really a pain!
I'm up and down off the bin, truck, tractors, and wagons;
Way before dark, my tail's really draggin'!
The moon is now out and stars are silver as tin,
And I'm still hauling grain from the field's to the bin.
Tired and shaking and almost in tears,
I question what I've done to deserve this, over the years.
I don't have to die and go to Hell, I'm already there.
Life on earth at harvest is near more than I can bear.

The Seasons Of Life

The winter is our gestation period.
The seeds are in the sack,
The babes are in the womb,
And we're all gaining strength.
Protected from the harshness of the elements
For when we will come into our own.

Soon, everything will be freed
From its secure confines.
Seeds will sprout to life
And send their roots into the warm, moist soil.
Tiny bodies will flop and wobble
Until the warm sunshine gives them strength,
And they seek the security of first nourishment.

Summer is the time of growth,
Or the time of stagnation.
Warm rains or hot dry winds and drouth.
Sickness, disease, injury; gains and glory.

And it will be in autumn
When we line up our labors;
And the auctioneer will tell us
If we can afford to die.

A Farm Sale

For Whatever reason we leave the land,
    There is something most people won't understand.
Why, to our profession have we remained so loyal?
    It's an intimacy we have had with the soil.

A lifetime is lined up and listed for sale.
    Alas, let them have my old shovel and pail.
And when the physical things are hauled away,
    The memories will be here to stay.

When it's 20° below I'll be able to stay where it's warm,
    And wait till it's nice to drive to the farm.
Then over the coffee, I can be the one,
    To tell those young bucks how it ought to be done.

I'll be able to drive through a gate that is way to narrow,
    And I won't have to straighten that worn out old harrow.
And maybe another thought will be a factor,
    I'm tired of jumping that darned old tractor.

It seems an awkward way to go,
    As we drag it out of the shed and into the snow.
And watching it all take place is trying.
    "Look," even the auctioneer is crying.

Where Did The Farmer Go ?

Where did the farmer go?
    He's not in his field going to and fro.
Maybe he's in bed, but that's all right,
    He was combining beans past midnight.

Where is he when time is fleeting?
    Perhaps at church or a School Board meeting.
Oh! Why didn't I think of it,
    Is he by the finisher, pumping out the pit?

Where did the farmer go?
    We've got a committee for him to chair.
I bet he's with his kids today
    Getting their projects to the fair.

It seems so very odd to me
    That there are no lots and fences.
What do you suppose his cattle do?
    Run free and take their chances?

Where did the farmer go?
    We'll all wonder where someday,
When the dollars flow to corporate hands
    And we help them haul away.

Oh yes, where did the farmer go?
    His exodus so complete.
His house, his barn, his church, his school.
    He even took Main Street.

Section VII

The Nature Of Things

Pull The Wool Over My Skies

Don't be fooled by a warm sunny day,
For spring is definitely not here to stay!
The geese overhead will be turning back south;
And the first robin will have frozen notes in his mouth.

The cows bred to calve on a warm, dry day,
Will be looking hard for their next bale of hay.
And as the snow and wind cause their instinctive huddle,
The first calf will be born in a cold water puddle.

The grass still green from the early fall snow,
Can't withstand its new bareness at 20° below.
In the morning it'll look like it's had too much starch,
And we will be reminded it is still the 7th of March.

Passing The Reins ?

    The earth bares itself
New and fresh in the spring
    And allows each of us
To do our own thing.

    To till and to plant
What and how we desire
    Each hoping that later
We'll have just fruits to admire.

    But sometimes our labors
Are to little avail
    If the rains come late
Or in the form of hail.

    Our being a hardy lot
Allows us to hold up our chin
    But our banker will decide
If we will try it again.

Fork In The Food Chain

What a relief
    When we spotted the thief
        Who took our calves in the night

Without question
    She was crossing the section
        Glancing from left to right

When she spotted our truck
    Out she struck
        As if suspecting her plight

Then the mangy old bitch
    Dropped in the ditch
        And disappeared from sight

Without a doubt
    From an earlier bout
        We knew which way she'd head

So we circled around
    Gaining ground
        Only to find the killer had fled

She'd given us the slip
    Made us bite our lip
        And left our faces red

But we won't stop
    Until we come out on top
        And her hide is on the end of our shed

Oh! Isn't It Pretty. What Is It?

These invaders they come amidst our crops
    What dare we call a weed.
We pull, we cut, we spray, we burn,
    Though, to something, they fulfill a need.

They're home, a perch, a shade from the sun
    As on our soils they feed.
They're food in excess so to renew themselves
    As they rape the earth with seed.

Appearing where they've never been before
    With their pods and buttons and burrs.
Some relying on their animal friends
    To transport them in their furs.

They even sneak up to our own backdoors
    Through a ride in our "best friend's" tail.
Others move on with the excess of rain
    Or through a jay, a pheasant, or quail.

Some open their wombs to the wind
    And over the fence they sail.
You see them everywhere but the endangered list.
    Somehow they do prevail.

SURPRISE

Maybe "mootta" or "toomta" ??
Or "amotto" or "motato" ??

It could ripen chartreuse,
Or periwinkle or puce.

It could be long and skinny,
Flat, square, or triangular shaped.

It'd still taste the same,
And no doubt bring me delight.

That first fruit of the season
And that first D-E-L-I-C-I-O-U-S bite!

Windrowing Alfalfa

In my windrower,
Whirring and bumping along,
I'm seeing a butterfly;
I'm humming a song.

The alfalfa, green,
Waves in front of me, so tall.
The big reel beckons it in.
Sickle makes it fall.

It's pulled in and crimped,
Mashed flat and spit out the back.
Made into corduroy wales.
There's no turning back.

The sun will dry it.
It will cure leafy and sweet.
We'll bale it in big bales,
For our cows to eat.

The moisture will come;
The alfalfa will grow tall.
I'll windrow it thrice before
Frost comes in the fall.

The Old Maple In The Middle Of The Farm

Grandpa planted it there:
    A symbol for all to see.
        Proudly in the center of his 160.

It divided the fields:
    You could see from the road;
        And it shaded the horses,
            Weary from the load.

In the corner of four fields
    There was shade for the cows,
        As they calmly swatted flies
            Beneath forty foot boughs.

If you watched you could see
    The lark and the sparrow,
        Fly down and perch on
            Grandpa's three section harrow.

When the way was clear,
    They'd drink from the tracks
        Where the cows had just stood.
            Then maybe a pheasant or quail
                Would show off its brood.

But the barbed wire choked
    And tore at its bark.
        The air-conditioned tractor
            Needed nowhere to park.

The lightning and the wind
    Actually meant it no harm.
    Now it's gone!

That old maple in the middle of the farm.

Shhhh, The House Is Bugged!

Right above the bedroom door,
    I see just one, now seven more.
I know that it is time to rise,
    When one lands quietly between my eyes.

As I reached for my toothbrush,
    In the midst of morning rush,
I see where two of them have nestled,
    To see how clean I left the bristles.

They do little but crawl in the sun,
    Gaining entrance, one by one.
When they finally do get inside,
    They don't even try to hide!

Are they here from a foreign land,
    Gaining numbers to make a stand?
All of them going by just one name,
    Wearing tiny disguises, all the same.

I think the reason for their being here
    Is to get us to close the cracks to colder air;
For when winter comes the wall is bare;
    And we don't even miss them as they disappear.

Leptocoris Trivittatus

On the windows,
On the doors,
On the cupboards,
On the floors!

In my dinner!
In my hair!
In my water!
In my chair!

These unwelcome guests!
These brassy invaders!
These brash intruders!
These abhorrent raiders!

Are they here for food?
Are they here to destroy?
Are they here for love?
Are they here to annoy?

Alas, that's not what
These strangers are after;
They're here for shelter
Underneath my rafter.

Amaranthus Retroflexus
(Tumbleweed)

I came to life and I have lived in one place all of my existence. Now I will break from my roots and be free to travel.

I will tumble to unknown destinations and sow the seeds of my likeness. Providing the elements of existence treat them favorably, they too may sprout and grow.

I will roll and bounce lightly with the wind at my back. Occasionally I will be confronted by insurmountable objects placed in my path by creatures who need not the wind to aid their travel, but can go against the winds at will.

I will wait patiently until what prevails will free me to chance another route, experience new horizons.

I will cross a road when I come to it, risking being crushed and ending it there; but I have no control.

At last, my mission completed, I will gather with my kind and await the forces that will decay me, and I will have sustained what I have perpetuated.

In Silent Servitude

      Oh mighty oak, what might your future be?
Will you fall to the forest floor like any common tree?
      After serving your environment past a century,
It seems a waste you can't endure for all to see.

      Is it your wish that among your own leaves you lay,
Never again in the soft breeze to sway?
      Oh, if someone could find you and haul you away,
Lest you fall victim to fungi, rot, and decay.

      For 100 years you've grown gnarled and hard,
Weathering the storms and droughts in God's back yard.
      But now the ravages of time are taking their toll,
Trying to soften your trunk, trying to consume your soul.

      Your flesh could become a school house floor,
Or in our old church, a new front door.
      Let the saws and the planes beneath your skin,
And you'll see the second phase of your existence begin.

The Little Raindrop

The rain started to freeze as the shadows lengthened and consumed the warmth of the day. As it was early for such a cold freezing rain, many of the trees still displayed their colorful fall umbrellas. This extended beauty would soon be their downfall. When the weight of the most recent raindrop became too much, their final bough came too low and they popped out of the spectacular fall scene.

Slightly disturbed but not alarmed when the lights flickered, we went about our lives as usual. Then it happened! Darkness saturated the house; the furnace stopped blowing; and last but most momentous of all failures, the picture on the TV melted away. We sat helpless as we watched it being sucked back into the cold darkness. As our clocks would later recount, time had suddenly stopped.

With our candles all packed neatly away somewhere and the flashlight batteries drained by the mechanical monkey, we decided to go to bed.

Morning came and it was cold and dreary; but we could handle that, just as we had in the past. We would simply call R.E.C. and ask them to restore power.

When their reply came back that it could be days before lines could be repaired, we came to the stark realization that:

Our water was at the bottom of a six inch well casing 500' beneath our feet.

Our food was in the refrigerator and it would keep for awhile if we didn't open the door.

Our warmth was confined to the L.P. tank behind the house.

Grain for the livestock was inaccessible but by an electrically driven auger.

The 1500 lb. hay bales could be moved only if we could get the big diesel tractor warm enough to start...

That little raindrop that we usually find ourselves praying for had brought us to our knees again.

The Safety of Similarity

I watched the deer from the closed back door
    As they came from the timber to eat and explore.
Then it dawned on me, they all were alike,
    No antlers adorned, not even a spike.

The buck was still the last to appear
    Letting the does assure that the way was clear.
He remembered watching his comrades fall
    Merely for their heads to adorn a wall.

Why does he hide in thicket and bush
    Giving the young bucks and does a push?
Being a coward is our first inclination.
    But it's his instinctive means of self-preservation.

For what defenses does he have left
    When his once stately weapon is now a cleft?
I guess God knew that in the spring of the year
    His ten point buck could just be a deer.

Tis in the fall when mating draws near
    That he needs his full armor in perfect repair.
But, it's to his discredit, his new grown crown,
    When the men from the city come to gun him down.

Walk Down The Lane One Time For Me

The frost made everything so pure, so white
    That it seemed to steal some time from the night
Yet the calm frosty quiet made me realize
    The earth lay resting peacefully before my eyes

The quiet ... the quiet ... as I stood so very still
    An occasional twig — snapping against its will
Freeing a barrage of diamonds to flutter down ... down
    Flirting with their kind before they reached the ground

The cottontail half darted from side to side
    Well knowing this whiteness left him nowhere to hide
Yet, even he let me feel as if I were alone
    As he stopped in the fencerow as still as a stone

To come, the most beautiful sight I'd ever lay eyes on
    As first rays of morn' peaked over the horizon
Ever so slowly erasing this work of art
    Baring the canvas to what it was in the start

Section VIII

Some Serious Selections

On Dad's Funeral Day

Now we lay him down to sleep
We pray you, Lord, his soul to keep
Since he died and did not wake
We pray you, Lord, his soul to take

Keep him, Lord, in your tender care
Watch over him while he is there
Let him know no fear or pain
Show him sunshine, Lord, instead of rain

There are others there that he once loved
Gone days ago to Your heavens above
Let them greet him and show him cheer
Guide him, Lord, till they are near

Keep him, Lord, in your tender care
And 'company him till we get there.

Shorted By Alzheimer's

I looked into your eyes
    But were you really there?
Behind the lines in your face
    And beneath your graying hair.

We know how you used to be,
    With your cunning and your wit.
You always used to be ready to go;
    Now all you do is sit.

We don't know how you feel or think,
    Somehow we know that you do.
One thing we hope you'll always realize
    And that's that we all love you.

On My Own

There's some land for sale,
    I wonder if I can pay for it and how.
        I bet Dad would know,
            But he is gone for now.
I'll have to wait to get his answer,
    But I think I know what it would be.
        "Son, you're not old enough,
            But I remember 'thirty-three'."

It's winter again,
    And we have roses to protect.
        Mom always said what her uncle did,
            The on that broke his neck.
Oh shoot, she's gone too,
    I guess I'm kind of late.
        If I can remember all of these questions,
        I can ask them at the Gate.

Where Are You Goin', Grandma?

Where are you goin', Grandma?
    Oh, Dad and I are going to a neighbor's today.
    His wife has been so sick.
    We know he's got lots of bills to pay,
    And he still has corn to pick.

Where are you goin', Grandma?
    Oh, I've got another Grandbaby they say,
    And his momma's feelin' a little meek.
    I guess I can catch a ride that way,
    So I'll help her out for a week.

Where are you goin', Grandma?
    Oh, the neighbor gave me these nice jars to use,
    And Dad went to town for lids.
    With this big garden, I couldn't refuse,
    We'll can things up for the kids.

Where are you goin', Grandma?
    Oh, they're holding the Bazaar at church today,
    And I said I'd bring some pie;
    The way the weatherman talks, we won't stay,
    We'll just have to watch the sky.

Where are you goin' Grandma?
    Oh, today's the picnic at Sunnyside,
    And I want to watch the kids play ball.
    My gosh, how this family has multiplied;
    And you know, I love 'em all!

Where are you goin', Grandma?
    Oh, to where the air is pure,
    And I can stay without a care.
    Don't worry, I'll be just fine Dear,
    And someday I'll see you there.

Ronnie

We've all known Curly
    Since he was a "big" little boy,
When all he had was
    A K-5 for a toy.

We've worked and we've played;
    We've danced through the night.
We'll remember his laughing
    In devilish delight.

We're thankful for those times,
    The hours we spend,
And wonder just why
    It all had to end.

So we're going to give
    A little oak tree,
And plant it where
    Everyone can see.

It can grow and broaden,
    Through thick and through thin,
And as we pass, remind us
    Of him and that grin.

1900 hrs E.S.T.   Jan 16,1991

There are many feelings we experience
As creatures of this earth.
        Some are taken with joy,
        Some are taken with mirth.

We have just come to know
What all of mankind abhors.
        That is the lump in our throats
        And the cold cringe on our skin
      That is **WAR!!**

Harvest Angels

Being a fall harvest day (about 1981), I was hauling corn from our combine on Louie's, to the bin. I had just pulled up to the auger to unload a 325 bu. gravity wagon when I saw Alan and Kris playing nearby. I told them firmly to stay away from the wagon and auger, that it was no place to be fooling around! I'd seen them heading to the house, and comfortable with that, I soon started the auger.

Unknown to me, they had circled back and gotten up on the load of corn. Because of the noise from the drying bin fan, the tractor, and auger, I hadn't heard them either. I opened the gravity wagon door, and only about ten bushels of corn had come out when I saw feet in the door hole! My heart jumped! At that instant too, Alan came around the wagon hollering, "Shut it off! Kris is in there!"

In a flash I had shut off the auger and was up on the wagon: Kris was face up against the unloading door side, completely entrapped in the corn, except for the top of her head sticking out! Corn was angled up three and a half feet above her head yet. I got in behind her and pulled corn away from her face, and she started spitting corn and crying. Even her arms and hands were trapped down under the corn and she was so scared! I told her to calm down, calm down, and quit crying, and we'd get her out.

(Corn weighs 56 lbs. a bushel and she had nearly 300 bu. of it — over three quarters of a ton — holding her against the side of the wagon.) I couldn't budge her! I dug as much away from her as I could, and decided I'd have to have Alan turn on the auger and let corn out until I could free her. Thank God, Alan was there to help me!

Sitting on the corn behind her head, I braced my feet and one arm up against the side of the wagon, and used my free hand to keep the corn brushed out of her mouth and face; and I held some of the weight of the corn away from her with my body as Alan augered the corn out.

It seemed an eternity... but we finally had enough corn out of the wagon to free her, and Alan shut everything off. Sobbing and shaking I squeezed her close, and then instinctively scolded them both saying, "Don't you ever do anything like that again!"

After we got out of the wagon, they went on to the house; and I went limp as a dishrag as the strength drained out of me. God and the harvest angels had helped save my little girl.

Lonely

No one to talk to,
No one to care,

No one to listen,
When I need to share.

No one to be near,

                          I sit alone in my chair.

Tears start to come,
           And I just sit and stare ...

Loneliness

Loneliness is

VAST

Infinite . . . .

E m p t y

Will anyone remember me?

Simply Renewed

One cold calm winter's day while walking the fields to get a head count of our cows, I happened upon a magical awe-inspiring site. It was in a secluded woodland area along a creek where all signs of human places were blocked from view. Nothing around me in all directions to see except simple things: like sparkling, snow covered rolling hills of corn stalks, pastures, and trees; snow drift creations; and rabbit track patterns; and tree limb designs against a vast blue sky.

A sensation of warmth washed over me and soaked clear to my soul. How calm ... quiet ... serene ... beautiful! Completely unlike the usual crazy stressful world I came from.

Just as I thought this was as beautiful as a place could be, a velvety red cardinal flitted past creating a striking brilliant contrast against the crisp white snow and the bare dark trees.

Still thirsty for more, I took a few more deliberate steps on the crusted snow, not wanting the sound to break the spell of this wonderland, but just wanting to drink in more.

I stopped stark still as I spotted a lone deer, just at the moment that he spotted me. He stood stately, less than twenty feet away. His ears were pricked to help him determine if I meant him harm. As we stood motionless, I marveled at the beauty of this creature. After we shared these moments of mutual observation, he stepped elegantly and quietly off among the trees, made a graceful, unstrained leap over a fence and disappeared.

While I stood there entranced, a crisp but kindly wind danced round a tree, tickled my cheeks, and made my nose tingle, as if to say, "remember me."

This magical woodland experience had cleansed my soul and renewed my spirits.

Someone touched me, I know He did ... to say,

"Slow down, remember Me."

Ode To Farmers

There's a place saved in heaven for farmers,
    For we work our hearts out down here.
        We love what the land has to offer,
            And hold its beauty and bounty so dear.

We see the roses differently,
    And we smell them differently too.
        We're not better than anybody else,
            We just do what we love to do.

We know the wrath of the weather;
    Adversity can keep a crop from our bin.
        We struggle and work often only to fail,
            But we're thankful we can try again.

We fight when things don't go our way;
    It's not in our nature to quit.
        We seldom stay down to wait for the count,
            Because we're tough and we have grit.

You see, hope is what we're made of;
    We live it everyday.
        And when that isn't quite enough,
            We're not afraid to pray.

Critical List

    We've all heard it said, "It won't happen to me."
Maybe a neighbor, a friend, somebody we knew;
    But eventually we're included on that fateful list,
Because these neighbors and friends have these thoughts too.

    A touch of the brake unexpectedly doubled my speed.
In a split second I landed with my wheels in the air.
    The steering column had me pinned.
Fuel and oil were dripping everywhere.

    Seven tons of iron were pinning me down.
Two hours later internal injuries were mapping my plight.
    The whole world would help if they knew where I was.
You can imagine how I felt when I heard my boy holler,
    "Dad, are you alright?"

    Then the tractor came off before the ambulance's arrival.
They called Life Flight and I went to Saint Joe.
    God and the trauma team assured my survival,
And I came out without a tag on my toe.

As I Saw It

It all happened so suddenly that in my mind I can't fully see the tractor rolling 180°, and coming to rest with me still barely inches from the position I was in before the upset. I can still hear the squishing sound as the steering column came to rest on my left leg... The deafening clank the loader made (when all of its pivots came simultaneously to the ends of their wear patterns) concealed from me the snap of my femur and pelvis. The dirt and debris, hitch pins and wrenches that gravity held to the deck around my feet were suddenly freed, and spread around me as I lay pinned.

My first thought is still as clear to me as it was that day, "This is it!" I remember saying to myself. I wasn't afraid as I always thought I would be, but I guess at that point, I hadn't had time to be.

Soon I realized that "it" wasn't what I had thought and I began to assess my situation. I could reach the fuel cap, so I took it off and let the gasoline run out and down the hill away from me. The steering wheel and center column lay squarely on my thigh. This and the two uprights of the loader supported the 8 Ton combined weight of the tractor and loader. My head and right arm were extended snugly under the left fender but there was no weight on them. The transmission oil was draining out of the gearshift opening in the deck on to me, but I couldn't stop that.

I was in the cattle lot 350 yards west, and out of sight of our house; and I had 90 cow-calf pairs grouped around the tractor eating the bale of Sudan grass off of the loader spear. I tried digging with a wrench beneath my leg; but decided if I was able to loosen the soil beneath it, I would only be lowering the fender onto my head. Finally I was resigned to the fact that I had to get someone's attention if at all possible. I found the twine that attached the drawbar pin to the back of the seat; and using the pin, I began pounding on the hollow gas tank.

About an hour and a half later, I had the gas tank caved in and my fingers were bleeding. I was getting so weak and numb that I could beat only a few times and I rested — and wondered — and asked, and then started over again.

It was getting late in my life when I heard our twelve year old son Jerod ask if I was all right. I hurriedly gave him instructions. I remember thinking, "don't make your own assessment and leave before I can tell you what I want you to do," but he listened and went for help.

Soon Karen came with the pickup and I sent her for the big tractor and chain. Jerod called my brother and the ambulances and tried the neighbors. Duane and Mike arrived and helped Karen pull the tractor up and over off of me. By then volunteer rescue people were here and they put in a call to Life Flight in Omaha.

The chopper landed right there in the cattle lot; and fourteen minutes after I was loaded, we were at St. Joseph Hospital in Omaha. I remained conscious until they put me under in the operating room.

Five operations and fourteen days later, I was moved out of intensive care to a room upstairs. I still had all of my parts, but they sure didn't work.

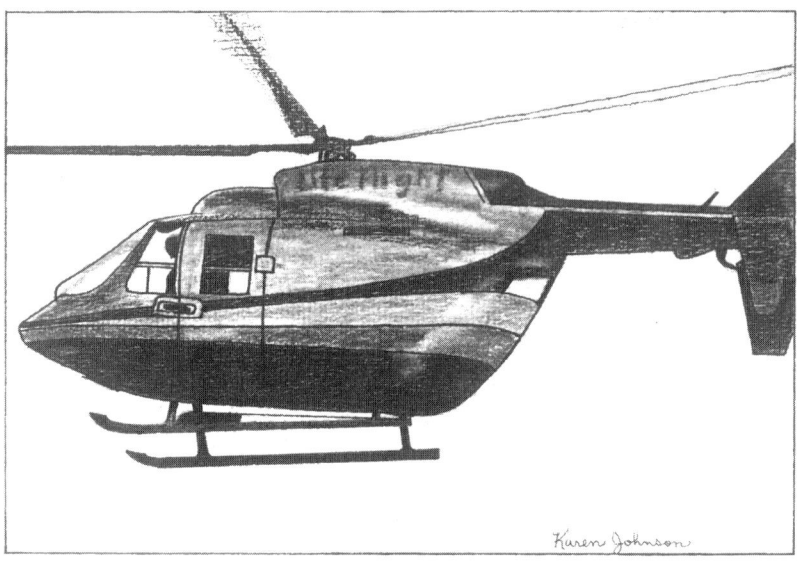

I'd like to express my sincerest gratitude to everyone whose mind I have crossed since my accident. This fall, when we tend to go one gear too fast, I hope I cross those same minds again, thus keeping someone else from getting seriously injured or killed. I'm one of the lucky ones.

I'm sure my attitude, being somewhat a clown,
    Has kept the pressures from dragging me down.
Modesty isn't something I took to town,
    As I traded in my calluses for a "one-sided" gown.

If they'd have told me how bad I was for sure,
    I think it would have been harder to effect a cure;
But thinking ahead to that harvesttime lure,
    Kept my attitude positive, my progress "pure."

As things level out, I'm beginning to understand
    What a blessing it was to run, to stand.
And ever so slowly I'm, beginning to heal and mend,
    I'm sure my fate is in someone else's hand.

I'm grateful to all who helped me out of my imprisoning lot,
    Every prayer helped me as much as a "shot."
Whether you've stopped, sent a card, or not,
    I know from all I've received a wishful thought.

Positively Yours

The wounds, the assessments,
    The pain, the suppressants,
The knives, the braces,
    The attention, the faces.

As I laid so very still,
    Allowing my wounds to heal,
Inactivity was consuming my whole,
    Trying to consume my soul.

Eventually, I realized the road I wanted to travel
    Might be longer than my means;
But not to make an effort,
    Was no where in my genes.

Just knowing I wasn't alone,
    Brought my goals somewhat nearer.
Though unknown, the hills and valleys:
    The journey, the rewards couldn't be clearer.

Epilogue

Bill: Things are moving faster in our world today and we tend to go with the flow, but wouldn't it be better if we backed off a little, looked, asked questions, and listened? I find myself wondering about things that happened in the lifetime of my parents and grandparents. I wasn't real interested when they were alive, but now it's too late.

We need to get our kids involved now and storytelling is a good medium to preserve their personal heritage for them. (Isn't it more gratifying to go to a museum or antique shop if we know something about what we're seeing? Doesn't knowing about the hardships of our ancestors make us more appreciative of what we have?) We are the storytellers, but what will we say? When it's our children's turn, what will they say?

Many people have gone through some very tough times out here on the farm; and one of the reasons for talking about it in our book is so folks might better realize what goes on behind the scenes and in the trenches of rural America. We manage to build equity in a favorable year, only to see it erode in a poor one. Our input costs continue to rise but our selling prices remain constant.

You experience high prices in the grocery stores, but they are very misleading in regard to the farmers share of these food dollars. For example, corn flakes are $1.89 for a 10 oz. box: that equates to $169.34 for a 56 pound bushel of corn, but we (the farmer) receive $2 for that bushel of corn.

We often hear, "Joe's got a new pickup; $2 corn must be working for him." If they only knew what Joe's old pickup had been through...

In our pickup we haul live calves, dead calves, feed, fencing, seed, chemicals, dirt, gravel, groceries, wheels and tires, air tanks, battery chargers and jumper cables. Junk, calf pullers, lariats, scour pills, ear tags, sand bags, sale bills, potatoes, cockleburs, coyote furs, shattercane, our walking cane, broken chains, parts and repairs.

We pull livestock trailers, weed sprayers, grain trailers, fertilizer spreaders, anhydrous tanks, hay wagons, machinery, cows out of the creek, and city folks out of the ditch.

Our pickup is a gate, a cutting horse, a cow chaser, and an errand runner.

You will see it at ASCS, SCS, the bank, the feed store, the grocery store, the elevator, the parts store, the salebarn, at farm sales, and sometimes just relaxing on main street.

When we get it cleaned up real good you may see it at school, church, or even the prom.

Both doors are caved in, the rear bumper is loose, the box is rusted out and the tailgate is gone. The windshield is cracked, the left window crank is gone, the defroster doesn't work, and the heater switch is broke off. There is no foam on the seat springs on the driver's side, the grill is wired on, and only one tail light works. The transmission slips, the valve covers leak, it misses on one cylinder until it gets warmed up, and it burns a quart of oil every two days.

But ... it's got a brand new oil filter and three pretty fair tires. The radio works and the cab is full of our valuable "stuff."

What will you give us for our old truck?

***

Karen: I ran across the following snippet in my journal of a couple summers ago: "Yard lights dot the horizon. The fields are black, but the sky at the horizon is distinguishable from the night of the fields by a lighter shade of dark. I was going to write, read, and relax in the summer night breeze (at the picnic table on our east porch); but a mosquito just bit me in the back, right through my shirt, and it hurt! So I'm going in to shower and try another way to end my day."

... This excerpt reminded me that when things don't go as you have planned, then just change your strategy! The secret is to stay positive and just carry on.

My Grandma Bornholdt used to say, "If the elevator to success is broken, take the stairs." If we could just foster these secrets in our children we could help them survive. Another way to help them is to arouse their interest, awareness, and caring for the people and things around them, and to stimulate and encourage their imagination and creativity whenever we can.

Shut off the Nintendos and TV's and make them some play dough. Teach them how to sew, cook, build bird houses, or make mudpies. Start them with a leaf, bug, or rock collection. Show them how to embroidery or whittle. Let them plant a flower garden or vegetable patch. (If you don't know how, learn with them.)

My mom taught me to sew when I was five years old and I've sewn ever since. Other than the time I accidentally ran the sewing machine needle right down through my little sister's index fingernail, sewing has given me a sense of accomplishment, and has been a satisfying, creative, stress-relieving outlet for me.

I taught my kids to cook when they were just big enough to stir a bowl of batter, or pat the pizza dough out in the pan. They not only can fend for themselves in the what's to eat department, but they can help me out with meals and lunches, and surprise us with cakes, pies, cookies, and muffins when they are so inclined.

Although as kids, my brother, sister, and I used our imaginations for most of our entertainment, movies at the theater were a welcome treat. I remember *Song Of The South, Old Yeller, Bambi, Cinderella*: movies that I either went away from "with a song in my heart" or that touched my heart with sadness and made me care. (Re-releases of such movies are still popular today!)

What feelings or values will movies like *Terminator II,* or *Rambo, Friday The 13th,* or *Faces Of Death* leave today's children with?

Making our own entertainment was part of our life style, as was wearing hand-me-downs, and working for our money. We learned to laugh and have fun, make do with what we had, to respect money and be conservative.

All in all, I've had to learn to do a lot of things in my life, and do them in the right order, and try to be aware all the time of what I was doing; so I didn't end up with a giant wob of straw between me and my rake.

Not to sweat the little things (at least for very long) helps me cope, and a good laugh is often the very best medicine to take away stress, lighten the mood, and help keep me positive.

I wonder ... will any of the stories, jokes, or poems in this book bring back memories for you, or make you laugh, or make you cry?

Glossary

abelskiver: a Danish food like a pancake, only made in a round ball shape, and eaten with syrup.

anhydrous: or anhydrous ammonia, a gaseous form of nitrogen used on farm fields for crop fertilizer.

ASCS: Agricultural Stabilization & Conservation Service. A division of the United States Government that handles the farm program.

bale accumulator: a small two-wheeled cart or trailer that is pulled behind our square baler. Two bales on edge, end for end are flipped up on it as they come from the baler until ten bales are made; then the trailer bed automatically raises; the bales slide off in a ten pack and can be picked up with a special loader attachment on a tractor and loaded onto a hay wagon.

auger: a piece of equipment used to move corn or beans from wagon to bin, for example. A flat steel spiral on a center shaft inside a tube is turned by a power shaft connected to a tractor and the grain is screwed up the auger by the turning of the spiral.

century farm: a farm that has been owned by members of the same family for 100 years or more. The Century Farms program started in Iowa in 1976. As of 1992, Shelby County had 123 and the Iowa total was 10,652 century farms.

choring or chored: the act of doing chores, like, "He cut his finger while choring" or, "We chored before going to town." Chores include the work involved with care and feeding of livestock, like feeding bales to cows, grinding feed for hogs or cattle, or watering cows.

cleaned: "a cow hasn't cleaned" or the placenta hasn't detached naturally as it usually should after a cow gives birth. Then a veterinary is called to physically remove the placenta after the birth of a calf, or "clean the cow."

combining: the process of using a big machine called a combine to cut or harvest plants of grain like corn, soybeans, oats, or wheat. The machine combines the process of cutting the plant and separating the grain from the plant. The grain is moved to a grain tank on the machine and the rest of the plant is expelled out the back of the machine and left on the field to enrich the soil; or as with wheat or oats, the stems can later be baled into straw for use as livestock bedding, or as landscape or crop mulch.

Co-op: refers to Farm Service Coop, owned by the people it serves. A cooperative that is a farmer's source for farm supplies.

cornstalk cigar: a stiff portion or section of a corn stalk about the size of a cigar that farmers & farm children sometimes put in their mouths to suck or chew on and pretend they're cigars.

cow "has feet sticking out": a calf is usually born front feet and head first, but if feet are showing from the cow's birth canal and the birth isn't progressing, it is a sign of a problem birth. The calf may not be positioned right, or may be too big to be born without assistance from either us or the vet.

crawler: Our 310 Case crawler is like a small Caterpillar or dirt dozer, with steel tracks instead of wheels.

cultivated: used a tractor and implement called a cultivator to remove unwanted grass and weeds from field crops.

cwt: hundred weight, as in $45 cwt for hog price is $45 per hundred pounds of the hogs' weight or 45 cents per pound.

dinner: farm people often refer to the noon day meal as dinner (not lunch), and the evening meal as supper. Lunch (snacks) is taken to the field to feed workers at about 4 to 5 p.m. to give them a boost of energy until supper, which in the busy season is eaten at 10 p.m. or later. Some farm folks who go out to work at sunup also have a forenoon lunch at 9 a.m. to tide them over with energy until dinner or the noon meal.

disking: using a tractor to pull an implement or disk over a field to kill small weeds and loosen up the soil to ready it for planting crops.

easy tree: a tree on the edge of our grove that had grown almost horizontally in pursuit of sunlight. We could easy walk up its trunk 25 feet.

farrowing: sows or female swine are raised to have pigs; and farrowing is the act of tending to them during and after the birth of their pigs.

Fs or Ag FS: Agriland Farm Service, a farm cooperative.

FB: Farm Bureau, an organization of farmers.

haybine: or windrower, a machine used to cut or mow alfalfa or forages. Some also crimp or flatten the plant stems to squeeze out the moisture and hasten the drying so the crop can be baled into bales or chopped for haylage.

haylage: a livestock feed made by chopping alfalfa (or other forage crops) and putting it in upright or pit silos to ferment.

haymow: (mow rhymes with cow) the area in a barn where hay is mowed or stored. To mow hay means to stack it in an orderly fashion in a building or haymow of a barn.

honey wagon: a cylindrical tank with wheels used to transport and spread liquid manure on crop ground. Sarcastically named for the not so sweet smell of the liquid manure.

IBP: Iowa Beef Packers buy cattle and hogs for processing into food products and other by-products.

incorporate: as to incorporate herbicides, is to work herbicides into the soil with a tractor and disk or field cultivator to kill weeds in the crops.

K-5: an International truck model of the 1940's era.

LaSalle Street: location of the Chicago Board of Trade.

Leptocoris Trivittatus: box elder bugs or McKinley bugs.

liquid manure: liquid livestock wastes, usually stored in a holding tank or manure pit. When spread on crop ground it adds nutrients that promote crop growth.

"made hay": harvested alfalfa or other forages and readied it for storage by baling it into small square bales (of 65-100 lbs. that are 16" x 18" x 40") or big round bales (of 1200-1600 lbs. that are 5' wide and 6' in diameter.)

PCA: Production Credit Association, now known as Farm Credit Services. They do just as the name says, provide credit for production of crops and livestock to farmers and ranchers.

pregged: when we've had the vet physically check a cow or cows to see if they are pregnant. If they are "open," not going to have a calf, they'll likely be culled from the breeding herd and sold.

pot: slang for a semitrailer used to haul livestock, with a "potbelly" hanging down between the trailer's wheels.

prolapse: when a sow or cow has a prolapse, their uterus is distended outside their body and requires repair by a vet.

pulled a calf: when we've physically taken hold of a calf who is having trouble being born (because of being to big, coming breech, or having his head or feet turned wrong) and pulled him out of the cow, hence assisted his birth.

pumping the pit: refers to pumping liquid manure out of our holding pit into a honey wagon for transport to the field where it serves as fertilizer to crops.

REA: Rural Electrification Association.

salebarn: a big "barn" or arena where farmers take livestock to sell, or go to buy livestock. Cattle, hogs, sheep, and other animals are shown in a ring to prospective buyers and auctioned off to the highest bidders. Hay, straw, and small equipment are bought and sold as well as livestock.

scours: diarrhea (especially harmful to young animals because they can quickly dehydrate and die).

shattercane: a noxious cane like weed that sheds its seeds readily when its heads dry and shatter.

silage: livestock feed made by chopping corn plants, ears and all, into small pieces and storing it in a pit or upright silo, where it ferments or ensiles.

skid: a flat wooden platform made from boards nailed across two round posts; bales were picked up by hand in a field, stacked on a skid and then the skid was pulled behind a tractor to haul the bales into the farm place.

springtooth: a piece of machinery pulled behind a tractor in a field to even the soil after disking, or to incorporate herbicide, or to kill small weeds before planting.

TGE: Transmissible Gastro Enteritis: a disease of swine marked by inflammation of the intestines and diarrhea, very often fatal to small pigs.

Tractors: we refer to our different ones by model numbers:
- 7000 Ford: 90 hp small tractor for lighter jobs.
- 830 Case: 1962 65 hp aka "old case." My trusty old favorite for grinding feed, pulling bale wagons, or smaller tasks.
- The loader 830: a second, little newer one, used to mount the loader for loading bales (the tractor Bill upset).
- 9600 Ford: 1976 135 hp, used for in between jobs, and used to mount the loader on.
- 9700 Ford: 1977 150 hp, aka "Big Ford," used for planting, disking, and bigger jobs.
- 1570 Case: 1977 185 hp, aka "Big Case."

"took cows to the stalks": we turn our cows into the corn stalks after a field is harvested, and they glean the field.

"turned boars out": put them with the sows or females to breed them. Gestation is 112 days.

"turned the bulls out": let them in the field with the cows to breed them. Cows calve in 9 months.

"walked beans": walked through the rows of soybean plants and cut out weeds or unwanted corn with a machete knife, spade, or sharp scythe-type hook.

windrowed: The process of using a windrower (ours has a 14' head with a sickle that cuts off the alfalfa, crimps it, and lays it in a 4' wide windrow behind the machine). The hay can then be picked up by a baler and made into bales or chopped with a chopper to make haylage.

***

The following figures were obtained from National Agricultural Statistics, a division of the United States Department of Agriculture:

* Iowa is the #1 hog producing state in the nation with 25,446,000 hogs produced in 1992 that provided gross income of $2,731,475,000.
* Iowa marketed 2,514,000 cattle and 75,000 calves in 1992 with

a value of production at $1,443,620,000.
* Iowa is the #1 corn producing state in the nation, with 1,903,650,000 bushels produced in 1992 with the value of the crop set at $3,712,118,000.
* Iowa is the #2 state in soybean production with 363,880,000 bushels of beans in 1992 with a value of $1,946,758.

***

These are figures for just four of Iowa's main farm products that not only mean food, but all of these pounds of meat and bushels of grain have to be shipped and processed which provides thousands of jobs for people, and adds billions of dollars to Iowa's economy. (Iowa farmers produce many more products besides beef, pork, corn, and beans but I'm using these four as examples because I am familiar with them.)

Farmers from all states of this nation, along with Iowa's farmers, produce a vast variety of products that add hundreds of thousands of jobs and many billions of dollars to our country's economy, as well as providing food and consumer products for people of this nation and abroad.

Hogs and cattle not only provide food in the form of pork chops, ham, and bacon; roast beef, sirloin, and ground beef; but valuable by-products from every part of them (including their bone, skin,& blood) are used in the manufacture of a variety of products. Such products as pharmaceuticals, cosmetics, glue, adhesives, gelatin, floor waxes, crayons, lubricants, anti freeze, cement, plastics, chalk, rubber, cellophane, insulation, pet foods, to name some. Art brushes are made from the hair. Their hides provide leather for shoes, coats, purses, and baseball gloves. Hogs give us porcine skin grafts for burn victims and heart valves for use in humans. Many people use these items everyday not knowing that cattle and hogs are a part of them.

As food, red meats have gotten a bum rap from the media in recent years. Beef and pork for example, are among the most nutrient dense of all foods which means they provide more <u>protein</u>, <u>vitamins</u>, and <u>minerals</u> per serving than most any other foods. Today's red meat is not high in fat or calories if you pick lean cuts and bake and broil rather than fry, and remember to drain the fat off of ground beef or ground pork after browning and before adding it to your recipes. Red meat is good for you. People have eaten it for years and years so how can it suddenly be bad for you?

Oil from soybeans is the major oil used to make salad oil, shortenings, margarines, mayonnaise, and salad dressings. Soybeans are used in such non-food products as printer's ink to print newspapers; and a soy diesel fuel is being developed.

Corn is also used in salad oils and margarines, and is made into corn flakes, corn meal for corn bread, and corn sweetener, which is widely used in soda pop and to sweeten other products. White corn like we grow is made into taco shells and white corn chips. Corn ethanol is blended into gasoline; and its starches are made into biodegradable plastic garbage bags and other containers. Corn and soybeans are far more than just feed for livestock.

Farmers nationwide provide numerous products besides just pork, beef, corn, and soybeans. The next time you use any of the products in the above article or sit down to a meal, think of the American farmers, won't you?

Title Index

(Initials following titles indicate whose work is whose.
KJ denotes pieces by Karen and BJ denotes pieces by Bill.)

1900 hrs E.S.T. Jan 16,1991	BJ
Amaranthus Retroflexus (Tumbleweed)	BJ
Another Threshing Story	BJ
As I Saw It	BJ
The Best Laid Plans Of Man And Cows Often Go Awry	KJ
The Breeze Blows By	BJ
Brighton No. 8	KJ
Cents Of Christmas	BJ
Consumed In The Night	BJ
Critical List	BJ
Cutting Remarks	KJ
Daffy Definitions	KJ & BJ
Daily Debut	BJ
Dance With Destiny	KJ
The Daus	BJ
Déjà Vu	BJ
Delicious?	KJ
A Derriere!	BJ
Dirt Farmer	BJ
The "Doctor"	KJ
Dress?	KJ
The Explorer	BJ
A Farm Sale	BJ
Figuring Income Taxes	KJ
First	BJ
First Exposure	BJ
Footprints	BJ
Fork In The Food Chain	BJ
For Sale:	BJ
A Fractured Fairy Tale	KJ
Gone	BJ
Grandmas And Grandpas	KJ
The Hands Of Time	BJ
The Harvest	BJ
Harvest Angels	KJ
Harvest Time ... Down Time	KJ
Hide! I Can't Let My Cornflakes Sog!	KJ

Hollering Up The Stairs	BJ
How This Book Came About And What's In It For You	KJ
How To Look, Listen, Laugh, And Survive	KJ
In	BJ
In Silent Servitude	BJ
I See You	BJ
It Must Come From Your Side	BJ
It's All Mine	BJ
It's Mine In Deed	BJ
Journal Journey	KJ
Journey Just Before Dawn	KJ
The Joys Of Being A Farm Wife And Mother	KJ
Just Twice A Day	BJ
The Key	BJ
Kidnapped	KJ
Kids Say And Do The Darnedest Things	KJ
Lean, Mean, Cuisine	KJ
Leptocoris Trivittatus	KJ
The Little Raindrop	BJ
Loneliness	KJ
Lonely	KJ
Making Memories At The Acova	KJ
Mary's Kitchen	BJ
My 4 Speed, Posi-traction, 4 x 4 Truck	BJ
My Kingdom,... Come	BJ
My Least Favorite Job	BJ
Mystery Lunch	KJ
The Night After Christmas	BJ
Ode To Farmers	KJ
Oh! It's Pretty. What Is It?	BJ
Oohhh, It's DRY	BJ
The Old Folks At Home	BJ
The Old Maple In The Middle Of The Farm	BJ
Omaha Stockyards	BJ
Once Upon A Farm	KJ
On Dad's Funeral Day	KJ
On My Own	BJ
Our Wishbook	BJ
Over The Hill	BJ
Passing The Reins ?	BJ
Peace Unquiet	BJ
A Piece Of The Rock	BJ

Pinnacles Of The Prairie	BJ
Positively Yours	BJ
Potluck	BJ
Potpourri	BJ
Pull The Wool Over My Skies	BJ
Ronnie	BJ
Rule Of Thumb	BJ
The Safety Of Similarity	BJ
Saturday Nights At The Acova	KJ
Savor It	BJ
The Scheme Of Things	BJ
The Seasons Of Life	BJ
See The Shape Things Are In	KJ
Shorted By Alzheimer's	BJ
Shhhh, The House Is Bugged	BJ
Simply Renewed	KJ
Sound Impressions	BJ
Sour Krauts And Wienies	BJ
Summer's A Better Time For Birthdays	KJ
SURPRISE	KJ
A Tale Of Old	KJ
A Tear, "So What"?	BJ
(Thank-you Poem)	BJ
Things Parents Used To Say	KJ
Things That Are Spotted	BJ
Thur Apr 12	BJ
Treasures	BJ
The Visitor	BJ
Walk Down The Lane One Time For Me	BJ
We're Pulling For You	KJ
When It Rains ———?	BJ
When The Dust Settles	BJ
Where Are You Goin', Grandma?	BJ
Where Did The Farmer Go?	BJ
Windrowing Alfalfa	KJ

Please direct your comments, questions, or suggestions concerning *Once Upon A Farm: How To Look Listen Laugh And Survive* to:

Karen & Bill Johnson
302 Ironwood Road
Avoca, Iowa 51521-3002

Hardbound copies of the book are available at the above address for $17.95 (plus 5% sales tax for Iowa residents). Please include $2.00 postage and handling per book for mailing.